TERRORISM IN AN UNSTABLE WORLD

Dr. Vijay Kumar Verma

MD PUBLICATIONS PVT LTD
NEW DELHI
www.mdppl.com

Published by :

MD Publications Pvt Ltd
'MD House', 11, Darya Ganj
New Delhi - 110 002
Phone : +91-11-41563325 (Customer Service)
+91-11-41562846 (Editorial)
E-mail (orders): contact@mdppl.com
Website: www.mdppl.com

ISBN: 978-81-7533-188-4

Published and Printed by Mrs. Rajni Gupta on behalf of **MD Publications Pvt Ltd** at Times Press, New Delhi.

Contents

Contents

PREFACE

Terrorism is the systematic use of terror and at present, there is no internationally agreed definition of terrorism. Common definitions of terrorism refer only to those acts which are intended to create fear (terror), are perpetrated for an ideological goal (as opposed to a lone attack), and deliberately target or disregard the safety of non-combatants.

Terrorism has been used by a broad array of political organizations in furthering their objectives; both right-wing and left-wing political parties, nationalistic, and religious groups, revolutionaries and ruling governments. The presence of non-state actors in widespread armed conflict has created controversy regarding the application of the laws of war.

The terms "terrorism" and "terrorist" (someone who engages in terrorism) carry strong negative connotations. These terms are often used as political labels, to condemn violence or the threat of violence by certain actors as immoral, indiscriminate, and unjustified or to condemn an entire segment of a population. Those labelled "terrorists" rarely identify themselves as such, and typically use other euphemistic terms or terms specific to their situation, such as separatist, freedom fighter, liberator, revolutionary, vigilante, militant, paramilitary, guerrilla, rebel or any similar-meaning word in other languages and cultures. The *Jihadi, mujaheddin,* and *fedayeen* are similar Arabic words which have entered the English lexicon.

Terrorism is a growing problem in this unstable world. A simple act of terrorism can cause tensions to break between two countries. Among the various potential threats, wars with neighboring countries, missile attacks on cites, biological and chemical terrorism, suicide bombings, and hostage taking are burning issues. But terrorism is revealing itself in new forms in this modern world, such as massacres, hijackings, attacks on U.S. troops, and hostage taking.

I am very grateful to Mr. Pranav Gupta, Director, MD Publications Pvt Ltd, New Delhi who has readily expressed his acceptance and supported me fully for completing this book.

Dr. Vijay Kumar Verma

1

Terrorism in an Unstable World

Introduction

Despite the drama surrounding Pervez Musharraf's lengthy resignation address yesterday, there was nothing particularly surprising about the Pakistani President's departure. The truth is that Mr Musharraf was doomed the moment his political base was wiped out in February's parliamentary elections. The former general's support in the country dried up some time ago, and the new coalition government was determined to use the impeachment process to get rid of him. This was a beleaguered politician bowing to the inevitable.

What has defined Mr Musharraf's rule more than anything else has been his relations with the West since the terror attacks of 11 September 2001. He presented himself as the world's sheriff in a volatile region, a stance that won him billions of dollars in US military aid. But doubts about the soundness of this investment have been creeping in over the years. Despite some early success in capturing some high-level al-Qa'ida operatives, President Musharraf has been unable to secure Pakistan's western border.

If Mr Musharraf's counter-terrorism achievements

have been a disappointment to his Western sponsors, his record as a democrat has simply been an embarrassment. After deposing a corrupt civilian government in a military coup in 1999, Mr Musharraf promised to restore democracy as soon as practically possible. Yet, despite shedding his army uniform last year, he has done nothing to strengthen the rule of law. By sacking the Chief Justice and imposing a state of emergency last year, he finally gave up all pretence of being a democrat. The challenges facing the civilian government in the post- Musharraf era are immense. Perhaps the most daunting will be bringing Pakistan's powerful intelligence services, the ISI, under political control. Rumours of secret co-operation between some in the ISI and the Taliban refuse to go away.

The second great security challenge is India. Relations with Pakistan's nuclear-armed eastern neighbour were actually quite good under Mr Musharraf, in large part because the President held Pakistan's army under tight control. But many question the ability of a civilian administration to exert the same level of influence over the generals. Almost as formidable as these challenges is the need to fix Pakistan's economy. Annual inflation is running at 28 per cent and high food prices are stoking popular discontent.

It is hard to be optimistic. The two parties of the coalition, the Pakistan People's Party and the Muslim League, both have a dreadful record of corruption and incompetence in office. And the one thing that has united them in recent months has been the determination to get rid of President Musharraf. It is hard to see what will hold them together now that he has departed.

If there is hope, it lies in Pakistan's increasingly assertive middle class and its outspoken press, both of which will demand honest and efficient government. It is also worth remembering that, despite the extreme image of Pakistan often projected to the outside world, the vast majority of Pakistanis do not favour fundamentalist religious parties.

If Pakistan's political leaders can find it within themselves to govern wisely, the materials are there to turn the country round.

It is hard to overstate the geo-political significance of Pakistan, this nuclear power situated in one of the most unstable regions on earth. We need to pray that President Musharraf's successors will do a better job of steering the country away from the abyss.

World's top nuclear threats

There wasn't a real nuclear threat in Iraq, and there isn't one currently in Iran. Instead, two other countries and one man in particular are on the worry radar of weapon proliferation expert Joseph Cirincione. North Korea has nuclear weapons. Pakistan has an unstable government, armed fundamentalist Islamic groups and material to build at least 30 nuclear weapons. And nuclear terrorism is as close as Osama bin Laden being able to get his hands on the enough of the right materials to build a bomb, according to Cirincione.

"Those are the more urgent threats," Cirincione, Director for Non-Proliferation at the Carnegie Endowment for International Peace told the Deseret Morning News.

A question that lingers is why the United States and its allies aren't doing more to address those threats, Cirincione added. One answer is that so much attention in the Middle East these days is focused on overlapping agendas that include interest in oil, Israel and a regional transformation – starting with Iraq – into a more democratic society, according to Cirincione. "So far, the results have not been good," he said of the latter.

The vision of a politically transformed Middle East, he said, is dying on the battlefield of Iraq and the process itself is proving more costly and complicated than anyone imagined. What people in this country still don't understand, Cirincione said, is that just prior to declaring war on Iraq, there was no intelligence that could confirm the presence of any weapons of mass destruction. The intelligence assessment at the time, he added, did not determine the decision whether to go to war — it was the decision to go to war, Cirincione said, that determined what the intelligence assessment should be.

"They saw Saddam as a threat that had to be removed," Cirincione said of senior officials in the Bush administration. The real threats Saddam Hussein did pose at the time, he added, were that he had a military force that was a threat to neighboring countries, that he could be a threat again to Israel and that he was already a threat to his own people.

Now Iran's leader is rattling cages, but the country is still at least five years away from being able to enrich enough uranium and develop enough technology to produce nuclear weapons, according to Cirincione, who said he is worried about how heated the rhetoric is getting on both sides of this issue. "Iran is not a nuclear bomb crisis — it's a nuclear diplomacy crisis," he added.

One key at this point, Cirincione said, is continued isolation of Iran and the support of Russia, China and India in that effort. "It's going to take time for that to work," he said. But in an action/reaction, dominoes-will-fall kind of scenario painted by Cirincione, military conflict could become reality in Iran without a weapons threat if the rhetoric and response boils over. He recalled World War I as a lesson in the context of how to handle Iran. "I'm very worried," he said, "about that situation with Iran right now."

Security in an Unstable World

Foreign Policy issues are too often discussed as though they occur in a vacuum. Commentators and academics theorize about policy options and strategic possibilities. International affairs are made to sound polite, esoteric and far removed from ordinary citizens. But the great issues of international politics do, in the end, impact directly on ordinary people across the globe. This can be seen clearly in the newly won freedom of the people of East Timor, and of Iraq.

- in the improved circumstances of families which have been lifted out of poverty by the benefits of economic globalization
- and in the desire of all Australians to be secured in a world changed fundamentally in the wake of September 11th and the Bali bombing.

This "real world" is where the Howard Government's foreign policy operates. What underpins our approach to foreign and trade policy is a determination to advance the national interest in a pragmatic and hard headed way. We look for outcomes not just empty form and posturing. We can not afford to be complacent and we can not afford to spend time and effort on processes and institutions that are marginal to our interests.

The Government has directed Australia's diplomatic and trade effort toward those relationships, institutions and issues that matter most to Australians and which will deliver results. Our approach has assumed an even greater importance in Australia's uncertain international environment. The challenges we face as a nation are complex and evolving rapidly. Our interests are global and not defined solely by geography.

The Government's two White Papers, In the National Interest and Advancing the National Interest set this out clearly. Australia's security is at risk from the threat of international terrorism and the spread of weapons of mass destruction. Instability and even state failure in our neighbourhood is a growing concern. Economic globalisation offers significant opportunities, but only if we continue to ensure strength in our institutions and pursue policies of further reform.

Australia's foreign and trade policies have to be focused sharply on achieving practical solutions to these urgent issues. For it is only through a strong and purposeful approach to the challenges of terrorism, weapons of mass destruction, regional instability and globalisations that we advance our national interests.

Terrorism

Australians are on the frontline in the war against global terrorism. We have no choice. We are a target because of what we believe in and what our society represents. Terrorists oppose the values we hold dear; our commitment to an open and tolerant society; and our commitment to democracy and freedom. Their goal is to form Taliban style states throughout the Islamic world and to end democracy and political and religious freedom.

The accused Bali bomber, Samudra, has said that democracy 'will never come true only by the Muslim system can society have a happy and prosperous society'. Samudra's vision of a Muslim system is one without the 'polluting' effects of media, secularism, and contact with women – despite him being found with a laptop laden with pornographic images. These terrorists have no more respect for the religion they purport to uphold than they do for the victims they target so ruthlessly and indiscriminately.

Their message and purpose is overwhelmingly negative and without hope. It is profoundly reactionary. Australia has played a leading role in the campaign against terrorism. I have always said the fight against terrorism would not be quick and it would not be easy. And that it can not be segmented into regional components for it is a global struggle in which connections between regions run deep. But we have made substantial progress in this fight. Australia's contribution of personnel and materiel helped drive al-Qaida and the pro-terrorist Taliban regime from Afghanistan.

Globally, nearly one half of al-Qaida's leadership has been captured or killed and over 3000 people connected to al-Qaida are in custody worldwide.

- the rest of al-Qaida is degraded and must now spend more time looking over their shoulder
- over US$100 million in terrorist assets have been frozen.

Our support and implementation of international controls over the movement of terrorists and their finances is helping to frustrate their operations. We have placed great emphasis on fighting terrorism in our region. This can be seen in close cooperation with our regional partners at the political level.

And importantly this has translated into closer ties between Australia's police, intelligence and security services and their regional counterparts which have helped to head off further attacks and combat the spread of extremist Islamic terrorist networks. The unprecedented joint investigation by Australian and Indonesian authorities has disrupted a significant terrorist network through the arrest, detention and current trial of the Bali suspects.

Our network of bilateral counter-terrorism MOUs is strengthening cooperation and information exchange on terrorist groups. The region is becoming a more difficult environment for terrorist groups. But al-Qaida, JI and other terrorist organisations retain a formidable capability. We, our Allies and our regional partners must – and do – remain alert to the persisting threat.

Weapons of Mass Destruction

Our greatest fear is of the consequences from terrorist groups or irresponsible states gaining access to nuclear, chemical and biological weapons. Documents and laboratories seized in Afghanistan show that al-Qaida has considered developing chemical and biological weapons.

And Osama bin Laden has declared openly that he would use such weapons if he had them.

Al-Qaida tried to gain access to crop dusters and hazardous chemicals in the United States in 2001. And recently police linked the discovery of deadly ricin toxin to suspected terrorists in the United Kingdom. While there is no evidence to suggest that terrorist groups have acquired nuclear weapons, reports suggest that groups linked to al-Qaida may have been looking to construct a radiation dispersal device – or so called dirty bomb.

We were reminded of this very real threat by the arrest in Bangkok of a Thai national attempting to sell radioactive materials from Russia only a week or so ago. Terrorists are not bound by the constraints – deterrence, denial and containment – to which even maverick states can be subject.

The only constraints on terrorists are the resources at their disposal to kill and terrify innocent civilian populations. It would be deeply unwise, therefore, to deny the potential link between the spread of nuclear, chemical and biological weapons and terrorism. The combination of these two developments would constitute the ultimate horror.

But, obviously, it is not just the risk that maverick states will pass such weapons to terrorists which concerns us. The proliferations of weapons of mass destruction, particularly to and from states that flout international norms are in themselves a grave threat to our security. Iraq was a striking example of our resolve to deal with this threat.

No-one could sensibly argue now that ridding Iraq of Saddam Hussein's barbarous regime and ridding the world of the threat posed by his weapons programs was the wrong thing to do. Yet Australia went into the conflict with the main Opposition Parties opposed to our involvement. The Labor Party's opposition was not based on outcomes or results – it was based on process.

That is, the Labor Party hid behind the French threat to veto any United Nations Security Council resolution – although it would abide by whatever policy decision the Security Council delivered with French acquiescence. Likewise, the Labor Party's response to the threat of nuclear weapons has been to call for the Canberra Commission on the Elimination of Nuclear Weapons to be reconvened.

The aims of the Commission were laudable, but its recommendations fell back on established processes and relied too much on multilateral institutions. In the current circumstances, that is simply not a viable course of action – politically or practically. The Government decided that Iraq had to disarm – it had to comply with the fourteen Security Councils.

Relative Balance in an Unstable World

If you are a writer, the assimilation of important experiences almost obliges you to write about them. Writing is how you explore what it means to you, how you come to possess it, and ultimately release it. I am a Somatic Traumatologist specializing in a relatively new field of Social Trauma. Trauma is defined by the American Psychiatric Association as a response to an overwhelming life event, as defined in the Diagnostic and Statistical Manual-IV. Trauma is a process of adaptation over time. According to this definition, Post-Traumatic Stress Disorder (PTSD) is a result of complex interrelationships among psychological, biological and social factors. The key word here is "response".

In individual trauma, the response is in the nervous system, not in the event. I would agree that this definition also works well for Somatic Traumatology: An emerging field of study involved in the development of innovative methods that include psycho physiological approaches toward identifying and realigning the conscious and unconscious bodily responses to overwhelm. In the realm of Social Trauma, however, I believe that we will need to expand these definitions to include the impact of unresolved trauma, not only on the individual, but upon those in relationship to traumatized people, as well as upon the larger field of local community, culture, nations, global community and Earth herself.

It is important to understand, in this respect, that unresolved trauma serves to perpetuate unresolved social issues for many generations of people who may be totally unaware of these dynamics. Since I am also a cultural historian, these generational dynamics are important to me as well. This has been with me, in way or another, for over a decade. During this process of bringing it into form, there were two important decisions to make. The first was whether to write a volume on social trauma for mental health professionals, or to write for any and all interested readers. My second decision was to choose between a personal or professional voice.

As you will see, I chose to write for any and all interested readers and from my own deeply personal perspective. This need to write about my developing understanding of collective overwhelm has emerged from an increasing awareness that trauma and its aftermath is both endemic and epidemic throughout our world. The psychosocial and economic impact continues to be costly. Recent research has shown that trauma victims are disproportionately likely to engage our social, medical, governmental and judicial systems.

Unfortunately, in the wake of the tragic events of September 11th, as our awareness of the magnitude of the issue increases, so do the limitations of the resources provided by our existing paradigms for treatment of post-traumatic stress responses. Given the increasing numbers of people identified as trauma survivors and the pressure of steadily rising health care costs; it is clear that we are moving in the direction of crisis. As the ancient Chinese proverb advises, "If we do not change directions, we are likely to wind up where we are going."

If we are to meet our oncoming challenges we will need to expand our understanding of trauma to include the kinds of overwhelm that extend beyond a traumatized individual. The concept of social trauma or those kinds of trauma that extend beyond the individual, into the community, cultures, nations and the Earth herself is still very new. With the frequency of natural and man-made disasters, contagious diseases, wars, revolutions, ethnic cleansing, terrorism and other forms of violence increasing all over the planet, treatment is often a question of real physical, social, cultural and political survival for the involved regions.

It is now imperative for us to understand that trauma is a global issue and that there is an urgent need to develop international, cross- cultural, cost effective trauma education and recovery programs based upon easily transmitted concepts. Over and over again, in many parts of the world, it has become clear that people in disastrous situations need immediate assistance with emergency medical care, food, water and shelter. However, "one size fits all" trauma-counseling programs will never really work because people often have highly individual and culturally specific responses to overwhelming life events.

Most trauma specialists experienced in the field would agree that reactions to catastrophes vary greatly due to the nature of the incident. We must also remain aware and respectful of individual differences, as well, in age, health status, coping styles, life assumptions and previous emotional problems. Over time, it has become increasingly clear that an understanding of trauma offers a valuable component for all of us who seek a greater understanding of the human condition. For this reason, this realm of inquiry needs to extend far beyond carefully described fields of psychiatry, psychology, sociology and even so-called psychohistory.

Over 30 years of experience in the study, treatment and teaching of trauma work, as well as graduate studies in humanities, history and art led to a perspective within which I understand and accept trauma as integral to human experience. As a historian, I have been deeply aware that the Greek verb historien means "to ask questions" and this has been a motivating factor in my study of trauma, as well. Humanistic studies and attention to history, as well as to current events, reveals that the kinds of overwhelm that we experience as "traumatic" in individual, community, national and international life, have always been with us in one form or another.

For Homo sapiens, trauma is "in the contract" so to speak, an often unavoidable component in the evolution of our understanding of ourselves, our world and the power of great and mysterious forces that shape our collective destiny. As a trauma specialist, moving beyond a focus on individual trauma into the larger realms of social trauma was a deeply personal process, for me as an individual, as a woman and also as a child of war. Readers are invited to come along on these inquiries which constellate around three major projects undertaken while I was a graduate student at the Western Institute for Social Research in Berkeley, California.

Working in the High Sierra Mountains with war trauma also led to a deeper understanding of the impact of any and all wars upon relationships, and families, that often continues to burden and disturb subsequent generations. It was here that I began to understand a need to take a closer look at war and gender issues which manifested as "Men, Women and War: And the War between Men and Women". These chapters carry some of my gender questions into another realm of exploration involving the healing potential in work with women and nature.

The Moon Rock experience, just at the edge of the Pacific Ocean, also served to expand my understanding of the cross-cultural potential of natural metaphors. Lessons learned there from my collaboration with a Brazilian shamana were to prove invaluable in preparing for the cross-cultural challenges of working with war trauma in Russia. The essential messages of the cross-cultural lessons offered by the natural world offer valuable resources for all of us working with trauma in private practice, clinics, official agencies or other settings.

My time in Russia offered many insights into the ongoing generational aftermath of war, revolution and man-made disaster. Over time, having learned from all three projects, it became increasingly clear that ALL social traumas, in essence, calls for creative ways to address both individual and collective overwhelm and the need to heal broken connections. In addition, all three projects served to emphasize the importance of "relative balance" and resiliency in all levels of trauma work.

It is my hope that by sharing some of these experiences that readers may become interested in possibilities for working with trauma which extend beyond the confines of medical models, state and government agencies and individual private practice. This book is an invitation to expand our thinking about trauma to include nature, shamanic wisdom, cross-cultural, non-verbal, kinesthetic methods, and an appreciation for the healing potential of community.

In keeping with my choice to retain a personal voice, I have foregone any emphasis on medical, psychological or other scientific explanations of trauma. Readers in search of a handbook or a textbook will not find those resources here. Those in search of that information will find excellent references in the extensive publications of Bessel Van der Kolk and his collaborators in Psychological Trauma and more recently Traumatic Stress: The Effects of Overwhelming Experience on Mind Body and Society.

More information on the somatic approach to an understanding and treatment of trauma is available in Peter

Levine's Waking the Tiger: Healing Trauma and in The Body Bears the Burden: Trauma Dissociation and Disease by Robert Scaer. I would refer those in search of self-help to Benjamin Colodzin's How to Survive Trauma. Gina Ross's Beyond the Trauma Vortex: The Media's Role in Healing Fear, Terror and Violence, carries Peter Levine's statement that "Trauma is the root of violence" into the realm of social activism.

Given the more contemplative nature of my approach as a trauma specialist and cultural historian, my piece of this unfolding collage remains with "connecting the dots", an ongoing process of exploring connections between our personal and familial destinies and the larger forces that shape human experience.

From Unstable Peace to Uneasy Settlements

From ancient times until the end of the Greek civil war in 1949, the area known as Macedonia was the field of recurring conquests, insurgencies, or terrorism sponsored by waxing and waning empires and neighboring states emerging out of the Ottoman Empire. Current Macedonia's first historical identity was as part of the much larger Kingdom of Macedonia believed to have been established in the 6th Century B.C. and expanded by Alexander the Great in the 4th Century B.C. For centuries thereafter, the territory known as Macedonia comprised a southern area now in Greece, Slavic Vardar Macedonia to the north, and eastern Pirin Macedonia within present-day Bulgaria. This area was taken over by the Roman Empire in 168 B.C., invaded by the Slavs in the 4th Century, captured by the Bulgars in the 9th, mostly absorbed into the Byzantine Empire in 1018, controlled by the Serb tsarist empire in the early 14th Century, and conquered by the Ottoman Empire in the Battle of Kosovo in 1389. The Ottoman Turks retained control until the early twentieth century.

A distinctly indigenous Macedonian national

consciousness did not arise until intellectuals from the area began to articulate the notion of a distinct local culture in the late nineteenth century. In 1893, a local political movement called the Internal Macedonian Revolutionary Organization (VMRO), fought for Macedonia's independence from the Ottoman Empire. This movement established a short-lived Republic of Krusevo in Macedonia, but their nationalist Ilinden Uprising in 1903 was quashed brutally by the Turks. As the Ottoman Empire declined, the ascendant Balkan states Serbia, Bulgaria and Greece supported guerrilla activity against the Turks on behalf of their respective nationalist causes, with several alliances shifting among them. In the First Balkan war of 1912, they expelled the Turks, agreed to divide the area, and granted independence to Albania.

Serbia was ceded the area comprising present-day Macedonia, but this was challenged in the Second Balkan War of 1913, when Bulgaria tried to annex the Serbian portion. Its defeat led to repartition of the larger area among Greece and Serbia, with a smaller eastern portion going to Bulgaria. As a result of World War I, the area of present-day Macedonia was placed under the Kingdom of Croats, Serbs and Slovenes, in which it was called South Serbia. Only when the Comintern created the Macedonian communist party within the Communist Balkan Federation in 1924 did the current boundaries begin to be regarded as a particular political jurisdiction. Yet during World War II, the Nazis captured Macedonia from Yugoslavia and gave its control to Bulgaria.

Course of the Conflict Pre-Existing Order

It was not until 1944 when Tito declared the existence of a "People's Republic of Macedonia," did the area first achieve some political and legal foundation. This action was taken in response to the demands of the increasingly self-conscious group of communists within the partisan movement who came from the Vardar area. It reduced Serbia's size, but retained control of Macedonia for Federal

Yugoslavia against Bulgarian and Greek interests. In 1946, the area became an autonomous republic with its own constitution within the new Socialist Federal Republic of Yugoslavia (SFRY). To link Yugoslavia while curtailing the Serbs' hegemony, who were sixty percent of the population, Tito granted more cultural autonomy and political authority to all the republics, including Macedonia.

Though that republic encompassed Albanians, Turks, and other groups, it was more tightly tied to the ethnic Macedonian majority, who were Orthodox, when Tito in 1967 revived an ancient bishopric that had existed at the southern city of Ohrid. This made the Macedonian Orthodox Church autocephalous. The 1974 Yugoslav Constitution bestowed yet more financial, judicial, and educational autonomy to the republics, and granted them authority over their own defense forces.

The collapse of communism was accompanied by economic decline throughout Yugoslavia, resulting in discontent directed toward the Federal government where Serbs were gaining greater influence. But Macedonia did not experience the same level of resentment toward the Serbs as was felt in the other republics. Most ethnic Macedonians at that time were pro-federation and shared with Serbia wariness toward the intentions of the ethnic Albanians who lived on both sides of their common border. Indeed, their first free parliamentary elections in November 1990 heard both Macedonian communists and nationalists approve of Albanian harassment, so the Albanians boycotted the election. Additionally, like Bosnia-Herze-govina, Macedonia was a poor republic that was heavily dependent on the federal redistributive policies coming from Belgrade, so President Kiro Gligorov was not inclined to secede.

Unstable Peace

In June, 1991, Gligorov proposed a loose confederal Yugoslavia, but by that time, Yugoslavia's de facto dissolution was proceeding through armed hostilities between Slovenia and Croatia, on the one hand, and the federal government in Belgrade, on the other. As a result, Macedonian leaders concluded they, too, must secede lest the Macedonians be left as a minority in a Serb-dominated rump Yugoslavia. In September, the government held a referendum in which 95% of the 72% eligible voters, including ethnic Macedonians living abroad, approved independence. Although the republic's Albanians as well as Serbs boycotted the referendum, the government declared sovereignty in November, held its first multi-party elections, and requested EC recognition and United Nations (UN) membership.

When Macedonia severed its ties to Yugoslavia, the potential for violent conflict increased not only with its former federal government, but several other fronts as well. This stemmed from its political identity being largely undefined in a new and uncertain environment of revived and contending nationalisms. Independence Day September 8, 1991 was a political apotheosis for Macedonian nationalists, culminating their own particular search for a sovereign state. But the fact that Macedonia had never before had its own exclusive government created considerable uneasiness. The Serbian, Albanian, as well as Bulgarian nationalisms that were also active in the region could upset the new country's uneasy internal ethnic relations and/or invite intrusions from a neighboring state.

As a pretense for aggressive actions against Macedonia, some of these nationalist movements could cite a past era when their ancestors had founded a political entity in the larger Macedonia region, and they could point to historical moments when opposed groups or states suppressed their cultural distinctiveness. Thus, the basic threat to Macedonian stability was not internal ideological, economic, or even cultural cleavages, but a more immediate matter of its future political control. How would a free-standing Macedonian state, in which about 64% of the population was ethnic Macedonian, relate to and integrate the several other ethnic groups living within and across its borders?

Three other Yugoslav republics were finding they could not reconcile the same kind of pressures, short of going to war. Although Macedonia thus faced threats on several sides, the most pressing question was how a contracted Yugoslavia, dominated by the Serbs, would react to Macedonia's independence. The Serbian political elite led by President Slobodan Milosevic had already been forced by Slovenia's break-away to give up trying to restructure the emerging post-communist Yugoslavia under Serbian hegemony. But another "Greater Serbia" vision, promoted by radical Serbian nationalists, favored uniting those areas inhabited by self-declared ethnic Serbs, such as the Krajina in Croatia, together with areas like Kosovo and Macedonia that had few Serbs but were regarded as part of Serbia historically.

The leader of the Serb Radical Party, Vojislav Seselj, said in 1991, "Three states will come out of Yugoslavia, Greater Serbia, Small Croatia, and even smaller Slovenia...And Macedonia has always been the Serb territory..Macedonians, Moslems, and Montenegrins are fictitious nations." Many Serbians referred to Macedonia by its interwar name, South Serbia, and still viewed Macedonians as having no distinct identity and their language as Bulgarian. The Serbian Church had never recognized the Macedonian Church. Yet in late 1991 and early 1992, despite increasing ethnic consciousness on both sides and the potential for tensions right after independence, no hostilities between Macedonia and Serbia broke out. Pursuing a policy it called "active neutrality," the Macedonian government pledged friendly relations with all neighbors.

After parliament voted that the Serbian-dominated Yugoslav army (JNA) should leave, Gligorov negotiated an agreement that removed it by April. But this peaceful departure was mainly possible only because Milosevic could not afford to keep troops both in Macedonia and fight the Bosnian war. He also reasoned that, left economically dependent and exposed to the depredations of what were known as the "three wolves" (Albania, Bulgaria, and Greece), Macedonia would crawl back to Serbian protection. This view was later reinforced by the collateral effects of the economic sanctions against the FRY of November 1991 and May 1992. Hence, although there appeared to be no immediate threat, because the JNA took every weapon and piece of equipment it could carry and destroyed the rest, the new Macedonian state was defenseless.

The negotiated pullout left Macedonia vulnerable in the face of possible Serb aggression, such as upon conclusion of the war in Bosnia. Also, Macedonia's efforts to be recognized by the U.S. and the EU and others as a sovereign state and thus deserving the protection called for under the UN Charter had been thwarted by the Greek government. Consequently, as soon as mid-1992, Macedonia and members of the international community began to fear that the war between Serbians and the Bosnian government might "spill over" into Macedonia. This might take the form of a direct Serbian attack on Macedonia, or intensified repression by the Belgrade government of the Albanian majority in Kosovo, a previously autonomous area in Serbia that borders Macedonia.

The latter could incite nearby Albania to come to their brothers in arms and/or a Kosovar uprising that could spur a large influx of refugees into Macedonia. Either event might unsettle the internal ethnic balance and destabilize the part-Albanian and fragile coalition government of the newly-independent, multi-ethnic and fledgling democracy. Its disintegration could also occur through subversion from the North. Ethnic Serbs in Macedonia were only two percent of the population and Milosevic had not claimed they were threatened as he had regarding the Serbs in Kosovo and

Bosnia. Yet, the radical Serbian nationalist Vojislav Seselj looked to exploit the discontent of Macedonia's Serbs, and Serbian elements are believed to have assisted cells of Serbian nationalists in Macedonia.

In short, although independence had provoked no immediate adverse reaction from Serbia, the longer the Bosnian war continued, Macedonia increasingly worried that changes in the Serbs' fortune might prompt them to recapture Macedonia or cause it to fall apart from within. The war in Bosnia thus focused the attention of U.S. and other governments to some extent on the wider region as well. In the fall 1992 they initiated several explicitly preventive initiatives. In late summer 1992, President Gligorov requested international observers to monitor the border with Serbia. In early fall, President Bush urged the Committee for Security and Cooperation in Europe (CSCE) to place observer missions in Macedonia, Kosovo, and other still peaceful areas of rump Yugoslavia. The idea was to discourage the aggravation of ethnic tensions and to alert the international community to the earliest signs of conflict.

The CSCE Council of Ministers (CoM) authorized the CSCE Spillover Monitoring Mission for Macedonia in September and gave it the job of monitoring the northern border. Its officials periodically visited Macedonia's leaders and neighboring capitals, including Belgrade, and paid visits where border incidents occurred, ensuring that their presence was known to local and international media. Visiting UN headquarters in early November, Gligorov also requested the deployment of a United Nations peacekeeping force to monitor the border. The co-chairs of the Steering Committee of the ICFY, Lord David Owen and Thorward Stoltenberg, suggested a fact-finding team be sent. In accordance with the team's recommendations, UN Secretary General Boutros-Ghali proposed the deployment of a battalion of approximately 700 men as an extension of the United Nations Protection

Force (UNPROFOR) in Croatia. Resolution 795 passed the Security Council with no opposition in December.

The world's first multilateral preventive deployment was put in place in January, 1993, composed of 500 Canadians, who were replaced in February by 700 Swedish, Norwegian, and Finnish troops. The force was organized into a separate command from UNPROFOR, with the name, United Nations Preventive Deployment Force (UNPREDEP) in March, 1995. By far the largest international mission in the country, the military contingent was 1,050-persons strong at its height in 1996, having been supplemented by U.S. troops in 1993. The deployment's mandate was to patrol the Macedonian side of the 240 kilometer-long Serbian and 180 km Albanian border, monitor and report developments that could threaten Macedonia, and "by its presence, deter such threats from any source, as well as help prevent clashes which could otherwise occur between external elements and Macedonian forces, thus helping to strengthen security and confidence in Macedonia."

Troops were positioned at a string of temporary observation posts, from which small patrols are sent out. The instructions to post commanders were to report the occurrence of specified threatening events, but retreat from any significant attack, returning fire only in self-defense. Border patrols approached intruders in non- threatening ways to inform them of the administrative line and request their return, which in most instances has occurred. The mission's civilian police supervised Macedonian police and civil authorities in border areas with large proportions of Serbs and Albanian minorities. Although the deployment of the OSCE mission UNPREDEP prevented the unstable relations between Serbia and Macedonia from developing into a crisis that could escalate into violence, it did not succeed in stabilizing them entirely.

As the war continued, there were further grounds for believing that changes in the Serbs' fortune might prompt them to recapture Macedonia or help it fall apart from within. FRY had not recognized the new state or agreed to an international border in place of the internal boundary. As late as 1994, Macedonia was still viewed in Belgrade as a seceding republic whose departure led it to economic disaster and to the risk of disintegration, due to the pressures from Albania and Bulgaria and the internal plotting of ethnic Albanians in Macedonia. Public comments by Serb leadership, combined with the fact that the Former Republic of Yugoslavia (FRY) had not recognized Macedonia or agreed to an official international border in place of the internal boundary, exacerbated Macedonia's fears.

In November 1993, for example, in a press conference with Greek Foreign Minister Michael Papaconstantinou, Milosevic referred to Macedonia in tenuous terms and spoke of a confederation with Greece. As late as 1994, Macedonia was apparently still viewed in Belgrade as a secessionist republic whose departure led it to economic disaster and to the risk of disintegration, due to both internal and external pressures. The pro-regime Belgrade press and Serbian ultra-nationalists continued to see "South Serbia" as going through a trying transition on the way to eventual reunion. After the 1994 census, the Serbian press rejected the results by claiming Macedonia actually had ten times the number of Serbs recorded. Many Serbians still viewed Macedonians as having no distinct identity and their language as Bulgarian.

Furthermore, the Serbian Church never recognized the Macedonian Orthodox archbishopric granted by Tito in 1967. Despite the presence of a deterrent force, the behaviour of Serbian border troops seemed to corroborate the notion of persisting Serbian designs on Macedonia. Small contingents of Serb forces would periodically penetrate the border, occupy a place for hours or days, and eventually retreat, but only after tensions sometimes arose and negotiations were required. In one instance, in June 1994, Serbian soldiers took over for several weeks a mountaintop in the northeast known as Hill 1703, which has an especially strategic vantage on Macedonia, Serbia and Bulgaria. Macedonia troops gathered in the area, but for awhile, the Serbs refused to leave or negotiate. Although the evidence is ambiguous as to whether or not the Serbs intended or were able to engage in more aggressive actions, clearly, Serb forces were at least testing the Macedonian government and the international peacekeeping force.

Conflict Abatement and Settlement

Although the Macedonia-FRY relationship remained uncertain and unstable from 1992 through 1995, it never reached the level of high tensions, low level violence, or open war. Aside from occasional border infractions, there were few instances of overt hostilities or even confrontation. Independence and the withdrawal of the JNA were negotiated bilaterally, yet deeper relations were not established because of the pressures of nationalists in Belgrade and pre-occupation with the Bosnia war. But neither did it enter anything like peaceful conflict through institutionalized bargaining and formal bi- lateral diplomacy. Then, following the Bosnian war Macedonian-FRY relations began to reflect more normal inter-state relations, at least minimally. Following the signing of the Dayton Accords in 1995, the FRY recognized Macedonia and economic traffic was fully restored.

The border issue was taken up by the Macedonian-FRY border commission, although it has proceeded very slowly because of Serb delays so an agreed boundary remains undecided. Macedonia was admitted to the OSCE, the Council of Europe, and the Partnership for Peace, and began receiving IMF and World Bank loans. The seemingly explosive situation in the Kosovo area added another pressure on Macedonia's territorial integrity and internal stability. The growing confrontation between Serbians and Albanians, particularly since the late 1980's potentially affected Macedonia because under Yugoslavia, Kosovo

Albanians were tied through family, economics, and frequent travel to those in Macedonia. Many highly educated Albanians studied at Kosovo's Prishtina University.

Were tensions to rise further there, masses of Albanian refugees might push into Macedonia and upset the ethnic Macedonian-Albanian balance. Thus, Kosovo's brethren Albanians in Macedonia and Albania might move through Macedonia against Serbia, possibly causing Serbia to attack. The escalation to civil war in Kosovo in 1998 increased the potential for destabilizing Macedonia that have been presented by Serbs directly and indirectly. For one thing, Macedonia has been put increasingly in the position of being an antagonist toward the rump Yugoslavia that is associated with the NATO policies. After the Macedonian government chose to recognise Taiwan as a sovereign state, having been offered economic aid, China vetoed the UN Security Council decision to renew the mandate of UNPREDEP when it came up for renewal in late 1998.

The mission was thus terminated, but in its stead, troops from the NATO alliance replaced those from UNPREDEP who had been patrolling its borders. After the bombing of Serbia commenced in March, 1999, Serb troops captured three US soldiers along the border and are holding them as prisoners of war. Since then, more NATO has arrived. Demonstrations against the NATO presence have apparently been attended by ethnic Macedonians as well as Serbs. Second, Macedonia's necessary reception of large numbers of Albanian refugees escaping the Kosovo conflict has not only placed on it a significant financial and logistical burden, but threatened to provoke its fragile internal ethnic Macedonian- Albanian modus vivendi.

Macedonian farmers protested violently against the use of their land for refugee camps, for example, and the forced nighttime expulsion of thousands of refugees from the temporary Blace camp and their deportation to other countries not only took the international humanitarian organizations by surprise, it threatened to provoke reactions from the Albanian citizens in Macedonia and their leaders in the government coalition. As a result, although NATO has pledged protection of Macedonia from external attack, that war may yet undo the value of the preventive measures that have been taken quite deliberately and been moderately successful so far, due to its weight on the domestic political fabric on which Macedonia's survival as a state has relied.

2

The United States and Islamic Radicals

U.S. Traded Freedom for Oil

When President George W. Bush used his State of the Union address to decry U.S. dependence on Middle Eastern oil, he made headlines. Two days later, when Donald Rumsfeld offered an apocalyptic rendering of the global war on terror—"they will either succeed in changing our way of life, or we will succeed in changing theirs"—few paid much attention. In the juxtaposition of the president's discovery and his defense secretary's call to arms lays the real story, casting in sharp relief the strategic conundrum facing the United States.

That Americans are "addicted to oil," relying increasingly on imports from what the president delicately called "unstable parts of the world," is manifestly true. The admission qualifies as noteworthy only in that it took Bush so long to acknowledge the problematic implications of this dependency.

Secretary of Defense Rumsfeld's extravagant depiction of the war on terror may also be true—but only so long as the United States persists in the very addiction that the president laments. End American dependence on Middle Eastern oil and the very notion of Islamic radicals posing a serious threat to our way of life becomes preposterous. End our dependence on Middle Eastern oil and the notion that the United States should take it upon itself to forcibly change their way of life becomes absurd. Terrorism won't disappear, but it will become a nuisance rather than a dire threat.

The dependency President Bush inveighs against didn't spring from nowhere. As with most addictions, it evolved over time, in plain view but incrementally. In its early stages, few Americans approved of this habit outright, but most persuaded themselves that it was manageable. So as our houses got bigger, our cars heavier, and our commutes longer, the amount of oil we import kept creeping up from one year to the next.

To their credit, every one of Bush's predecessors going back to Richard Nixon has warned against the consequences of permanent energy dependence. None did so more presciently than Jimmy Carter in his much-derided "Crisis of Confidence" speech of July 1979. "Down that road," he cautioned, "lies a mistaken idea of freedom, the right to grasp for ourselves some advantage over others. That path would be one of constant conflict, ending in chaos." Restoring self-sufficiency, on the other hand, might enable Americans to "seize control again of our common destiny."

Despite such admirable talk coming from on high, U.S. policies after 1979—Carter's included—served only to undercut further America's control over its own fate. Feeding the daily habit of cheap gas took precedence over longer-term considerations. As our appetite for oil increased so too did our exertions in the Middle East. As the U.S. military presence in the Persian Gulf grew, especially beginning with Operation Desert Storm in 1991, so too did the costs of maintaining our habit. While no one noticed, the pain involved in cleaning up our act had become too great to contemplate. Only now we are beginning to glimpse the results. By blithely abdicating control of our destiny, we forfeited our freedom of action. Oil now calls the tune to which the self-proclaimed world's sole superpower is obliged to dance.

Leave it to Donald Rumsfeld to spell out the implications. If we take him at his word, the United States now finds itself with no choice but to transform the politics, culture, and mores of the Islamic world—for surely, it is these things that constitute their "way of life." If Rumsfeld gets his way, that is, the enterprise that the Pentagon now refers to as "the Long War" will not end with Iraq. Indeed, it has barely begun.

Yet Iraq alone, in addition to taking the lives of over 2,200 American soldiers, is currently draining some $4.5 billion per month from the U.S. Treasury, with no end to those expenditures in sight. The Nobel Prize-winning economist Joseph Stiglitz projects that the war's total cost may reach $2 trillion. U.S. military spending this year will easily exceed a half-trillion dollar, a figure that will only increase in the years to come.

This is money that we don't have: continuing to indulge our oil habit means plunging ever deeper into debt. But like the sorriest dopester, we cling to the tacit assumption that our line of credit is endless and that the bills will never come due. Bush has considerable firsthand experience with dependency. In his memoir A Charge to Keep, he writes candidly of wrestling with a drinking problem. On his own personal day of reckoning, Bush took responsibility for that problem and vowed to "drink no more." Had he not done so, by his own testimony, Bush today would be hanging out at some bar back in Houston rather than occupying the Oval Office?

As America's collective day of reckoning draws near, going cold turkey is not a practical option. But neither is demanding that "their" way of life change to accommodate our addiction. In that way lies only the constant conflict and chaos that Jimmy Carter foretold, not to mention moral complications beyond calculation. In Bush's personal story is the beginning of wisdom: preserving what you value most requires the will to abandon self-destructive habits. Preserving the American way of life requires that we first regain control of it. We must change. Though not yet fully recognized, this is the real challenge of our times.

The events of September 11, 2001 shook the foundations of the world's only superpower. Approximately 3,000 lives were lost in the tragic attacks on American soil. The United States quickly determined that the radical Islamic group al Qaeda bore responsibility for the horrendous act. Since then, President George W. Bush has vowed to fight terrorism until the threat to the U.S. is completely eradicated. Adopting a proactive policy, the U.S. attacked the al Qaeda base in Afghanistan in October 2001, forcing the Taliban regime that harbored al Qaeda from power. Despite an outright victory in the war against the Taliban and al Qaeda, Afghanistan remains unstable and al Qaeda continues to operate around the world.

The situation is not much different in Iraq where U.S. military force has toppled the regime of Saddam Hussein. Successful al Qaeda terrorist attacks around the world following American military action in both Afghanistan and Iraq highlight the difficulty of devising a strategy to combat even one radical Islamic group, let alone eradicating the threat from all groups. As military operations against both al Qaeda forces in Afghanistan and elements of Saddam Hussein's late regime in Iraq continues, and speculation concerning an expansion of America's current war against terrorism increases, the world hopes that the end to this campaign will bring long-lasting peace. Application of the concept of Game Theory to the conduct of the war on terrorism, however, indicates that one should not be optimistic about future prospects for peace between the U.S. and radical Islamic groups.

Game Theory

Unlike games that one observes in the sporting world, "games of theory" are interactive exercises that require one to think strategically. A "game" is a competitive situation where opposing players try to make moves according to particular strategies that promise to yield the best "payoffs" for them. A fundamental premise of a game is that a single player cannot dictate the outcome. The strategies of all the players involved in the game determine the outcome. "Game Theory" is thus a study of decision-making in a situation where there is either a combination of conflict and cooperation or total conflict between the players.

A "game" can consist of two or more players. For the purpose of this discussion, two clearly defined players will be used, the U.S. and radical Islamic groups, both of whom are willing to resort to violence as a means of achieving their objectives. According to the tenets of Game Theory, there are two major types of games: sequential and simultaneous. In a sequential game, one finds a strict order of play; one player makes a move and the other has a chance to study it before reacting. This creates a situation where one player makes a move in consideration of future consequences. A sequential game that continues over several plays is known as an iterated game. In this particular game, there can be evolution of cooperation between the players, as, over time, they realize the possibility of a mutually beneficial strategy.

A simultaneous game, on the other hand, is one in which both players make decisions that are implemented at the same time and are independent of the other player's actions. The knowledge of any previously employed strategy of the opponent is not available in this situation. As a consequence both players have to base their moves on what they think the other player is likely to do. In this discussion, the "game" is sequential. The U.S. has complete knowledge of a move made by radical Islamic groups and takes that into account before making a decision. Similarly, a U.S. move towards radical Islamic groups is not covert and can be studied by the radicals before they take any further action.

The games structured in Game Theory can also be divided into two categories based on the final outcome: zero-sum and non-zero sum games. A zero-sum game is one in which a gain for one player automatically results in an equivalent loss for the other. The total sum of the payoffs for the players taking part in the game is always zero or some constant. Unlike zero-sum games, non-zero sum games are ones in which a gain for one player does not automatically imply a loss for the other. In this situation, there is no relationship between the payoffs for different players and the sum of the payoffs is neither zero nor a constant. In the case of the U.S. versus radical Islamic groups, the game is of a non-zero nature, as are most games in the real world.

The following discussion will try to demonstrate that merely one or even a few victories for either side will not completely ensure the eradication of the other. It may be clear at this point that the U.S. is the better defined of the two players. Its opponent in this game, "radical Islamic groups," needs to be defined to afford a fair discussion. These groups do not include every single Muslim radical group present in the world today. Rather, they include only those groups that are inclined to resort to violence as a means to harm U.S. interests in their quest to achieve their objectives. It is also assumed that the radical Islamic groups included in this study have preferences in line with the established parameters of this game. They may be "state sponsored" but so long as they are willing to use violence against the U.S. to further their cause and have preferences in accordance with the set perimeters of the game they are categorized as the "player" opposing the U.S. in this game.

The players in every game implement strategies. The term "strategy" refers to a course of action followed to achieve a desired objective. The players are bound to use a combination of different strategies to achieve their desired "outcome." An outcome is deemed favorable if it pushes the player closer to his goal. An outcome leads to a "payoff" in a game. A "payoff" constitutes the reward obtained by pursuing a particular strategy and is affected by the strategy implemented by the opposing player. A favorable outcome depicts a positive payoff while an unfavorable outcome reflects a negative payoff for a player.

A "payoff matrix," or "payoff table," is used to depict mathematically the payoffs that each player can achieve for every possible combination of the available strategies. Each individual cell in the payoff matrix lists the payoffs expected by the players when the combination of the strategies associated with the particular cell is implemented. The payoffs in the game being developed are based on assigning integer values to established parameters. These parameters depict particular situations that can logically be expected to occur for the two sides in the real world. The single integer that depicts the final payoff value for each combination of strategies is calculated by summing up the individual values assigned to each parameter for the particular combination.

The values assigned to the parameters are arbitrary. The numbers are important in relative terms, and it is the relative magnitude of the final payoffs that depicts one strategy being preferable for a particular player than some other. It is also important to examine another concept fundamental to Game Theory: the "Nash Equilibrium." Game Theory operates under the logical assumption that in any game, the players involved will constantly try to pursue a strategy that would offer them the highest payoff. In the following game model, it is evident that both the U.S. and the radical Islamic groups would want to pursue the strategy that would provide the highest payoff for them regardless of the payoff their strategy would bring to the opponent.

In a sequential game, however, the strategy adopted by one player will be governed not only by the urge to achieve the highest payoff, but it also will be modified by the strategy employed by the other player. Hence, neither player is able to follow the strategy they would have followed in the absence of the other player and have to choose alternate strategies that would serve them best in light of the strategies pursued by the opponent.

This causes both players to abandon their most preferable strategies. They thus end up pursuing a set of strategies that each player believes yields the best payoff for each one individually given the strategy employed by the other player. This set of strategies is known as the "Nash Equilibrium" for the particular game. In short, this term refers to a position in which neither player might like to be optimally, but which neither is inclined to alter unilaterally on account of its dependency upon the strategy of the other player.

Bearing in mind the current situation in the conflict between radical Islamic groups and the U.S., it is now necessary to evaluate the conflict's outcome and impact on the world's future. In so doing, one must define the objectives of the two sides and list the strategic alternatives available to them. The U.S. seeks to eradicate threats posed to it by radical Islamic groups. This would entail continuing its interventionist policy in the Muslim world and maintaining a physical presence in Muslim countries. Radical Islamic groups are bent on removing American presence from the Muslim world and forcing the U.S. to abandon its manipulation of the affairs of Muslim countries.

These objectives are those that have never been stated publicly by either of the players in question, but careful examination of the motives of both sides based on past actions can be used to determine their respective objectives. Based on public pronouncements, the American campaign against radical Islamic groups seeks to eliminate "terrorism" and enhance freedom in the world. Similarly, radical Islamic groups have proclaimed that their goal is to create an environment where Islam can be practiced without oppression or fear.

Strategic Alternatives Available

For the purpose of this game, both players have three strategic alternatives. The U.S. might withdraw its presence from Muslim countries and refrain from interfering in their affairs. It could also continue its pre-September 11, 2001 policy of maintaining its presence in the Muslim world and manipulation of the affairs of Muslim countries. In adopting this strategy, the U.S. does not employ military force to achieve its objectives. Finally, the U.S. could use military force to destroy networks of radical Islamic groups or to retaliate against any acts of violence against U.S. interests. In contrast, radical Islamic groups might abandon acts of violence completely.

They could apply pressure through Muslim masses and governments of Muslim countries, and continue threatening the U.S. with violent attacks. The actual attacks are not conducted in this strategy. Finally, radical Islamic groups might conduct violent attacks against U.S. interests. To be sure, there are many more strategic alternatives available to both sides in the real world. The alternatives presented here are undoubtedly the most significant and the discussion will be limited to them. Having determined the strategic alternatives available to both players in this game, a payoff matrix depicting all possible combinations of strategies can be created.

Each cell in the table signifies a combination of strategies that might be implemented. As described earlier, the actual set of strategies pursued will represent the "Nash Equilibrium" for the game provided it is not a strategy that is preferable to both players, regardless of what the other player does. To arrive at final payoff values for both players, it is necessary to set the criterion for assigning individual integer values to each combination of strategies depicted in the matrix.

- Get the other party to accede to all demands and thus win the game: +, - 100.
- Completely give up goals and quit the game: +, - 100.
- A situation created that provides a realistic opportunity for either player to inflict further loss upon the opponent after an initial loss has been inflicted: +, - 50.
- A situation where the opportunity to cause further loss to the opponent (mentioned in the above scenario) after an initial loss has actually been realized by some action of the player: +, - 100.
- Any uncertainty or element of mistrust involved in a situation: +, - 50.
- A situation that provides a chance for propaganda to be employed by either player to gain support for future actions: +, - 50.
- Reaction of the supporters of both sides for every combination of strategies: +, - 100.
- An act that might gain something for the player in the short run but is likely to have dire consequences in the future: +, - 50.

(N.B. A partial gain or loss in any of the above scenarios will be assigned half of the payoff points listed for the particular scenario.)

From the U.S. Perspective

Withdraw presence and abandon manipulation/Give up acts of violence: In this instance, the U.S. would abandon its bases in the Muslim world and refrain from manipulating the affairs oı Muslim countries. Radical Islamic groups, in turn, would agree to give up acts involving violence. This would be an ideal situation, enhancing world peace and offering a permanent solution to the ongoing conflict. The execution of the agreement to stop all acts of violence, however, cannot be guaranteed. The U.S. would always doubt that radical Islamic groups would refrain from attacking American interests since most of them operate as small independent cells rather than under a central command. Under these circumstances, there would he ever-present uncertainty for the U.S.

Withdrawing its presence from Muslim countries and abandoning manipulation of Muslim affairs would constitute U.S. abandonment of its objective. The international community at large, and U.S. allies in particular, hopeful of achieving long-lasting peace at the end of this conflict, are likely to support this scenario (+50). CUMULATIVE PAYOFF: -100

Withdraw presence and abandon manipulation/Apply pressure and threaten U.S.: This would involve a situation where the U.S. would have to withdraw from the Muslim world and refrain from intervening in the affairs of Muslim countries. Here, the U.S. would give in to the demands of radical Islamic groups due to some unforeseen problem that makes it impossible for them to continue its presence in and manipulation of the Muslim world (-100). U.S. allies would view this as a sign of American weakness (-50). Radical Islamic groups could take advantage of this weakness by pressing for acceptance of further demands which might eventually force the U.S. to somewhat alter its policies (-50). CUMULATIVE PAYOFF: -200

Withdraw presence and abandon manipulation/ Conduct acts of violence: This might involve a situation where the U.S. agrees to withdraw its forces from the Muslim world, partly as a cosmetic measure (-100). U.S. allies will again see this as giving in to the demands of radical Islamic groups (-50). In this scenario, radical Islamic groups will actually conduct an attack against American interests even after the U.S. carried out its withdrawal, inflicting further loss upon it (-100). CUMULATIVE PAYOFF: -250

Maintain presence and manipulation/Give up acts of violence: The U.S. would continue to maintain its current presence in Muslim countries and manipulation of Muslim affairs (+100) while radical Islamic groups unilaterally cease to pursue their objectives through the use of violence. This scenario is unlikely to arise in the real world because Muslim radicals view death or "martyrdom and the attendant promise of heaven" as preferable to surrender. This, in fact, is a major factor that helps Islamic radicals enlist support for their cause from Muslim governments and Muslim masses. U.S. allies are sure to view this as a positive event (+50). CUMULATIVE PAYOFF: +150

Maintain presence and manipulation/Apply pressure and threaten U.S.: The U.S. would continue to maintain its presence and constantly intervene in Muslim countries (+100) while radical Islamic groups continue to press for acceptance of their demands. This is the situation the world has been facing for quite some time now. This no-win situation is trying the patience of the international community at large, and all but a few hard-liners want an end to this state of affairs. (-50). CUMULATIVE PAYOFF: +50

Maintain presence and manipulation/Conduct acts of violence: In this scenario, the U.S. maintains its physical presence in and manipulation of the affairs of Muslim countries (+100). Radical Islamic groups continue to voice their demands but also use force in an attempt at coercion. The pressure and attacks would represent losses for the U.S. (-100). U.S. allies would surely denounce such terrorist acts as they did after the attack of September 11, 2001. They would want to see the U.S. react in light of the Bush administration's strong commitment to take decisive action in these matters. But this situation presumes no attempt by the U.S. to counter the attacks militarily.

If the current administration decides to retreat from its promises to take a firm stance against terrorism worldwide, it is likely to lose credibility at home and abroad. Such an event is likely to induce a negative reaction from U.S. allies (-50). This exceptional situation would arise only if the U.S. was desperate to win the support of the Muslim masses in order to regain moral legitimacy following its controversial intervention in Iraq or elsewhere in case of a similar intervention in the future. This approach could be interpreted as a weakness of the U.S. and could pave the way for future concessions to radical Islamic groups (-50).

Those groups would take advantage of the opportunity and threaten to, if not actually conduct, another attack, thus creating great uncertainty in the U.S., as has been the case since the events of September 11, 2001(-50). CUMULATIVE PAYOFF: -150

Use military force/Give up acts of violence: In this scenario, the U.S. would use military force to eliminate radical Islamic groups. For the radicals to give up their objectives, the U.S. would have to destroy them completely (+100). U.S. allies would view this as a move by the U.S. to establish a peaceful world and support its cause, as they did in the operation against al- Qaeda in Afghanistan (+50).

This possibility, however, represents a utopian state, as the U.S. would never be sure that it had extinguished all radical Islamic groups. This problem is fueling discussion in the U.S. to expand military intervention to other countries after finishing its anti-terrorist campaigns in Afghanistan and Iraq. Thus, the uncertainty of the extent of success, and of what to expect in the future will always exist (-50). CUMULATIVE PAYOFF: +100

Use military force/Apply pressure and threaten U.S.: Here, the U.S. would use force against radical Islamic groups in an attempt to demolish them. The radicals would respond by threatening attacks against U.S. interests. This is likely to happen in every conflict between the two sides, as was evident in the early days of the operation in Afghanistan. Radical Islamic groups realize that they do not have the capability to win a military conflict against superior U.S. military force, and thus are likely to resort to threats of attacks against U.S. interests. For such threats to be deemed credible, radical Islamic groups would have to be strong enough to at least carry out some of them. Thus, the objective from the U.S. perspective would not have been achieved.

Reaction from U.S. allies would be mixed; some would support America's use of force while others would be more concerned about the possibility of the threatened attacks (0). An uncertain atmosphere would prevail due to continuous threats of future attacks, as has been the case in the U.S. since September 11, 2001 (-50). CUMULATIVE PAYOFF: -50

Use military force/Conduct acts of violence: In this instance, the threat of attacks would materialize in retaliation to the use of military force by the U.S. The threatened attacks would obviously make clear that the initial military campaign by the U.S. failed to eliminate all radical Islamic groups. This would again create an uncertain atmosphere (-50). Additionally, U.S. allies would be extremely wary of the consequences of any future military assault on the radicals knowing that it would potentially lead to a retaliatory attack. They would press the U.S. to adopt alternate means to achieve its objective (-50). CUMULATIVE PAYOFF: -100

From the Perspective of Radical Islamic Groups

Withdraw presence and abandon manipulation/Give up acts of violence: In this situation, the U.S. would agree to remove its presence from the Muslim world and refrain from intervening in the affairs of Muslim countries (+100). Radical Islamic groups, in turn, would cease all violent attacks against U.S. interests. Yet, they would not trust the U.S. to fulfill its promises (-50). Supporters of radical Islamic groups would see this as a victory for the radicals (+50). They would view this as submission by the U.S. to the demands of the radicals and hence would agree to abandon the use of violence to achieve their objectives. CUMULATIVE PAYOFF: +100

Withdraw presence and abandon manipulation/Apply pressure and threaten U.S.: This again represents an unlikely scenario where the U.S. might withdraw its presence from the Muslim world and abandon its interventionist policy in Muslim countries in the face of some unforeseen pressure (+100). Radical Islamic groups, capitalizing on the weakness of the U.S. apparent from its unilateral withdrawal, would apply pressure on the U.S. to accept further demands (+50). Supporters of radical Islamic groups are likely to welcome this development and would surely perceive this as a sign of American weakness (+50). This scenario might provide the radicals with an opportunity to publicize to the world the fact that the U.S. withdrawal, in effect, offers proof of victory and acceptance of their "just cause" (+50). CUMULATIVE PAYOFF: +250

Withdraw presence and abandon manipulation/ Conduct acts of violence: The U.S. would give up its objectives due to domestic pressures or a promise from radical Islamic groups to abort violent attacks against American interests (+100). The radicals, however, would renege on their promise and conduct such an attack. This would signify added loss for the U.S. after having given up its objective in the first place (+100). Radical Islamic groups might lose the support of their own masses for having indulged in blatant fraud and having unnecessarily invited the possibility of retaliation from the U.S. (-50). CUMULATIVE PAYOFF: +150

Maintain presence and manipulation/Give up acts of violence: In this case, the U.S. would maintain its presence in the Muslim world and continue its manipulation of the affairs of Muslim countries, paying no heed to the demands of radical Islamic groups (-100). Simultaneously, radical Islamic groups would give up their objectives due to either lack of unity or extreme financial constraints. This situation, which is unlikely to occur, would signify total defeat for radical Islamic groups, shocking and disappointing their supporters (-50). The U.S. could, at a later time, capitalize on the weakness of the radicals and attempt to eliminate them completely in an effort to achieve its ultimate goal (-50). CUMULATIVE PAYOFF: -200

Maintain presence and manipulation/Apply pressure and threaten U.S.: The U.S. would persist in its interventionist policy and presence in the Muslim world (-100) while radical Islamic groups would continue to threaten the U.S. This is the situation the world witnessed for a long time before September 11, 2001. Both parties continue to accuse the other of damaging its interests. The radicals, conscious of the military superiority of the U.S., continue to threaten violence. Mere threats, however, cannot be assigned a payoff, as they do not signify a gain or loss for either side. Supporters of both sides oppose this scenario. In fact, allies of radical Islamic groups would view this situation as representing a lack of concrete progress towards the achievement of their aims (-50). CUMULATIVE PAYOFF: -150

Maintain presence and manipulation/Conduct acts of violence: In this scenario, radical Islamic groups, frustrated by the lack of achievement through mere threats, would conduct an attack against American interests. The U.S., despite the attack, would maintain its presence and continue its intervention in Muslim countries, thus preventing the radicals from achieving their goal (-100). Radical Islamic groups would then conduct an extensive propaganda campaign to portray to the world how the attacks are actually a last resort to achieve their objective (+50). This is the current policy being pursued by al Qaeda leadership. They have been largely successful in their propaganda campaign and al Qaeda membership is believed to be on the rise since the 2001 attacks.

While the Muslim masses are likely to oppose the violent attacks, they might actually be convinced of U.S. bias and might see this as the only recourse to achieve their goals. The likelihood that allies of radical Islamic groups would support such a move increases as the U.S. expands the scope of its current military interventions. Consequently, supporters of radical Islamic groups can be expected to back the radicals' future actions (+50). CUMULATIVE PAYOFF: 0

Use military force/Give up acts of violence: The U.S. would either initiate an extensive and successful military campaign against radical Islamic groups in order to achieve its ultimate objective of destroying them or it would retaliate to counter extreme threats from the radicals. In this scenario, it is assumed that at the end of American military action the radicals' network would be crippled to the point where they would be unable to stage a comeback (-100). Supporters of radical Islamic groups would be shocked by their defeat (-50). The loss of life and materials incurred by the radicals, however, would be an effective propaganda tool and is sure to win support from the Muslim masses (+50). This support would be essential to recruit men into the radicals' forces, a necessity after the losses incurred by the radicals due to successful use of force by the U.S. Yet, the loss of financial prowess would prevent radical Islamic groups from staging a comeback (-50). CUMULATIVE PAYOFF: -150

Use military force/Apply pressure and threaten U.S.: This situation was witnessed in the early days of the American military operation in Afghanistan. The U.S. would use military force and inflict severe damage upon the militarily weak radical Islamic groups while maintaining its interventionist policy in the Muslim world (-100). The U.S. might actually be successful in achieving its ultimate objective of wiping out the radicals if it pursued a comprehensive campaign (-50). Radical Islamic groups would be left with no option but to continue threatening the U.S. with attacks. Their supporters would be disheartened by their defeat (-50). Sympathy due to loss of life in the conflict might at the same time be used as an effective propaganda tool and help the radicals in securing future financial and personnel support (+50). CUMULATIVE PAYOFF: -150

Use military force/Conduct acts of violence: Radical Islamic groups will be strong enough to conduct an attack on U.S. interests and will do so, as they did on September 11, 2001. This would not ensure achievement of their objectives, but it would incite a reaction from the U.S. The U.S. military campaign could be extensive enough to engulf all radical Islamic groups, unlike the operation targeted solely against the al Qaeda network in Afghanistan, and thus create a situation that could cause extensive damage to the radicals' network (-50).

The U.S. would maintain its presence in and continue its manipulation of Muslim countries (-100). The U.S. military campaign, however, would provide an opportunity for the radicals to die for their cause and provide ground for effective anti-U.S. propaganda (+50). The reaction of the Muslim masses can be expected to be the same as that witnessed in the wake of the September 11, 2001 attacks. While they would support the radicals in their fight against the U.S. military assault, they would also deem the initial attacks on the U.S. unnecessary, and ultimately detrimental to the radicals and their cause (0). CUMULATIVE PAYOFF: -100

Filling the Matrix

Having assigned payoffs to the possible combinations of strategies that can be implemented; the payoff matrix can be filled as follows:

Radical Groups

Give up acts Pressure and Conduct acts of

U.S. of violence threaten violence

Withdraw

presence and (-100,+100) (-200,+250) (-250,+150)

abandon

manipulation

Maintain

presence and (+150,-200) (+50,-150) (-150,0)

manipulation

Use (+100,-150) (-50,-150) (-100,-100)

military force

An examination of the matrix clearly indicates that the ideal strategy for the U.S. is to maintain its presence in and continue its manipulation of the affairs of Muslim countries while forcing radical Islamic groups to abort attempts at attacking American interests. Radical Islamic groups gain the most by pressuring the U.S. to give in to their demands and by threatening the U.S. with attacks without actually conducting them. Such a strategy would force the U.S. to withdraw its presence from the Muslim world and to abandon its manipulation of Muslim countries.

Ideally, the world would like to see this conflict resolved peacefully. The most effective way of attaining this goal is for the U.S. to withdraw its presence from the Muslim world and refrain from manipulating the affairs of Muslim countries, and for the radicals to renounce all acts of violence against the U.S. This combination is depicted in the cell labeled withdraw presence and abandon manipulation, give up acts of violence in the matrix above. Yet, since this combination does not bear the highest payoff for either side, neither player would strive to attain this balance, at least in the short run.

To illustrate this point, one should view the situation from the perspective of both sides. For the U.S., the ideal situation is depicted in the cell labeled maintain presence and manipulation, give up acts of violence. Starting from this cell, where the U.S. manages to maintain its presence and interventionist policy in the Muslim world, radical Islamic groups, instead of abandoning acts of violence, would rather conduct a violent attack against U.S. interests. They would do so because this yields the highest payoff for them, given the strategy of the U.S. (cell labeled: maintain presence and manipulation, conduct acts of violence.). In the event of an attack, the U.S. would obtain the highest payoff by engaging in a military struggle against the radicals (cell labeled: use military force, conduct acts of violence).

From the perspective of radical Islamic groups, the combination of strategies that bears the highest payoff is depicted in the cell labeled: withdraw presence and abandon manipulation, pressure and threaten. In this scenario, the radicals would threaten to attack the U.S. in an attempt to force the U.S. to give up its objective. The U.S., in turn, would strive to maintain its physical presence and interventionist policy in Muslim countries, again highlighting the highest possible payoff for the U.S., given the strategy adopted by the radicals (cell labeled: maintain presence and manipulation, pressure and threaten). Radical Islamic groups, in retaliation, would conduct attacks against U.S. interests (cell labeled: maintain presence and manipulation, conduct acts of violence) leading to military retaliation by the U.S. (cell labeled: use military force, conduct acts of violence).

It thus appears that the driving forces in this conflict, in accordance with strategies that yield the highest payoff for each player, push the situation towards the balance described by the cell labeled use military force, conduct acts of violence in the matrix. Still, it should be noted that no matter which starting point one chooses, the conflicting objectives of the U.S. and radical Islamic groups would lead the equilibrium towards the situation depicted by use military forcing and conducting acts of violence.

The cell labeled use military force, conduct acts of violence in the matrix represents the "Nash Equilibrium" for this game. Once the two sides reach this point, neither would be inclined to give up its stance, since, in view of the radicals' strategy to conduct violent attacks on the U.S., the highest payoff for the U.S. is achieved by conducting a military campaign against the radicals. Likewise, in the face of a military attack on the radicals, continuing violence against the U.S. would yield the highest payoff for radical Islamic groups. It is important to note that neither party would have wanted to arrive at this balance in the matrix had they been acting of their own accord. The conflicting interests of the two sides, however, pull them towards this situation.

The attack on September 11, 2001, followed by American military retaliation in Afghanistan, is likely to initiate a cycle of violence. It is hard to see the U.S. abandoning its promise to combat "terrorism" actively anytime in the near future. A retaliatory attack on the U.S. will be followed by a military assault on radical Islamic groups and vice-versa. To break this cycle of violence, either one of the two sides would have to be completely annihilated, or there would have to be evolution of cooperation over time in this game.

Complete annihilation of either side is a near-impossible goal. Whereas the U.S., with its superior military capabilities, may be able to conduct successful military campaigns against the most prominent radical Islamic groups, there will almost certainly be others that will remain untackled. The evolution of cooperation between the two sides over time also appears unlikely. American physical presence and intervention in the affairs of Muslim countries will continue to stir anti-U.S. sentiment among Muslim masses and ensure the emergence of new anti-American radical Islamic groups. Since radical Islamic groups are unlikely to possess the unity and financial strength to subdue the U.S. in the near future, the latter is unlikely to change the policy of direct U.S. involvement in the Muslim world.

The evolution of cooperation is equally unrealistic in this game. As the Folk Theorem suggests, if the U.S. and radical Islamic groups continue in this tit-for-tat equilibrium long enough, they could finally move towards a different mutually beneficial strategy. This is possible if each party can convince the other of a devastating response in case the other decides to break the cooperation and cheat them. For an iterated game to witness the evolution of cooperation, however, the two sides have to be certain of the others' reaction, the reactions must be frequent enough that the two players are not solely concentrating on the current benefits of a move but are also concerned about the next action of the player, and players should not discount benefits of future actions heavily.

In this particular game, these conditions are unlikely to be met, at least for the foreseeable future. The multiplicity of radical Islamic groups ensures that the U.S. cannot know which particular group is responsible for a particular retaliation. Furthermore, there will never be any guarantee that the retaliation from either side will be prompt. Finally, as both sides are desperately trying to achieve decisive victory in the near future, they have discounted future benefits heavily.

Consequently, the U.S. will continue to struggle to "ensure freedom" in the Muslim world and radical Islamic groups will continue to fight for the "just cause" of removing evil from the world. In the process, millions of innocent lives will be lost and billions of dollars will be wasted. It is impossible to see the ultimate goals of either side being realized. Yet there is one certainty: continued warfare between the U.S. and the radical Islamic groups. The world will not be a peaceful place anytime soon. That conclusion, as bleak as it may seem, is very convincing.

3

Threats to Globalisation in an Unstable World

What happens to globalisation in this new era of turmoil and conflict? The question is inevitable after three years of falling stock markets, sputtering economies, slowing world trade, accounting scandals, new threats of terrorism - and, of course, impending war. As the just-retired (if somewhat relieved) head of one of the world's leading insurance companies put it: "A lot fewer companies are going to go global in the next five years than in the past 10."

"Globalisation" was one thing that, in recent years, could really turn out a crowd. The very invocation of that word seemed to draw hundreds of thousands of protesters to international conclaves and summits of heads-of-state. This was a pretty powerful effect for a rather abstract, five-syllable word like "globalisation".

But globalisation had come to symbolise things that some people just do not like - such as markets, competition, capital flows, expanding trade, and capitalism itself. All these were among the key attributes of the 1990s, when world trade doubled, the Third World transformed itself into emerging markets, borders and boundaries came down, and countries became less poor by engaging with the world economy.

Despite all the criticism and the real issues that need to

be addressed in a more interconnected world, globalisation has proved to be a primary avenue to higher standards of living around the world. One of the most important themes to emerge out of Commanding Heights* is the central role of international trade in reducing poverty in developing countries. Just 35 years ago, Singapore was so poor that its future as a country was in question. It chose to cast its fate with the world economy. The result of its per capita income in 2001 was slightly higher than that of Britain.

Since the fall of the Berlin Wall, we have been living in a Second Age of Globalisation. But it's hard not to have a certain degree of unease when one considers what happened to the First Age. In the late 19th and early 20th centuries, world trade was growing at 33 per cent per year, the pound sterling was the foundation of global commerce, and technologies such as the steam engine and the telegraph were shrinking the planet. It seemed unstoppable, and yet it all came to an end in 1914 with the Guns of August. It took 75 years to put a truly global economy back together again.

Frederick von Hayek, the Austrian-born economist, was - as much as anyone - the inspiration for the market revolution of the last quarter century; he was the man whose book Margaret Thatcher would slam down on the table when she wanted to tell people what she believed. But, in making Commanding Heights, we were haunted by the pithy judgment he delivered on the cataclysm of the First World War, which had destroyed the world in which he had grown up in Vienna: "We didn't know how fragile our civilisation was."

Do we know how fragile this Second Age of Globalisation is? It is now all too painfully clear that, in the aftermath of the Cold War and the quick end of the Gulf War, there was much too much overconfidence about security. It was thought that traditional conflict was no longer a threat beyond a localised or regional area. The point is that globalisation works better in a time of peace and stability.

It is facilitated by openness and trust.

But the times today are less peaceful, and openness is considered not a virtue but vulnerability. Terrorism uses the tools of globalisation - travel, communications, and flows of funds - to attack the global economy. As Osama bin Laden announced several months ago, al-Qaeda intends to target the "hinges" of the world economy. War is imminent with Iraq, with unknown consequences for the Middle East. North Korea is gearing up to produce one nuclear weapon a month. The stresses of instability are evident in many other countries, from Indonesia to Venezuela.

The effects of the shift can be measured in the rising direct costs of security, whether military spending by governments or unanticipated costs for companies to secure their facilities. They show up in the slowdowns and complexity faced by companies shipping their goods - and the requirement to turn up at airports three hours before flight time to go through complex security procedures.

But the higher costs and burdens range over the entire span of the economy. They affect what may well be the most important commodity of all in a market economy: confidence - the willingness of consumers to buy and, more pertinently, the confidence of business to invest. Right now, the weakness of business confidence is one of the biggest checks on any economic rebound. Caution has, for the time being, replaced confidence. Postponement has superseded decision, and time horizons have been decidedly foreshortened.

Yet, with all that said, the question is not whether this period of globalisation is over. After all, the internet is not going to disappear; computers are not going to get slower. Even if world trade did not grow at 1990s rates in 2002, it still managed almost 3 per cent.

So the real question is: "What kind of globalisation will we be looking at in the future?"

It can be an open and relatively smoothly operating

system, facilitating the expansion of trade and knowledge, the movements of people, and rising standards of living. This would be a world in which the Doha "development round" of trade expansion brings the benefit of international commerce to developing countries.

But it can also be a more fractured system, fragmented and disrupted by poor economic performance, financial crises, new government intervention and over-regulation. Or there may be the kind of loss of legitimacy and respect for markets that corporate malfeasance and under funded pensions can generate.

Globalisation can be fragmented in a different way, by what threatens now: conflict, war, weapons-proliferation, and pervasive terrorism. Trade is disrupted. The barriers go up. More virulent nationalism emerges, perhaps even that much-feared clash of civilisations. Facing geopolitical risk and uncertainty, businessmen and women avoid the economic risk that is inherent when one invests in the future.

All this adds to the urgency for countries to do the "right things" in terms of strengthening their own economies and bolstering the institutions and co-operation required for a healthy international economy. That is a very important part of the agenda. But it won't be enough. For there is still the price to be paid for assuming, during the 1990s, that security would take care of itself.

The World's Top 10 Most Unstable Entities [mh]

Jane's, an IHS company (NYSE:IHS) has launched a new online service that assesses the stability of every country, territory and political entity around the world. Jane's Country Risk Ratings uses multiple weighted factors affecting country stability in distinct categories: political, social, economic, external and military and security.

"Today's global climate of insecurity and terrorism requires an in-depth, independent analysis of stability around the world," said Christian Le Mière, Managing

Editor of Jane's Country Risk. "These ratings assess stability and allow comparisons on an entity-by-entity or regional basis, which is valuable for business and defense organizations' decision making."

The inaugural Jane's Country Risk Ratings, published this month, list the 10 least stable entities, with number one being the least stable, as:

1. Gaza and West Bank
2. Somalia
3. Afghanistan
4. Sudan
5. Cote d'Ivoire
6. Haiti
7. Zimbabwe
8. Chad
9. Democratic Republic of Congo
10. Central African Republic

The Gaza Strip and West Bank—divided between two rival governments for more than a year—ranks as the most unstable entity in the world. A lack of control over its borders, frequent incursions of its territory by Israel, low levels of law and order, poor domestic security and worsening public health combine to place it in the top spot.

Iraq is not among the ten most unstable countries. It ranks 22nd from the least stable entity. Although it suffers from high levels of daily, non-state organised violence, the country's rating is bolstered by other elements that contribute to stability.

Its government is relatively secure and maintains control over areas of its territory, its economy is more or less resilient and the population remains relatively healthy. Stability in Afghanistan was shown to be far more elusive, according to the ratings. It currently ranks as the fourth most unstable entity in the world.

Gaza and West Bank

The War on Terrorism, or War on Terror, is the common term for the military, political, legal and ideological conflict against Islamic terrorism and Muslim militants and specifically used in reference to operations by the United States, since the September 11, 2001 attacks. The stated objectives of the war are to protect US territory, break up terrorist cells in the US, and disrupt the activities of the international network of terrorist organizations made up of a number of groups under the umbrella of al-Qaeda. Both the term and the policies it denotes have been a source of ongoing controversy, as critics argue it has been used to justify unilateral preemptive war, human rights abuses and other violations of international law.

War on Terrorism

Militant organizations — chiefly al-Qaeda — carried out attacks on the US and its allies throughout the last few years of the twentieth century. The 1993 World Trade Center bombing by Al-Qaeda was the first of many attacks upon US targets during this period. Subsequent attacks included the 1996 Khobar Towers bombing in Saudi Arabia, and the 1998 United States embassy bombings in Tanzania and Kenya. Also in 1998 came the World Islamic Front declaration of 23 February 1998, entitled *"Jihad Against Jews and Crusaders"*, which described the actions of Americans as conflicting with "Allah's order".

Led by Osama Bin Laden, a radical Islamist, Al-Qaeda formed a large base of operations in Afghanistan, which had been ruled by the Islamist extremist regime of the Taliban since 1996. Following the bombings in Kenya and Tanzania, US President William Clinton launched Operation Infinite Reach, a bombing campaign in Sudan and Afghanistan against targets the US asserted were associated with al-Qaeda. The strikes failed to kill al-Qaeda's leaders or their Taliban supporters (targets included a civilian pharmaceutical plant in Sudan that produced 90% of the region's malaria drugs).

Next are the 2000 millennium attack plots which included an attempted bombing of Los Angeles International Airport. In October 2000 the USS Cole bombing occurred, followed in 2001 by the September 11 attacks. The 2001 attacks (on the World Trade Center, the Pentagon and United 93 crash) led to an invasion of Afghanistan dubbed Operation Enduring Freedom which removed the Taliban from power and ended al-Qaeda's use of the country as a base.

In 2001 the United Nations Security Council adopted resolution 1373 which obliges all states to criminalize assistance for terrorist activities, deny financial support and safe haven to terrorists and share information about groups planning terrorist attacks. In 2005 the Security Council also adopted resolution 1624 concerning incitement to commit acts of terrorism and the obligations of countries to comply with international human rights laws. Although both resolutions require mandatory annual reports on counterterrorism activities by adopting nations, the United States and Israel have both declined to submit reports.

The phrase "War on Terrorism" was first widely used by the Western press to refer to the attempts by Russian and European governments, and eventually the U.S. government, to stop attacks by anarchists against international political leaders. Many of the anarchists described themselves as "terrorists," and the term had a positive valence for them at the time. When Russian Marxist Vera Zasulich shot and wounded a Russian police commander who was known to torture suspects on 24 January 1878, for example, she threw down her weapon without killing him, announcing; "I am a terrorist, not a killer."

The phrase gained currency was when it was used to describe the efforts by the British colonial government to end a spate of attacks by Jews in the British Mandate of Palestine in the late 1940s. The British proclaimed a "War on Terrorism" against Jewish groups such as Irgun and Lehi, and anyone perceived to be cooperating with them. The Jewish attacks, Arab attacks and revolts, and the subsequent British crackdown hastened the British evacuation from Palestine. The phrase was also used frequently by US President Ronald Reagan in the 1980s, to describe his campaigns against Libya and Nicaragua.

On September 20, 2001, during a televised address to a joint session of congress, former President George W. Bush launched his war on terror when he said, "Our war on terror begins with al Qaeda, but it does not end there. It will not end until every terrorist group of global reach has been found, stopped and defeated." Bush did not say when he expected this would be achieved. US President Barack Obama has signaled an end to the "war on terror", by stating that "Afghanistan is where the war on terror began, and that is where it must end", in stark contrast to Bush's open-ended and ambiguous language.

Operative Definition in U.S. Foreign Policy

The United States has defined terrorism under the Federal Criminal Code. Chapter 113B of Part I of Title 18 of the Code defines terrorism and lists the crimes associated with it. In Section 2331 of Chapter 113b, terrorism is defined as:

> "...activities that involve violent... or life-threatening acts... that are a violation of the criminal laws of the United States or of any State and... appear to be intended (i) to intimidate or coerce a civilian population; (ii) to influence the policy of a government by intimidation or coercion; or (iii) to affect the conduct of a government by mass destruction, assassination, or kidnapping; and ...if domestic...(C) occur primarily within the territorial

> jurisdiction of the United States...if international...(C) occur primarily outside the territorial jurisdiction of the United States..."

With respect to defining his policy known as the War on Terror, President Bush has stated that:

"...today's war on terror is like the Cold War. It is an ideological struggle with an enemy that despises freedom and pursues totalitarian aims....I vowed then that I would use all assets of our power of Shock and Awe to win the war on terror. And so I said we were going to stay on the offense two ways: one, hunts down the enemy and brings them to justice, and takes threats seriously; and two, spread freedom."

British Objections to the Phrase "War on Terrorism"

The Director of Public Prosecutions and head of the Crown Prosecution Service in the UK, Ken McDonald — Britain's most senior criminal prosecutor — has stated that those responsible for acts of terror such as the 7 July 2005 London bombings are not "soldiers" in a war, but "inadequates" who should be dealt with by the criminal justice system. He added that a "culture of legislative restraint" was needed in passing anti-terrorism laws, and that a "primary purpose" of the violent attacks was to tempt countries such as Britain to "abandon our values." He stated that in the eyes of the UK criminal justice system, the response to terrorism had to be "proportionate, and grounded in due process and the rule of law":

> "London is not a battlefield. Those innocents who were murdered...were not victims of war. And the men who killed them were not, as in their vanity they claimed on their ludicrous videos, 'soldiers'. They were deluded, narcissistic inadequates. They were criminals. They were fantasists. We need to be very clear about this. On the streets of London there is no such thing as a war on terror. The fight

against terrorism on the streets of Britain is not a war. It is the prevention of crime, the enforcement of our laws, and the winning of justice for those damaged by their infringement."

At the time that the "War on Terror" became a national catchphrase in the U.S., many British people cynically compared America's new found spur 'against' terrorism with America's previous actions regarding tacit 'support' for terrorism in Ireland. The political wing of the Irish Republican Army, a recognized terrorist organization, openly raised money in the United States for their cause.

Ostensibly the money was raised for the families of those imprisoned on terrorist offences, but U.S. politicians were long made aware that this was the major source of funding for the IRA's terrorist activities. In January 2009, the British foreign secretary, David Miliband, wrote "ultimately, the notion is misleading and mistaken" and later said "Historians will judge whether [the notion] has done more harm than good".

Stated U.S. Objectives

The Bush Administration has defined the following objectives in the War on Terrorism:

1. Defeat terrorists and destroy their organizations.
2. Identify, locate and destroy terrorists along with their organizations.
3. Deny sponsorship, support and sanctuary to terrorists.
    1. End the state sponsorship of terrorism.
    2. Establish and maintain an international standard of accountability with regard to combating terrorism.
    3. Strengthen and sustain the international effort to fight terrorism.
    4. Working with willing and able states.

   5. Enabling weak states.
   6. Persuading reluctant states.
   7. Compelling unwilling states.
   8. Interdict and disrupt material support for terrorists.
   9. Eliminate terrorist sanctuaries and havens.
4. Diminishing the underlying conditions that terrorists seek to exploit.
   1. Partner with the international community to strengthen weak states and prevent (re)emergence of terrorism.
   2. Win the war of ideals.
5. Defend U.S. citizens and interests at home and abroad.
   1. Implement the Nation Strategy for Homeland Security.
   2. Attain domain awareness.
   3. Enhance measures to ensure the integrity, reliability, and availability of critical physical and information-based infrastructures at home and abroad.
   4. Integrate measures to protect U.S. citizens abroad.
   5. Ensure an integrated incident management capability.

4

Campaigns and Theaters of Operations

This extension of Operation Enduring Freedom, titled OEF-HOA, was initiated in response to the September 11 attacks on the United States. Unlike other operations contained in Operation Enduring Freedom, OEF-HOA does not have a specific terrorist organization as a target. OEF-HOA instead focuses its efforts to disrupt and detect terrorist activities in the region and to work with host nations to prevent the reemergence of terrorist cells and activities.

In October 2002, the Combined Joint Task Force - Horn of Africa (CJTF-HOA) was established in Djibouti at Camp Le Monier. It contains approximately 2,000 personnel including U.S. military and Special Operations Forces (SOF) and coalition force members, Combined Task Force 150 (CTF-150). Task Force 150 consists of ships from a shifting group of nations, including Australia, Canada, France, Germany, Italy, Netherlands, Pakistan, New Zealand, Spain and the United Kingdom. The primary goal of the coalition forces is to monitor, inspect, board and stop suspected shipments from entering the Horn of Africa region and areas of Operation Iraqi Freedom.

Included in the operation is the training of selected armed forces units of the countries of Djibouti, Kenya and Ethiopia in counterterrorism and counterinsurgency tactics.

Humanitarian efforts conducted by CJTF-HOA include rebuilding of schools and medical clinics as well as providing medical services to those countries whose forces are being trained.

The program expands as part of the Trans-Saharan Counter Terrorism Initiative as CJTF personnel also assist in training the forces of Chad, Niger, Mauritania and Mali. However, the War on Terror does not include Sudan, where over 400,000 have died due to state-sponsored terrorism. On July 1, 2006, a Web-posted message purportedly written by Osama bin Laden urged Somalis to build an Islamic state in the country and warned western states that his al-Qaeda network would fight against them if they intervened there.

Somalia has been considered a "failed state" because its official central government was weak, dominated by warlords and unable to exert effective control over the country. Beginning in mid-2006, the Islamic Courts Union (ICU), an Islamist faction campaigning on a restoration of "law and order" through Sharia Law, had rapidly taken control of much of southern Somalia.

On December 14, 2006, the U.S. Assistant Secretary of State Jendayi Frazer claimed al-Qaeda cell operatives were controlling the Islamic Courts Union, a claim denied by the ICU. By late 2006, the UN-backed Transitional Federal Government (TFG) of Somalia had seen its power effectively limited to Baidoa, while the Islamic Courts Union controlled the majority of Southern Somalia, including the capital of Mogadishu. On December 20, the Islamic Courts Union launched an offensive on the government stronghold of Baidoa, and saw early gains before Ethiopia intervened in favor of the government.

By December 26, the Islamic Courts Union went into a "tactical retreat" towards Mogadishu, before again retreating as TFG/Ethiopian troops neared, leading them to take Mogadishu with no resistance. The ICU then fled to Kismayo, where they are currently fighting Ethiopian/TFG forces in the Battle of Jilib.

The Prime Minister of Somalia claims that 3 terror suspects from the 1998 Embassy Bombings are being sheltered in Kismayo. On 30 December 2006, al-Qaeda deputy leader Ayman al-Zawahiri called upon Muslims worldwide to fight against Ethiopia and the TFG in Somalia. On January 8, 2007, the U.S. launched a strike in Somalia against the suspects using AC-130 gunships.

Europe

Beginning in October 2001, Operation Active Endeavour is a naval operation of NATO started in response to the 9/11 attacks. It operates in the Mediterranean Sea and is designed to prevent the movement of terrorists or weapons of mass destruction as well as to enhance the security of shipping in general. The operation has also assisted Greece with the prevention of illegal immigration.

Middle East

Iraq

Iraq had been listed as a State Sponsor of Terror by the United States since 1990, and maintained poor relations with the United States since the Gulf War. The regime of Saddam Hussein in Iraq proved a continuing problem for the UN and Iraq's neighbors in its refusal to account for previously known stockpiles of chemical and biological weapons, its violations of UN resolutions, and its support for terrorism against Israel and other countries.

After the 1991 Gulf War, the US, French and British militaries began patrolling the Iraqi no-fly zones to protect Iraq's Kurdish minority and Shi'ite Arab population – both of which suffered attacks from the Hussein regime before and after the 1991 Gulf War – in Iraq's northern and southern regions, respectively.

Tensions were high throughout the 1990s, with the United States launching Operation Desert Fox against Iraq in 1998 after it failed to meet demands of "unconditional cooperation" in weapons inspections. In the aftermath of Operation Desert Fox during December 1998, Iraq announced that it would no longer respect the no-fly zones and resumed its efforts in shooting down Allied aircraft.

Air strikes by the British and Americans against Iraqi anti-aircraft and military targets continued over the next few years. Also in 1998, President Clinton signed the Iraq Liberation Act which called for regime change in Iraq on the basis of Saddam Hussein's possession of weapons of mass destruction, oppression of Iraqi citizens and attacks upon other Middle Eastern countries.

After the September 11 attacks, the U.S. government claimed that Iraq was a threat to the United States because Iraq could begin to use its previously known Weapons of Mass Destruction to aid terrorist groups.

The George W. Bush administration called for the United Nations Security Council to send weapons inspectors to Iraq to find and destroy alleged weapons of mass destruction and for a UNSC resolution. UNSC Resolution 1441 was passed unanimously, which offered Iraq "a final opportunity to comply with its disarmament obligations" or face "serious consequences."

Resolution 1441 did not authorize the use of force by member states, thus Resolution 1441 had no effect on the UN Charter's prohibition on the use of force by member states against fellow member states. Saddam Hussein subsequently allowed UN inspectors to access Iraqi sites, while the U.S. government continued to assert that Iraq was being obstructionist.

In October 2002, a large bipartisan majority in the United States Congress authorized the president to use force if necessary to disarm Iraq in order to "prosecute the war on terrorism." After failing to overcome opposition from France, Russia, and China against a UNSC resolution that would sanction the use of force against Iraq, and before the UN weapons inspectors had completed their inspections which were deemed to be fruitless by the U.S. because of Iraq's alleged deception, the United States assembled a "Coalition of the Willing" composed of nations who pledged support for regime change in Iraq.

On March 20, 2003, the invasion of Iraq was launched in what the Bush Administration said were the "serious consequences" spoken of in UNSC Resolution 1441. Saddam Hussein's regime was quickly toppled and on May 1, 2003, George W. Bush stated that major combat operations in Iraq had ended. However, an insurgency arose against the U.S.-led coalition and the newly developing Iraqi military and post-Saddam government.

Elements of the insurgency were led by fugitive members of Saddam's Ba'ath regime, who included Iraqi nationalists and pan-Arabists. Most insurgency leaders are violent Islamists and claim to be fighting a religious war to reestablish the Arab Islamic Caliphate of centuries past.

After months of brutal violence against Iraqi civilians by Sunni and Shi'ite terrorist groups and militias — including Al-Qaeda in Iraq -- in January 2007 President Bush presented a new strategy for Operation Iraqi Freedom based upon Counter-insurgency theories and tactics developed by General David Petraeus. The Iraq War troop surge of 2007 was part of this "new way forward" and has been credited with a widely recognized dramatic decrease in violence by up to 80%, and a more controversial possible increase in political and communal reconciliation in Iraq.

Lebanon

In July 2006, following the killing of three Israeli soldiers and the taking prisoner of two more by Hezbollah, Israel invaded southern Lebanon, intent on the destruction of

Hezbollah. The conflict lasted over a month and caused the deaths of between 845 and 1300 Lebanese and 163 Israelis (119 military and 44 civilian) and wounding thousands more Israelis and Lebanese.

Both the Lebanese government (including Hezbollah) and the Israeli government have agreed to the terms of the ceasefire agreement created by the United Nations that began at 0500 on August 14, 2006. While the conflict is associated with the longer running Arab-Israeli conflict, prior to the declaration of the ceasefire, Israel stated it was fighting a war against terror, the U.S. government stated the conflict was also a front in the "War on Terror" and President Bush reiterated it in a speech the day the ceasefire came into effect.

In 2007 a conflict began in northern Lebanon after fighting broke out between Fatah al-Islam, an Islamist militant organization, and the Lebanese Armed Forces on May 20, 2007 in Nahr al-Bared, a Palestinian refugee camp near Tripoli. The conflict evolved mostly around the Siege of Nahr el-Bared, but minor clashes had also occurred in the Ain al-Hilweh refugee camp in southern Lebanon and several terrorist bombings took place in and around Lebanon's capital Beirut.

The terrorist group has been described as a militant jihadist movement that draws inspiration from al-Qaeda. The U.S. provided military aid to Lebanon during the conflict. On September 7, 2007 Lebanese Forces captured the camp and then declared victory. In May 2008, Lebanon's 17-month long political crisis spiralled out of control. The unrest saw fighters from Shi'a movements Hezbollah and Amal opposing pro-government gunmen, including fighters loyal to the Sunni Future Movement Party, in several areas of the capital. The government was U.S.-backed while the Shiite militants were armed and financed by Syria and Iran. The fighting led to the fall of Beirut and the eastern Aley area to opposition forces.

Saudi Arabia

The latest wave of attacks in Saudi Arabia started with the bombing in Riyadh on 12 May 2003 by al-Qaeda terrorists. The attacks are targeting the Saudi security forces, the foreign workers, and tourists (mostly Western).

Gaza Strip/West Bank

The Fatah-Hamas conflict began in 2006 and has continued, in one form or another, into the middle of 2007. The conflict is between the two main Palestinian factions, Fatah and Hamas, with each vying to assume political control of the Palestinian Territories. The majority of the fighting is occurring in the Gaza Strip, which was taken over by Hamas in June 2007. Fatah is United States backed whereas Hamas, despite being considered a terrorist organization by the United States, United Nations and the European Union, won the first free and democratic elections held in the Palestinian territories.

Following Hamas's violent takeover of the Gaza Strip during the Battle of Gaza Israel imposed a blockade of the territory. What ensued was a series of rocket attacks by Hamas against southern Israel and small military operations against the rocket teams by the IDF. This culminated by the end of December 2008, after a six-month truce ended between Israel and Hamas. Rocket attacks intensified and Israel responded with heavy air strikes on December 27, 2008.

At least 225 people were killed on the first day of the Israeli attack, 140 of the Hamas militants according to the IDF. Following a week of air raids Israeli troops started ground operations and attacked the Gaza Strip on January 4, 2009. The attack cut Gaza into three parts and by January 13, 9333 Palestinians (around 485 civilians) and 13 Israelis (10 soldiers) were killed. By some the conflict had been considered, just like the 2006 Lebanon war, as a proxy war between Israel's Western allies and Iran for the Middle East.

Central Asia/South Asia

India

The recent rise in prominence of several Pakistan and Kashmir-based terror groups, such as Lashkar-e-Toiba, Jaish-e-Mohammed, Hizbul Mujahideen and others in Kashmir has created grave problems for the country. Major terrorist incidents in India carried out by Islamic groups include the 1993 Mumbai bombings, as well as terrorism in Kashmir such as Wandhama massacre, Kaluchak massacre, Chittisinghpura massacre and others.

Other deadly terrorist attacks in the rest of the country include:

- The 2001 Indian Parliament attack.
- Akshardham Temple attack.
- 29 October 2005 Delhi bombings.
- 2005 Ram Janmabhoomi attack in Ayodhya.
- 2005 Jaunpur train bombing.
- 11 July 2006 Mumbai train bombings.
- 2006 Varanasi bombings.
- The 2007 Samjhauta Express bombings.
- Hyderabad bombings.
- Jaipur bombings.
- Bangalore bombings.
- 2008 Ahmedabad bombings.
- 13 September 2008 Delhi bombings.
- 2008 Assam bombings.
- And the 26 November 2008 Mumbai attacks.

In the aftermath of the 2001 Indian Parliament attack, tensions between India and Pakistan increased as India blamed Pakistan for not doing enough to contain anti-India terrorist groups based there. This resulted in massive troop build-ups along the Indo-Pakistani international border by both India and Pakistan resulting in fears of a nuclear war.

However, international diplomacy helped reduce tensions between the two nuclear weapons-armed states. Pakistan was also suspected to be behind the 2008 Indian embassy bombing in Kabul. Kashmiri insurgents, who initially started their movement as a pro-Kashmiri independence movement, have gone through a radical change in their ideology. They now portray their struggle as a religious one.

Research and Analysis Wing, India's premier external intelligence agency, observed the growing link between Islamic terrorist groups based in Afghanistan and Kashmiri insurgents. Al-Qaeda also lends ideological and financial support to terrorism in Kashmir; with Osama bin Laden constantly demanding that jihad be waged against India and Islamic fundamentalist groups disseminating propaganda in many countries against India with rhetoric like "idol worshipers and Hindus" who "occupy Kashmir".

The government and military of India have taken numerous counter-terrorist measures to combat rising terrorism in the country. Some of these measures have been criticized by human rights groups as being too draconian, particularly in Kashmir.

However, increased vigilance by Indian security forces has had a positive impact with the number of terrorist attacks declining sharply in 2007. India is considered to be one of main allies in the war on terrorism and has worked closely on counter-terrorism activities and training with several countries such as United States, Japan, China, Australia, Israel, United Kingdom, and Russia.

India has been criticized over its anti-terrorist operations in Jammu and Kashmir, the heavy-handed response to unrest in which 40 people - the vast majority unarmed civilian protesters - were killed by Indian armed forces could lead to the "Talibanisation of the Kashmiri separatist struggle."

Afghanistan

In October 2001, in the wake of the September 11 attacks on the United States, US and UK forces (with some coalition allies) invaded Afghanistan to remove al-Qaeda forces and oust the Taliban regime which had control of the country.

On September 20, 2001 George W. Bush delivered an ultimatum to the Taliban regime to turn over Osama bin Laden and al-Qaeda leaders operating in the country. The Taliban demanded evidence of bin Laden's link to the September 11 attacks and, if such evidence warranted a trial, they offered to handle such a trial in an Islamic Court.

On October 7, 2001 the official invasion began with British and American forces conducting aerial bombing campaigns. Waging war in Afghanistan has been of a lower priority for the U.S. government than the war in Iraq. Admiral Mike Mullen, Staff Chairman of the Joint Chiefs of Staff, said that while the situation in Afghanistan is "precarious and urgent," the 10,000 additional troops needed there would be unavailable "in any significant manner" unless withdrawals from Iraq are made. However, Admiral Mullen stated that "my priorities . . . given to me by the commander in chief are: Focus on Iraq first. It's been that way for some time. Focus on Afghanistan second."

Pakistan

The Saudi- born Zayn al-Abidn Muhammed Hasayn Abu Zubaydah was arrested by Pakistani officials during a series of joint U.S. and Pakistan raids during the week of March 23, 2002. During the raid the suspect was shot three times while trying to escape capture by military personnel. Zubaydah is said to be a high-ranking al-Qaeda official with the title of operations chief and in charge of running al-Qaeda training camps. Later that year on September 14, 2002, Ramzi Binalshibh was arrested in Pakistan after a three-hour gunfight with police forces.

Binalshibh is known to have shared a room with Mohammad Atta in Hamburg, Germany and to be a financial backer of al-Qaeda operations. It is said Binalshibh was supposed to be another hijacker; however the U.S. Citizenship and Immigration Services rejected his visa application three times, leaving him to the role of financier. The trail of money transferred by Binalshibh from Germany to the United States links both Mohammad Atta and Zacarias Moussaoui.

On March 1, 2003, Khalid Shaikh Mohammed was arrested during CIA-led raids on the suburb of Rawalpindi, nine miles outside of the Pakistani capital of Islamabad. Mohammed at the time of his capture was the third highest ranking official in al-Qaeda and had been directly in charge of the planning for the September 11 attacks.

Escaping capture the week before during a previous raid, the Pakistani government was able to use information gathered from other suspects captured to locate and detain Mohammed. Mohammed was indicted in 1996 by the United States government for links to the Oplan Bojinka, a plot to bomb a series of U.S. civilian airliners.

Other events Mohammed has been linked to include: ordering the killing of Wall Street Journal reporter Daniel Pearl, the USS Cole bombing, Richard Reid's attempt to blow up a civilian airliner with a shoe bomb, and the terrorist attack at the El Ghriba synagogue in Djerba, Tunisia. Khalid Shaikh Mohammed has described himself as the head of the al-Qaeda military committee.

Amidst all this, in 2006, Pakistan was accused by NATO commanding officers of aiding and abetting the Taliban in Afghanistan; but NATO later admitted that there was no known evidence against the ISI or Pakistani government of sponsoring terrorism. However in 2007, allegations of ISI secretly making bounty payments up to CDN$ 1,900 (Pakistani rupees. 1 lakh) for each NATO personnel killed surfaced.

The Afghan government also accuses the ISI of providing help to militants including protection to the recently killed Mullah Dadullah, Taliban's senior military commander, a charge denied by the Pakistani government. India meanwhile continues to accuse Pakistan's Inter-Services Intelligence of planning several terrorist attacks in Kashmir and elsewhere in the Indian republic, including the 11 July 2006 Mumbai train bombings, which Pakistan attributes it to "homegrown" insurgencies.

Many other countries like Afghanistan and the UK have also accused Pakistan of State-sponsored terrorism and financing terrorism. The upswing in American military activity in Pakistan and neighboring Afghanistan corresponded with a drastic increase in American military aid to the Pakistan government.

In the three years before the attacks of September 11, Pakistan received approximately $9 million in American military aid. Three years after, the number increased to $4.2 billion, making it the country with the maximum funding post 9/11.

Such a huge inflow of funds has raised concerns that these funds were given without any accountability, as the end uses not being documented, and that large portions were used to suppress civilians' human rights and to purchase weapons to contain domestic problems like the Balochistan unrest Pakistan has stated that India has been supporting terror groups within FATA and Balochistan with the aim of creating unrest within the country which has also been blamed for the diversion of funds.

Waziristan

In 2004 the Pakistani Army launched a campaign in the Federally Administered Tribal Areas of Pakistan's Waziristan region, sending in 80,000 troops. The goal of the conflict was to remove the al-Qaeda and Taliban forces in the region.

After the fall of the Taliban regime many members of the Taliban resistance fled to the Northern border region of Afghanistan and Pakistan where the Pakistani army had previously little control. With the logistics and air support of the United States, the Pakistani Army captured or killed numerous al-Qaeda operatives such as Khalid Shaikh Mohammed, wanted for his involvement in the USS Cole bombing, Oplan Bojinka plot and the killing of Wall Street Journal reporter Daniel Pearl. However, the Taliban resistance still operates in the Federally Administered Tribal Areas under the control of Haji Omar.

Southeast Asia

Indonesia

In 2002 and again in 2005, the Indonesian island of Bali has been struck by suicide and car bombings that killed over 200 people and injured over 300. The 2002 attack consisted of a bomb hidden in a backpack exploding inside of "Padds's Bar," a remote controlled car bomb exploding in front of the "Sari Club" and a third explosion in front of the American consulate in Bali.

The 2005 attack consisted of 2 suicide bombings, the first near a food court in Jimbaran, the second in the main square of Kuta. The group Jemaah Islamiyah is suspected by Indonesian authorities of carrying out both attacks.

On September 9, 2004, a car bomb exploded outside of the Australian embassy in Jakarta, killing 10 Indonesians and injuring over 140 others; despite conflicting initial reports there were no Australian casualties. Foreign Minister Alexander Downer reported that a mobile phone text message was sent to Indonesian authorities before the bombing warning of attacks if Abu Bakar Bashir was not released from prison.

Abu Bakar Ba'asyir was imprisoned on charged of treason for his support of the 2002 and 2005 Bali bombings.

Currently Jemaah Islamiyah is suspected of carrying out the attacks and Noordin Mohammed Top is a prime suspect. Top is a bomb maker and explosions expert for Jemaah Islamiyah.

Philippines

In January 2002 the United States Special Operations Command, Pacific deployed to the Philippines to advise and assist the Armed Forces of the Philippines in combating terrorism. The operations were mainly focused on removing the Abu Sayyaf Group (ASG) and Jemaah Islamiyah (JI) from their stronghold on the island of Basilan.

The United States military has reported that they have removed over 80% of the Abu Sayyaf Group members from the region. The second portion of the operation was conducted as a humanitarian program called "Operation Smiles." The goal of the program was to provide medical care and services to the region of Basilan to prevent the ability for members of the terrorist groups to reestablish themselves.

North America

United States of America

A $40 billion emergency spending bill was passed by the United States Congress, and an additional $20 billion bail-out of the airline industry was also passed. The Justice Department launched a Special Registration procedure for certain male non-citizens in the U.S., requiring them to register in person at offices of the Immigration and Naturalization Service.

In addition to military efforts abroad, in the aftermath of 9/11 the Bush Administration increased domestic efforts to prevent future attacks. A new cabinet level agency called the United States Department of Homeland Security was created to lead and coordinate federal counterterrorism activities.

The USA PATRIOT Act removed legal restrictions on information sharing between federal law enforcement and intelligence services and allowed for the investigation of suspected terrorists using means similar to those in place for other types of criminals. A new Terrorist Finance Tracking Program monitored the movements of terrorists' financial resources (discontinued after being revealed by The New York Times newspaper). Telecommunication usage by known and suspected terrorists was studied through the NSA electronic surveillance program.

Political interest groups have alleged that these laws remove important restrictions on governmental authority, and are a dangerous encroachment on civil liberties, possible unconstitutional violations of the Fourth Amendment. On July 30th, 2003, the ACLU filed the first legal challenge against Section 215 of the Patriot Act, claiming that it allows the FBI to violate a citizen's 1st Amendment rights, 4th Amendment Rights, and right to due process, by having the ability to search business, bookstore, and library records in a terrorist investigation - without disclosing to the individual that records were being searched. Also, governing bodies in a number of communities have passed symbolic resolutions against the act.

In a speech on June 9, 2005, Bush said that the USA PATRIOT Act had been used to bring charges against more than 400 suspects, more than half of whom had been convicted. Meanwhile the American Civil Liberties Union (ACLU) quoted Justice Department figures showing that 7,000 people have complained of abuse of the Act.

DARPA began an initiative in early 2002 with the creation of the Total Information Awareness program, designed to promote information technologies that could be used in counterterrorism. This program, facing criticism, has since been defunded by Congress.

Various government bureaucracies which handled security and military functions were reorganized. Most notably, the Department of Homeland Security was created to coordinate "homeland security" efforts in the largest reorganization of the U.S. federal government since the consolidation of the armed forces into the Department of Defense.

The Office of Strategic Influence was secretly created after 9/11 for the purpose of coordinating propaganda efforts, but was closed soon after being discovered. The Bush administration implemented the Continuity of Operations Plan (or Continuity of Government) to ensure that U.S. government would be able to continue in catastrophic circumstances.

Since 9/11, Islamic extremists made various attempts to attack the US homeland, with varying levels of organization and skill. For example, in 2001 vigilant passengers aboard a transatlantic flight to Miami prevented Richard Reid (shoe bomber) from detonating an explosive device. Other terrorist plots have been stopped by federal agencies using new legal powers and investigative tools, sometimes in cooperation with foreign governments.

Such thwarted attacks include;

- A plan to crash airplanes into the U.S. Bank Tower (aka Library Tower) in Los Angeles;
- The 2003 plot by Iyman Faris to blow up the Brooklyn Bridge in New York City;
- The 2004 Financial buildings plot which targeted the International Monetary Fund and World Bank buildings in Washington, DC,
- The New York Stock Exchange and other financial institutions;
- The 2004 Columbus Shopping Mall Bombing Plot;
- The 2006 transatlantic aircraft plot which was to involve liquid explosives;
- The 2006 Sears Tower plot;
- The 2007 Fort Dix attack plot; and

- The 2007 John F. Kennedy International Airport attack plot.

To date, no attacks by Islamic terrorists on the US homeland have been successful since September 11, 2001. Recently the House of Representatives passed a bill enacting many of the recommendations of the 9/11 Commission, something the Democrats campaigned on as part of their "100 hour plan." The bill passed in the House 299-128 and is currently still being considered in the U.S. Senate. So far funding has not been appropriated for the enactments.

United Kingdom

Several terrorism attacks and plots have occurred in the U.K. These include the 7/7 and 21/7 bombings of London in 2005 which killed 57 people and injured about 700. Many Britons died in the 9/11 attacks on the United States also.

The worst terrorist incident in the United Kingdom is the Pam Am flight from London Heathrow to the USA. It is called the Lockerbie Bombing and was over Scotland, U.K. in 1988 which killed over 200 US and UK citizens.

In 2005 on July 7th several British Muslim men from Leeds, England traveled to London and detonated several bombs in the London Underground System killing 57 people. The men of the 7/7 attacks left a video warning the U.K. government and people that more attacks were to come.

Exactly 2 weeks later on the 21st of July 2005, more British Muslim terrorists traveled to London and tried to detonate more bombs on the London Underground. Since the July 2005 attacks the U.K. has attemptedly been attacked several times but so far all attempts by Islamic Terrorists have failed as security and intelligence is far too high.

In August 2006, a major plot involving the bombings of several U.S. and U.K. airliners flying transatlantic from several U.K. airports to the U.S. was foiled by US and UK intelligence. If the attack comes off, it would have caused a large number of deaths, most likely on a higher scale than 9/11.

Several men were arrested in cities across the United Kingdom and have since been sentenced in the U.K. This plot has caused mass security changes on airports all round the EU and US, at the moment it has stopped people from taking any drink on the plane and all liquids must be below a certain amount of mm's and must be placed in a see through bag.

Canary Wharf in London is one of the world's largest financial districts and Scotland Yard has said it is a potential target by Islamic terrorists.

In July 2007, just as Ex Prime Minister Tony Blair resigned and Gordon Brown was sworn in as the Prime Minister, and the UK was in chaos after flooding. British Muslim doctors planted several car bombs in Central London, one by the Tiger nightclub in the West End which was found by an ambulance crew.

The men then drove several hundred miles to Glasgow, Scotland and the next day, drove an jeep full of gas bottles into the main terminal entrance of Glasgow International Airport and set it on fire one of the terrorist's had a bomb wrapped around his waist, he was tackled to the ground and arrested.

He later died in hospital from severe burns caused by setting the jeep on fire. The other terrorist was sentenced to life in prison after being tried in the U.K. No member of the public was hurt in the attacks. It caused mass fear. The U.K. has not been attacked by terrorists successfully since the 7/7 London bombings.

South America

Colombia

Following the September 11 attacks the United States government increased military aid to Colombia. In 2003,

98 million dollars were spent for new Pentagon training and equipment for the Colombian military. The purpose of which was to help the Colombia government fight the FARC rebel group which is regarded by the U.S. as a terrorist group. It has also been alleged that the Communist rebel group has connections to the drug cartels of South America.

International Military Support

The first wave of attacks was carried out solely by American and British forces. Since the initial invasion period, these forces were augmented by troops and aircraft from Australia, Canada, Denmark, France, Italy, Netherlands, New Zealand and Norway amongst others. In 2006, there were about 33,000 troops in Afghanistan.

On September 12, 2001, less than 24 hours after the attacks in New York City and Washington, NATO invoked Article 5 of the North Atlantic Treaty and declared the attacks to be an attack against all 19 NATO member countries. Australian Prime Minister John Howard also declared that Australia would invoke the ANZUS Treaty along similar lines.

In the following months, NATO took a wide range of measures to respond to the threat of terrorism. On November 22, 2002, the member states of the EAPC decided on a Partnership Action Plan against Terrorism which explicitly states that "EAPC States are committed to the protection and promotion of fundamental freedoms and human rights, as well as the rule of law, in combating terrorism." NATO started naval operations in the Mediterranean Sea designed to prevent the movement of terrorists or weapons of mass destruction as well as to enhance the security of shipping in general called Operation Active Endeavour.

The invasion of Afghanistan is seen as the first action of this war, and initially involved forces from the United States, the United Kingdom, and the Afghan Northern Alliance.

Support for the United States cooled when America made clear its determination to invade Iraq in late 2002. Even so, many of the "coalition of the willing" countries that unconditionally supported the U.S.-led military action have sent troops to Afghanistan, particular neighbouring Pakistan, which has disowned its earlier support for the Taliban and contributed tens of thousands of soldiers to the conflict. Pakistan was also engaged in the Waziristan War. Supported by U.S. intelligence, Pakistan was attempting to remove the Taliban insurgency and al-Qaeda element from the northern tribal areas.

The International Security Assistance Force

December 2001 saw the creation of the NATO-led International Security Assistance Force (ISAF) to assist the Afghan Transitional Administration and the first post-Taliban elected government. With a renewed Taliban insurgency, it was announced in 2006 that ISAF would replace the U.S troops in the province as part of Operation Enduring Freedom.

The British 16th Air Assault Brigade (latter reinforced by Royal Marines) formed the core of the force in Southern Afghanistan, along with troops and helicopters from Australia, Canada and the Netherlands. The initial force consisted of roughly 3,300 British, 2,000 Canadian, 1,400 from the Netherlands and 240 from Australia, along with Special Forces from Denmark and Estonia (and small contingents from other nations).

Criticisms of U.S. Objectives and Strategies

The War on Terrorism as Indefinite and Indeterminate

Policy experts have criticized the "War on Terrorism" as an irresponsible metaphor, arguing that "war" must by definition be waged against nations—not against broad and controversial categories of activity such as "terrorism". Cognitive linguist George Lakoff writes:

> "Literal—not metaphorical—wars are conducted against armies of other nations. They end when the armies are defeated militarily and a peace treaty is signed. Terror is an emotional state. It is in us. It is not an army. And you can't defeat it militarily and you can't sign a peace treaty with it."

Dr. David Kilcullen, a counterinsurgency and counterterrorism advisor to Gen. David Petraeus and U.S. Secretary of State Condoleezza Rice, has asserted that:

> "We must distinguish Al Qa'eda and the broader militant movements it symbolises – entities that use terrorism – from the tactic of terrorism itself. In practice, as will be demonstrated, the 'War on Terrorism' is a defensive war against a world-wide Islamist jihad, a diverse confederation of movements that uses terrorism as its principal, but not its sole tactic."

Francis Fukuyama, a prominent former neoconservative, has made the similar point that "The term "war on terrorism" is a misnomer, resulting in distorted ideas of the main threat facing Americans today. Terrorism is only a means to an end; in this respect, a "war on terror" makes no more sense than a war on submarines."

The term "terrorism" has been also been characterized as unacceptably vague. The United Nations Office on Drugs and Crime observes:

> "The lack of agreement on a definition of terrorism has been a major obstacle to meaningful international countermeasures. Cynics have often commented that one state's "terrorist" is another state's "freedom fighter".

Opponents critical of this inherent subjectivity point out that governments such as Iran, Lebanon, and Venezuela consistently use the term "terrorism" to describe actions taken by the United States. In an article published in October 29, French Army officer LTC Jean-Pierre Steinhofer described war on Terror as a "semantic, strategic and legal perversion. Terrorism is not an enemy, but a method of combat."

Further criticism maintains that the War on Terrorism provides a framework for perpetual war; that the announcement of such open-ended goals produces a state of endless conflict, since "terrorist groups" can continue to arise indefinitely. President Bush has pledged that the War on Terrorism "will not end until every terrorist group of global reach has been found, stopped, and defeated." During a July 2007 visit to the United States, newly appointed British Prime Minister Gordon Brown defined the War on Terror, specifically the element involving conflict with Al Qaeda, as "a generational battle".

The War on Terrorism as Counterproductive

A number of security experts, politicians, and policy organizations have claimed that the War on Terrorism has been counterproductive: that it has consolidated opposition to the U.S., aided terrorist recruitment, and increased the likelihood of attacks against the U.S. and its allies. In a 2005 briefing paper, the Oxford Research Group reported that

> "Al-Qaida and its affiliates remain active and effective, with a stronger support base and a higher intensity of attacks than before 9/11. ...Far from winning the 'war on terror', the second George W. Bush administration is maintaining policies that are not curbing paramilitary movements and are actually increasing violent anti-Americanism."

The South African *Mail & Guardian* describes research commissioned by the British Ministry of Defence which concluded:

- "The war in Iraq ... has acted as a recruiting sergeant for extremists across the Muslim world ... Iraq has served to radicalise an already disillusioned youth and al-Qaeda has given them the will, intent, purpose and ideology to act."

Peter Bergen and Paul Cruickshank, research fellows at the Center on Law and Security at the NYU School of Law, have argued that the "globalization of martyrdom" potentiated by the Iraq War "has generated a stunning sevenfold increase in the yearly rate of fatal jihadist attacks, amounting to literally hundreds of additional terrorist attacks and thousands of civilian lives lost."

The 2007 National Intelligence Estimate issued the following among its "key judgments":

- "The Iraq conflict has become the —cause cèlèbre for jihadists, breeding a deep resentment of US involvement in the Muslim world and cultivating supporters for the global jihadist movement. Should jihadists leaving Iraq perceive themselves, and be perceived, to have failed, we judge fewer fighters will be inspired to carry on the fight."

On September 19, 2008, the *RAND* Corporation presented the results of a comprehensive study for "Defeating Terrorist Groups" before the United States House Armed Services Committees. RAND's testimony began with the thesis statement "the United States cannot continue conducting an effective counter-terrorism campaign against al- Qa'eda without understanding how terrorist groups end."

Their conclusions included strong proposals for strategic policy changes. "[The U.S. military] should generally resist being drawn into combat operations in Muslim countries where its presence is likely to increase terrorist recruitment." and recommended, "ending the notion of a 'war' on terrorism" and "Moving away from military references would indicate that there was no battlefield solution to countering terrorism." In conclusion the RAND study advised: "By far the most effective strategy against religious groups has been the use of local police and intelligence services, which were responsible for the end of 73 percent of [terrorist] groups since 1968."

Double Standards

Others have criticized the U.S. for double standards in its dealings with key allies that are also known to support terrorist groups, such as Pakistan. Afghan President Hamid Karzai has repeatedly stated that in the "war against terrorism," "the central front is Pakistan"; Pakistan has also been alleged to provide Taliban operatives with covert support via the ISI. These accusations of double dealing regard civil liberties and human rights as well as terrorism.

According to the Federation of American Scientists, "[i]n its haste to strengthen the "frontline" states' ability to confront transnational terrorist threats on their soil, and to gain the cooperation of regimes of geo-strategic significance to the next phases of the "War on Terrorism", the administration is disregarding normative restrictions on U.S. aid to human rights abusers." Amnesty International has argued that the Patriot Act gives the U.S. government free rein to violate the constitutional rights of citizens. The Bush administration's alleged use of extraordinary rendition, secret prisons, and torture have all fueled opposition to the War on Terrorism.

Decreasing International Support

In 2002, strong majorities supported the U.S.-led War on Terrorism in Britain, France, Germany, Japan, India, and Russia. By 2006, supporters of the effort were in the minority in Britain (49%), France (43%), Germany (47%), and Japan (26%). Although a majority of Russians still supported the War on Terrorism, that majority had decreased by 21%. Whereas 63% of the Spanish population supported the War on Terrorism in 2003, only 19% of the population indicated support in 2006. 19% of the Chinese population supports the War on Terrorism, and less than a fifth of the populations of Turkey, Egypt, and Jordan support the effort. Indian support for the War on Terrorism has been stable.

Andrew Kohut, speaking to the U.S. House Committee on Foreign Affairs, noted that, according to the Pew Research Center polls conducted in 2004, "majorities or pluralities in seven of the nine countries surveyed said the U.S.-led war on terrorism was not really a sincere effort to reduce international terrorism. This was true not only in Muslim countries such as Morocco and Turkey, but in France and Germany as well. The true purpose of the war on terrorism, according to these skeptics, is American control of Middle East oil and U.S. domination of the world."

Stella Rimington, former head of the British intelligence service MI5 has criticised the war on terror as a "huge over reaction", and had decried the militarization and politicization of the U.S. efforts to be the wrong approach to terrorism. David Milliband, UK foreign secretary, has similarly called the strategy a "mistake".

Abuse of Power

The War on Terrorism has been viewed by some as a pretext for reducing civil liberties. The NSA electronic surveillance program and DARPA's Total Information Awareness were two examples of post-September 11th government monitoring programs. Though overtly intended to target terrorist behaviour, critics worried fears about government monitoring might lead people to self-censorship.

A controversy also erupted concerning National Security Letters, issued by the federal government and not subject to prior judicial review. These letters demanded information the government asserted was relevant to a terrorism investigation, but also contained a gag order preventing recipients from revealing the existence of the letter. Critics contend this prevents public oversight of government investigations, and allows unreasonable search and seizure to go unchecked. The American Civil Liberties Union complained that Section 505 of the USA PATRIOT Act removed the need for the government to connect recipients to a terrorism investigation, widening the possibility for abuse.

The Protect America Act of 2007 was also controversial for its lack of judicial review. In October 2008, British PM Gordon Brown used the Anti Terrorist Act to freeze Icelandic holdings in Great Britain during the Icelandic financial crisis. Iceland's prime minister Geir Haarde protested against what he described "a terrorist law being applied against us", calling it "a completely unfriendly act". Iceland is a founding member of NATO.

Role of U.S.Media

Researchers in the area of communication studies and political science have found that American understanding of the war on terror is directly shaped by how the mainstream news media reports events associated with the war on terror. In *Bush's War: Media Bias and Justifications for War in a Terrorist Age* political communication researcher Jim A. Kuypers illustrated "how the press failed America in its coverage on the War on Terror." In each comparison, Kuypers "detected massive bias on the part of the press." This researcher called the mainstream news media an "anti-democratic institution" in his conclusion.

"What has essentially happened since 9/11 has been that Bush has repeated the same themes, and framed those themes the same whenever discussing the War on Terror," said Kuypers. "Immediately following 9/11, the mainstream news media (represented by CBS, ABC, NBC, USA Today, New York Times, and Washington Post) did echo Bush, but within eight weeks it began to intentionally ignore certain information the president was sharing, and instead reframed the president's themes or intentionally introduced new material to shift the focus."

This goes beyond reporting alternate points of view, which is an important function of the press. "In short," Kuypers explained, "if someone were relying only on the mainstream media for information, they would have no idea what the president actually said. It was as if the press was reporting on a different speech." The study is essentially a "comparative framing analysis". Overall, Kuypers examined themes about 9-11 and the War on Terror that the President used, and compared them to the themes that the press used when reporting on what the president said.

"Framing is a process whereby communicators, consciously or unconsciously, act to construct a point of view that encourages the facts of a given situation to be interpreted by others in a particular manner," wrote Kuypers. These findings suggest that the public is misinformed about government justification and plans concerning the war on terror.

Others have also suggested that press coverage has contributed to a public confused and misinformed on both the nature and level of the threat to the U.S. posed by terrorism. In his book, *Trapped in the War on Terror* political scientist Ian S. Lustick, claimed, "The media have given constant attention to possible terrorist-initiated catastrophes and to the failures and weaknesses of the government's response." Lustick alleged that the War on Terror is disconnected from the real but remote threat terrorism poses, and that the generalized War on Terror began as part of the justification for invading Iraq, but then took on a life of its own, fueled by media coverage.

Media researcher Stephen D. Cooper's analysis of media criticism *Watching the Watchdog: Bloggers As the Fifth Estate* contains many examples of controversies concerning mainstream reporting of the War on Terror. Cooper found that bloggers' criticisms of factual inaccuracies in news stories or bloggers' discovery of the mainstream press's failure to adequately check facts before publication caused many news organizations to retrack or change news stories.

Cooper found that bloggers specializing in criticism of media coverage advanced four key points. Firstly, that mainstream reporting of the war on terror has frequently contained factual inaccuracies. In some cases, the errors go uncorrected; moreover, when corrections are issued they usually are given far less prominence than the initial coverage containing the errors. Secondly, they claimed that the mainstream press has sometimes failed to check the provenance of information or visual images supplied by Iraqi "stringers" (local Iraqis hired to relay local news). Next, they argued that story framing is often problematic; in particular, "man-in-the-street" interviews have often been used as a representation of public sentiment in Iraq, in place of methodologically sound survey data; and lastly, that mainstream reporting has tended to concentrate on the more violent areas of Iraq, with little or no reporting of the calm areas.

Military Decorations

Since 2002, the United States military has created several military awards and decorations related to the "War on Terrorism" including:

- "Global War on Terrorism Expeditionary Medal"
- "Afghanistan Campaign Medal"
- "Iraq Campaign Medal"
- "Global War on Terrorism Service Medal"

The U.S. Department of Transportation created two awards related to the "War on Terrorism" which are authorized to be worn on U.S. military uniforms:

- "9-11 Medal"
- "9-11 Ribbon"

NATO has also created military decorations related to the "War on Terrorism":

- Article 5 NATO Medal
- Non-Article 5 ISAF NATO Medal

Casualties

There is no widely agreed on figure for the number of people that have been killed so far in the "War on Terrorism" as it has been defined by the Bush Administration to include the war in Afghanistan, the war in Iraq, and operations elsewhere. Some estimates include the following:

- Iraq – 62,570 to 1,124,000
    - Opinion Research Business (ORB) poll conducted August 12-19, 2007 estimated 1,033,000 violent deaths due to the Iraq War. The range given was 946,000 to 1,120,000 deaths. A nationally representative sample of approximately 2000 Iraqi adults answered whether any members of their household (living under their roof) were killed due to the Iraq War. 22% of the respondents had lost one or more household members. ORB reported that "48% died from a gunshot wound, 20% from the impact of a car bomb, 9% from aerial bombardment, 6% as a result of an accident and 6% from another blast/ordnance."
    - Between 392,979 and 942,636 estimated Iraqi (655,000 with a confidence interval of 95%), civilian and combatant, according to the second Lancet survey of mortality.
    - A minimum of 62,570 civilian deaths reported in the mass media up to 28 April 2007 according to Iraq Body Count.
    - 4000 U.S. military dead (2008 26 March). 22,401 wounded in action, of which 10,050 were unable

to return to duty within 72 hours. 6,640 non-hostile injuries and 18,183 diseases (both requiring medical air transport).

- Afghanistan — between 1,300 and 49,600
    - According to Marc W. Herold, up to 3,600 civilians were killed as a result of U.S. bombing.
    - Joshua Muravchik of the American Enterprise Institute and Carl Conetta of the Project on Defense Alternatives question Herold's heavy use of the Afghan Islamic Press, "suspicious" tallies of other news agencies, and statistical errors in Herold's study. Conetta's study puts total civilian casualties between 1000 and 1300.
    - A Los Angeles Times study put the number of collateral dead between 1,067 and 1,201.
    - According to Jonathan Steele of *The Guardian* between 20,000 and 49,600 people may have died of the consequences of the invasion.
- Somalia - 7,000+
    - In December 2007, The Elman Peace and Human Rights Organisation said it had verified 6,500 civilian deaths, 8,516 people wounded, and 1.5 million displaced from homes in Mogadishu alone during the year 2007.

5

Global Progress against Terrorism

Counterterrorism requires complex, comprehensive and collaborative strategy. International gains against terrorist cells in 2007 highlight the continuing need for a complex, comprehensive and collaborative strategy against terrorism.

"Working with allies and partners across the world, we've created a less permissive operating environment for terrorists, kept leaders on the move or in hiding and degraded their ability to plan and mount attacks," said State Department counterterrorism coordinator Dell Dailey upon the April 30 release of *Country Reports on Terrorism 2007*.

An annual report developed jointly by the State Department and the National Counterterrorism Center (NCTC), *Country Reports on Terrorism 2007* provides Congress with information on progress in the fight against al-Qaeda and other U.S.-designated foreign terrorist groups active in the Americas, Africa, Europe, the Middle East and Asia. In 2007, there were 14,499 terrorist attacks worldwide, according to the report, a slight decrease from 14,570 in 2006. But progress against terrorism cannot be measured by numbers alone, says NCTC Deputy Director Russ Travers.

"Last year, almost 9,400 police officers were injured or killed. We also saw a growth in the number of attacks against schools," Travers said. "We also have reporting indicating upwards of 2,400 children were killed. The number is undoubtedly far higher, but that's [what] we can document."

Terrorism Remains Complex Threat

Since 2001, improvements in border and transportation security, new banking and legal codes and expanded intelligence cooperation among nations have weakened terrorists, said Dailey, citing foiled terrorist plots in the United Kingdom, Germany and Denmark in 2007.

But terrorism remains a complex threat, Dailey added. Cells operating from safe havens in unstable corners of the world are working to circumvent new security measures by forging alliances with regional affiliates and waging an increasingly Internet-based propaganda campaign to exploit local grievances and recruit a new generation of youth onto the path of radicalism.

"The terrorists' message of hate and death holds no promise for anyone's future," Dailey said.

Countering radicalization is a top priority, said Dailey, and is taking a variety of forms, from Colombia's delivery of services and security in confronting the Revolutionary Armed Forces of Colombia, to Saudi Arabia's initiative to rehabilitate former radicals, to the newly elected Pakistani government's renewed effort to bring peace and security to its tribal regions bordering Afghanistan.

Comprehensive Attention to State Sponsors

Confronting terrorism also means continued attention to state sponsors of terrorism Iran, Syria, Sudan, Cuba and North Korea, Dailey said. Iran's Revolutionary Guard Corps actively provided arms, training and support to Shia militias in Iraq during 2007, said Dailey, as well as to Palestinian militants and Lebanon's Hezbollah. It also aided militant groups in Afghanistan that target civilians and NATO-led peacekeepers.

As many as 90 percent of foreign fighters entering Iraq arrived through Syria, Dailey said, while Cuba has provided aid to the FARC, among others, and North Korea has yet to resolve questions about past bombings and kidnappings. While Venezuela is not officially considered a state sponsor of terrorism, its recent moves in support of the FARC are a cause for concern, he added.

In the case of Iran and North Korea, a comprehensive approach to counterterrorism overlaps international concerns about the potential spread of chemical, biological and even nuclear weapons to terrorists. "All nations that fail to live up to their counterterrorism and nonproliferation obligations deserve greater scrutiny as potential facilitators of [weapons of mass destruction] terrorism," Dailey said.

International Collaboration Progressing

Terrorists transcend international boundaries, making regional and global cooperation a must, said Dailey, as seen in 2007 in successes by the Philippines and Indonesia in confronting, respectively, the terrorist groups Abu Sayyaf and Jemaah Islamiyah, as well as in Africa, where Mauritania and Somalia confronted al-Qaeda-linked insurgencies.

The United States is encouraging a collaborative approach to counterterrorism through its Regional Strategic Initiative, an effort to bring together diplomats and U.S. government experts with their foreign counterparts across a region to share information and work together against terrorists by providing aid and development assistance, health care and education or police and military training to give states the tools they need to safeguard their citizens. "Over time, our global and regional cooperative efforts will reduce terrorists' capacity to harm us and our partners, while local security and development assistance will build our partners' capacity," Dailey said.

The Nuclear Option and the "War on Terrorism"

The wars on Afghanistan and Iraq are part of a broader military agenda, which was launched at the end of the Cold War. The ongoing war agenda is a continuation of the 1991 Gulf War and the NATO led wars in Yugoslavia (1991-2001). The war on Iraq has been in the planning stages at least since the mid-1990s. A 1995 National Security document of the Clinton administration stated quite clearly that the objective of the war is oil "to protect the United States' uninterrupted, secure U.S. access to oil."

In September 2000, a few months before the accession of George W. Bush to the White House, the Project for a New American Century (PNAC) published its blueprint for global domination under the title: "Rebuilding America's Defenses." The PNAC is a neo-conservative think tank linked to the Defense-Intelligence establishment, the Republican Party and the powerful Council on Foreign Relations (CFR) which plays a behind-the-scenes role in the formulation of US foreign policy.

The PNAC's declared objectives are:

- defend the American homeland;
- fight and decisively win multiple, simultaneous major theater wars;
- perform the "constabulary" duties associated with shaping the security environment in critical regions;
- transform U.S. forces to exploit the "revolution in military affairs;"

Deputy Defense Secretary Paul Wolfowitz, Defense Secretary Donald Rumsfeld and Vice President Dick Cheney had commissioned the PNAC blueprint prior to the 2000 presidential elections.

The PNAC outlines a roadmap of conquest. It calls for "the direct imposition of U.S. "forward bases" throughout Central Asia and the Middle East "with a view to ensuring economic domination of the world, while strangling any potential "rival" or any viable alternative to America's vision of a 'free market' economy". Distinct from theater wars, the so-called "constabulary functions" imply a form of global military policing using various instruments of military intervention including punitive bombings and the sending in of US Special Forces, etc.

New Weapons Systems

The PNAC's "revolution in military affairs" (meaning the development of new weapons systems) consists of the Strategic Defense Initiative, the concurrent weaponization of space and the development of a new generation of nuclear weapons. The Strategic Defense Initiative, (Star Wars), not only includes the controversial "Missile Shield", but also a wide range of offensive laser-guided weapons with striking capabilities anywhere in the world, not to mention instruments of weather and climatic warfare under the High Altitude Auroral Research Program (HAARP).

Recent scientific evidence suggests that HAARP is fully operational and has the ability of potentially triggering floods, droughts, hurricanes and earthquakes. From a military standpoint, HAARP is a weapon of mass destruction. Potentially, it constitutes an instrument of conquest capable of selectively destabilizing agricultural and ecological systems of entire regions. Also contemplated is the Pentagon's so-called FALCON program. FALCON is the ultimate New World Order weapons' system, to be used for global economic and political domination. It can strike from the continental US anywhere in the World.

It is described as a "global reach" weapon to be used to "react promptly and decisively to destabilizing or threatening actions by hostile countries and terrorist organizations". This hypersonic cruise weapon system tc be developed by Northrop Grumman "would allow the U.S. to conduct effective, time-critical strike missions on a global basis without relying on overseas military bases. FALCON would allow the US to strike, either in support of conventional forces engaged in a war theater or in punitive bombings directed against countries that do not comply with US economic and political diktats.

The "Pre-emptive" Use of Nuclear Weapons

The Bush Administration has adopted a first strike "pre-emptive" nuclear policy, which has now received congressional approval. Nuclear weapons are no longer a weapon of last resort as during the Cold War era. In a classified Pentagon document (Nuclear Posture Review) presented to the US Senate in early 2002, the Bush Administration established so-called "contingency plans" for an offensive "first strike use" of nuclear weapons, not only against the "axis of evil" (Iraq, Iran, Libya, Syria and North Korea), but also against Russia and China.

The pre-emptive nuclear doctrine contained in the Nuclear Posture Review is supported by the Republican Party and Washington's conservative think-tanks:

"The Pentagon must prepare for all possible contingencies, especially now, when dozens of countries, and some terrorist groups, are engaged in secret weapon development programs."

While scaling back – in agreement with Russia — on the number of nuclear warheads, the Pentagon's objective is not only to 'modernize' its nuclear arsenal, but also to establish "full spectrum dominance" in outer space. With advanced surveillance equipment and space weaponry, the U.S. would be able to inflict force locally and instantly anywhere in the world, directly from orbiting satellites, using an appropriate level of pain and doing so with impunity.

The US, Britain and Israel have a coordinated nuclear weapons policy. Israeli nuclear warheads are pointed at major cities in the Middle East. The governments of all three countries stated quite openly, in the months leading up to the war on Iraq, that they were prepared to use nuclear weapons "if they are attacked" with so-called "weapons of mass destruction." Barely a few weeks following the entry of the US Marines into Baghdad in April 2003, the US Senate Armed Services Committee gave the green light to the Pentagon to develop a new tactical nuclear bomb, to be used in conventional war theaters, "with a yield [of up to] six times more powerful than the Hiroshima bomb".

The "Privatization" of Nuclear War

This green light decision of the Senate Armed Services Committee was followed a few months later by a major redefinition of US policy pertaining to nuclear weapons. On August 6, 2003, the day the first atomic bomb was dropped on Hiroshima, 58 years ago, a secret meeting was held with senior executives from the nuclear industry and the military industrial complex at Central Command Headquarters at the Offutt Air Force Base in Nebraska.

"More than 150 military contractors, scientists from the weapons labs, and other government officials gathered at the headquarters of the US Strategic Command in Omaha, Nebraska to plot and plan for the possibility of "full-scale nuclear war" calling for the production of a new generation of nuclear weapons—more "usable" so-called "mini-nukes and earth penetrating "bunker busters" armed with atomic warheads."

The new nuclear policy explicitly involves the large defense contractors in decision-making. It is tantamount to the "privatization" of nuclear war. Corporations not only reap multibillion-dollar profits from the production of nuclear bombs, they also have a direct voice in setting the agenda regarding the use and deployment of nuclear weapons.

The Nuclear weapons industry, which includes the production of nuclear devices as well as the missile delivery systems, etc., is controlled by a handful of defense contractors with Lockheed Martin, General Dynamics, Northrop, Raytheon and Boeing in the lead.

It is worth noting that barely a week prior to August 6 meeting, the National Nuclear Security Administration (NNSA) disbanded its advisory committee which provides an "independent oversight" on the US nuclear arsenal, including the testing and/or use of new nuclear devices. Meanwhile, the Pentagon had unleashed a major propaganda and public relations campaign with a view to upholding the use of nuclear weapons for the "defense of the American Homeland."

In an utterly twisted logic, nuclear weapons are presented as a means to building peace and preventing "collateral damage". The Pentagon has intimated, in this regard, that the 'mini-nukes' (with a yield of less than 5000 tons) are harmless to civilians because the explosions 'take place under ground'. Each of these 'mini-nukes', nonetheless, constitutes – in terms of explosion and potential radioactive fallout – a significant fraction of the atom bomb dropped on Hiroshima in 1945.

Formally endorsed by the US Congress in late 2003, the mini-nukes are considered to be "safe for civilians". Once this assumption has been built into military planning, it constitutes a consensus, which is no longer the object of critical debate. Decisions pertaining to the use of these nuclear weapons will be based on the prior "scientific" assessments underlying this consensus that they are "not dangerous for civilians".

The propaganda campaign stipulates that the mini-nukes are harmless. Based on this premise, the US Congress has given the "green light": this new generation of nuclear weapons is slated to be used in the next phase of the war, in "conventional war theaters" (e.g. in the Middle East and Central Asia) alongside conventional weapons.

In December 2003, the US Congress allocated $6.3 billion solely for 2004, to develop this new generation of "defensive" nuclear weapons. The overall annual defense budget is in excess of 400 billion dollars, more than the entire Gross Domestic Product (GDP) of the Russian Federation.

Nuclear Weapons and the "War on Terrorism"

To justify pre-emptive military actions, the National Security Doctrine requires the "fabrication" of a terrorist threat, —i.e. "an outside enemy." It also needs to link these terrorist threats to "State sponsorship" by so-called "rogue states."

Spelled out in the 2002 National Security Strategy (NSS), the preemptive "defensive war" doctrine and the "war on terrorism" against Al Qaeda constitute essential building blocks of the Pentagon's propaganda campaign. In the wake of September 11, 2001, the nuclear option is intimately related to the "war on terrorism."

The objective is to present "preemptive military action" —meaning war as an act of "self-defense" against two categories of enemies, "rogue States" and "Islamic terrorists", both of which are said to possess weapons of mass destruction:

"The war against terrorists of global reach is a global enterprise of uncertain duration. ...America will act against such emerging threats before they are fully formed.

...Rogue states and terrorists do not seek to attack us using conventional means. They know such attacks would fail. Instead, they rely on acts of terror and, potentially, the use of weapons of mass destruction (...)

The targets of these attacks are our military forces and our civilian population, in direct violation of one of the principal norms of the law of warfare. As was demonstrated by the losses on September 11, 2001, mass civilian casualties is the specific objective of terrorists and these losses would be exponentially more severe if terrorists acquired and used weapons of mass destruction.

The United States has long maintained the option of preemptive actions to counter a sufficient threat to our national security. The greater the threat, the greater is the risk of inaction- and the more compelling the case for taking anticipatory action to defend ourselves, (...). To forestall or prevent such hostile acts by our adversaries, the United States will, if necessary, act preemptively."

This "anticipatory action" under the NSS includes the use of tactical nuclear weapons, which are now classified as in theater weapons alongside conventional weapons. Nuclear weapons are presented as performing defensive functions to be used against so-called "rogue states" and terrorist organizations, including Al Qaeda,

The propaganda ploy emanating from the CIA and the Pentagon consists in presenting Al Qaeda as capable of developing a nuclear device. According to a report entitled "Terrorist CBRN: Materials and Effects" by the CIA's Intelligence Directorate (released 2 months prior to the August 2003 "Hiroshima day" meeting in Nebraska):

"Al Qaeda's goal is the use of [chemical, biological, radiological or nuclear weapons] to cause mass casualties...

[Islamist extremists] "Have a wide variety of potential agents and delivery means to choose from for chemical, biological and radiological or nuclear (CBRN) attacks," said the four-page report titled."

Amply documented, the "war on terrorism" is fabricated.

The nuclear threat emanating from Al Qaeda is also fabricated, with a view to justifying Washington's pre-emptive nuclear policy. Needless to say, the September 11 2001 terrorist attacks have served to galvanize public opinion, particularly in the US, in support of the pre-emptive war doctrine.

While the media has its eyes riveted on Islamic terrorists and Al Qaeda, the threats to global security resulting from Washington's pre-emptive nuclear doctrine are barely mentioned. Deafening Silence: the August 6 2003 "Hiroshima Day" meeting in Nebraska was not covered by the mainstream media. In the wake of September 11, 2001, the "war on terrorism" constitutes a cover-up of the broader objectives underlying US military and economic expansionism. The central objective is to eventually destabilize Russia and China.

War and the Economy

The articulation of America's war agenda coincides with a worldwide economic depression leading to the impoverishment of millions of people. The economic crisis is the direct result of a macro-economic policy framework under IMF-World Bank-WTO auspices. More generally, trade deregulation, privatization and downsizing under the neoliberal policy agenda have contributed to the demise of the civilian economy. The recession hits the civilian sectors of economic activity. It tends to support the growth of the military industrial complex.

The shift towards a war economy is has resulted in massive austerity measures applied to all areas of civilian expenditure including public investment in infrastructure and social programs. While the civilian economy plummets, extensive financial resources are funneled towards America's war machine. In North America and the European Union, State resources which had previously been tagged to finance health and education have been redirected towards defense.

The war economy will not resolve the mounting tide

of unemployment. This new direction of the US economy geared towards the military industrial complex, will generate hundreds of billions of dollars of surplus profits, while contributing very marginally to the rehabilitation of the employment of specialised scientific, technical and professional workers laid-off in recent years in the civilian sectors of economic activity.

This redirection of the US economy is motivated by geopolitical and strategic objectives. The most advanced weapons systems are being developed by America's military-industrial complex with a view to achieving a position of global military and economic dominance, not only in relation to China and Russia, but also in relation to the European Union, which Washington considers a potential encroachment.

Behind America's so-called "war on terrorism" is the militarization of vast regions of the world. Since the 1999 war in Yugoslavia, an Anglo-American military axis has developed based on a close coordination between Britain and the U.S. in defense, foreign policy and intelligence. The defense industries of the US, Britain, Canada and Israel are increasingly integrated.

Under the Trans-Atlantic Bridge, an agreement signed in 1999, British Aerospace Systems Corporation (BAES) has become increasingly integrated into the system of procurement of the US Department of Defense. In turn, Israel, although not officially part of the Anglo-American axis plays a central strategic role in the Middle East on behalf of Washington.

Europe versus America

A rift in the European defense industry has occurred. There are serious divisions within NATO. While Britain is firmly aligned with the US, France and Germany have joined hands in the development of a European based weapons arsenal, which challenges the hegemony of the US.

Franco-German integration in aerospace and defence production since 1999 constitutes a response to U.S. dominance in the weapons market. The latter hinges upon the partnership between America's Big Five and Britain's defence industry under the trans-Atlantic bridge agreement.

In 1999, in response to the alliance of British Aerospace with Lockheed Martin, France's Aerospatiale-Matra merged with Daimler's Deutsche Aerospace (DASA) forming the largest European defence conglomerate. And the following year, the European Aeronautic Defence and Space Co. (EADS) was formed integrating DASA, Matra and Spain's Construcciones Aeronauticas, SA.

The Franco-German alliance in military production under EADS means that Germany (which does not officially possess nuclear weapons) has become a de facto producer of nuclear technology for France's nuclear weapons program. In this regard, EADS already produces a wide range of ballistic missiles, including the M51 nuclear-tipped ballistic submarine-launched ICBMs for the French Navy.

War and globalization go hand in hand. The powers of the Wall Street financial establishment, the Anglo-American oil giants and the U.S.-U.K. defense contractors are indelibly behind this process, which consists in extending the frontiers of the global market system. The purpose of America's New War is to transform sovereign nations into open territories (free trade areas), both through military means, as well as through the imposition of deadly "free market" reforms.

The objective behind this war is ultimately to re-colonize not only China and the countries of the former Soviet block, but also the entire Middle Eastern region and the Indian peninsula. Concurrently, Washington's objective is to exert global dominance in military affairs, overshadowing the military capabilities of its European "allies". The development of America's nuclear arsenal including the pre-emptive use of nuclear weapons in conventional war theaters is an integral part of this process.

6

War against Terrorism

The advent of twenty-first century is not good for humanity. War is the major characteristic of the modern age. Today, few words are as politically or emotionally charged as "terrorism" but it is still not clear what exactly "terrorism" is. Generally speaking, "terrorism" is the use of politically-motivated violence or terror by state or non-state actors and groups. It is a derisive and subjective term with negative connotations applied to one's enemies and opponents. What may be "terrorism" to one could be a "freedom struggle" for the other. Interestingly, for example, the American definition of "terrorism" is "intimidation of governments" which is totally converse to the word's original meaning given in the Oxford Dictionary, i.e. "government by intimidation" into "intimidation of governments." State terrorism, like terrorism, is also controversial and there is no generally accepted definition.

Often acts that critics describe as terror, supporters defend as legitimate defence against perceived threats. Generally, the definition of terrorism does not extend to states in direct and open military conflict, if the actions of their armed forces are within the laws of war. Despite all this descriptive uncertainties, one thing is clear that "terrorism" is not all about individuals or about a neglected country like Afghanistan or for that matter, countries like Pakistan, Iran, Iraq and North Korea which in today's geopolitical global environment arouse concern in some quarters only for "subjective" reasons. War is an act of aggression between two or more nations. While terrorism is a relative term and every country uses it according to its perception in the contemporary world politics.

If we look into the definitions of terrorism given in different sources of international politics, we can deduce that 'terrorism is an act of aggression or violence that creates fear among innocents' or it may be called as 'killing, maiming, threatening and inflicting brutalities upon innocents.' Hence, Terrorism is all about bullying and "terrifying" the weaker, and any such behaviour at the level of states. In fact at individual level the west usually believes that terrorism is the weapon of the weaker against a stronger and a powerful enemy to have a psychological edge. It may be accepted at individual level that such and such individual commit that act of violence. Contrary to this, my hypothesis is that terrorism is an act of the stronger, as a weaker can rarely commit an act of violence due to its poor resources.

This hypothesis is in the perspective of prevailing American state terrorism against the weaker nations. In the modern world, developing countries like Afghanistan, Iran, Iraq, Pakistan and North Korea are politically and economically so unstable that they can hardly have any urge or capacity to employ terrorism for achieving their objectives. No weak or unstable country can abet or cause an act of terrorism. The fear of "fierce" retaliation in case the target of an act of terrorism is a super power is itself a strong inhibiting factor for any weak or unstable country to abet or cause any act of terrorism. It is quiet understandable that Pakistan and Afghanistan are not able to support any terrorist activity. Afghanistan has nothing to loose while Pakistan can never afford to abet terrorism, as it is a land of skillful, talented, hardworking and peaceful people. History has a vindication in this perspective that Pakistan had never indulged in any terrorist activity since its birth.

Therefore, terrorism is such an aggressive activity that mostly lies with the stronger not with the weaker. So Afghanistan and Pakistan are not under a cloud as far as terrorism or abetting terrorism is concerned owing to their impoverished political systems and meager economies. One certainly can argue that the stronger nations by their might commit aggression against the less powerful nations for which they try to justify their acts of naked aggression disguised by the civilized slogans like 'human rights,' 'peace,' 'democracy' etc. but collective or individual terrorism is generally resorted by those who do not have resources to do otherwise. America and Israel along with their allies are stronger in the world not only economically and militarily but also in technological sophistications. Media is also a big weapon in their hands. The South Asia does not have a strong media that could compete with the credibility of the western media.

India is the only country in the region that has a media of great influence but unfortunately, that does not represent the whole South Asia. Put some simple questions to any sane person that who is stronger in the world. Who has quality arms in the world? Whose economy is stronger than the rest of the world? Who is killing innocents in the world? The answer will be 'America, Israel and its allies.' Now, it becomes easier to understand the reality of war against terrorism. After incidences like 9/11 in the U.S. and 7/7 in the U.K., the western powers are fighting a war against so-called terrorism. It is useless to know the history of terrorism as it is not appreciating aspect of human life we must concentrate upon the ongoing so- called war against terrorism and its impact on the world especially on South Asia.

After appreciating the meanings of war and terrorism, it becomes very trouble-free for every normal person to realize that war against terrorism is not against terrorism but it is a war for terrorism that based on monopolization of world economic resources by America and its allies and then delivering those resources according to the heart of the west. Benjamin R. Barber writes in his celebrated treatise *Jihad VS. McWorld* in these words, "When other domains wrest sovereignty away from the state, whether they are religious or economic, the result is kind of totalitarian coordination-in the Middle Ages it was theocratic; in this age of McWorld it is economistic."

Today increasing population and manufacturing of sophisticated weapons of mass destruction have increased the competition among nations for gaining economic resources. There are fewer resources and more competitors. After the disintegration of Soviet Union in 1991, America started thinking that it was the only power in the world and announced its new world Order for its dominance. In 1989, Berlin Wall was demolished. The East and the West Germany were reunited officially in 1990. That was the first sign of division of centre of power in the world community after the end of Cold War. In 1990s nuclear detonation by India pronounced it another power in the process. Pakistan also joined the nuclear club by following suit. China is emerging as an economic giant. Iran is going to be nuclear very soon. Japan is a technological hub in the world. Therefore, in such circumstances American dream of dominance in the community of nations seems doubtful. The centre of power has been divided among America, Australia, Brazil, Britain, Canada, China, France, Germany, India, Italy, Japan, and revived Russia. The world has become uni-multipolar rather unipolar.

The phenomenon of globalization is serving as a catalyst for monopolization of economic resources for industrialized world. Economic globalization has started a never-ending competition in the world. Hoffmann says, "Economic globalization has caused inequality among states as well as within countries. Therefore, such inequalities are creating deprivations among few states and provoking them against the dominant powers in the world. In this perspective, we believe that this war for terrorism is preplanned; America initially used Saddam Hussein for entering in the Middle East. Saddam waged war against Kuwait and America came for unconditional support and compelled Iraq to withdraw its forces from Kuwait. In the twenty first century, America has decided to stay in the Middle East for controlling political geography of the region for a considerable time. Owing to its hegemonic designs, America waged war against 'cyber terrorism' in 2001, sensing a threat of being impoverished in future.

The U.S. so-called war against terrorism is in fact a source of bullying the weaker nations of the world. In the absence of any central force and futility of the U.N. in prevailing circumstances has pushed the modern world in to a kind of a state of nature. Barber quotes Leviathan and says, "For there is no international state and thus no guarantor or discoverer of an international good. The international disorder remains a kind of state of nature among nations and it is marked by a "war of all against all." Therefore, contemporary world is experiencing the state of nature where South Asia is the most vulnerable region. Pakistan and Afghanistan are nations that are politically and economically unstable since their birth. Afghanistan has been a buffer state between ancient Czar of Russia and England in the nineteenth century. In the twentieth century, America used it for the collapse of Russia.

In the twenty first century America is utilizing the same to control China, Iran, the Middle East, Central Asia, Pakistan and India under the umbrella of NATO forces. In Afghanistan, out of 18000 troops of NATO American troops are almost 17000. This is increasing day by day to stay longer in the region as Afghanistan has given a base to America in the North of Kabul. So it is crystal clear that who is controlling the region. As far as war against terrorism is concerned, it may be a justification for America to live in the region. America is the creator of Taliban and its blue-eyed boy Osama Bin Laden in Afghanistan during Russian intervention in 1980s. It may be using its subjects (Osama Bin Laden, Mullah Umer and al-Qaeda) for the fulfillment of its dream for controlling the maximum economic fruits of the world. It is in fact not a war against terrorism but a war for terrorism in which American hegemony is the final destiny.

The Final Report of the National Commission on Terrorist Attacks upon the United States has published that is giving very poor information about the collapse of World Trade Centre and debacle of Pentagon. In an article published in 2004, named as *Whitewash as Public Service: How The 9/11 Commission Report defrauds the nation,* Harpers Magazine writer Benjamin DeMott wrote, "The plain, sad reality — I report this following four full days studying the work — is that The 9/11 Commission Report, despite the vast quantity of labor behind it, is a cheat and a fraud. It stands as a series of evasive maneuvers that infantilize the audience, transform candor into iniquity, and conceal realities that demand immediate inspection and confrontation . . . At the core of all these failures lies a deep wariness of earnest, well-informed public debate." Therefore, it is clear that report was itself vague and based on subjectivity. In the same way, report by Iraq study group is again full of misconceptions and even explaining the helplessness of Americans. It says "The situation in Iraq is grave and deteriorating.

There is no path that can guarantee success, but the prospects can be improved." This is how this report starts. It also exposes the fakeness and vagueness in the final findings. Here we have an historical analysis to know about powerful nations' behaviour when they were stronger than the others were. What America is doing today for ruling over the world was done by Muslims in 640s A.D. Hazrat Umar's (RA) generals conquered Azerbaijan, Egypt, Iran, Iraq, Jordan, Khurasan, Kirman, Palestine, Seistan, and

Syria, and included them into the Muslim empire. If you ask any non Muslim about those conquests he may pronounce them a cruel act of history. Since non Muslims have their own perception. Empirical analysis discloses that in the third century Alexander the great conquered the world, in the fifth century Roman and Byzantine Empires came into existence, in the sixth century Muslims ruled over the world until the thirteenth century.

Changeiz Khan and Mongols emerged in the thirteenth century and ruled for three centuries. In the sixteenth century Spanish rose in the world, the seventeenth century was of Dutch conquerors, the nineteenth century was of British Empire and in the twentieth century Zionism conquered the world through its multinational corporations. Consequently, the twenty first century can be considered a sharing between capitalism and Zionism. These details give us a valid point that any nation when had power in the form of religion, economy, politics, or culture at any stage of history that did make conquests and made itself prosperous and dominant. Being a Muslim we can say that Muslim ventures were based on morality, while, the contemporary western ventures are based on selective morality. Since, the people of the west are not convinced with the notion of war against terrorism. Midterm elections of Senate held in America at the end of 2006 in which donkey defeated elephant is a categorical proof of peoples' disliking for war against terrorism. Ruling over the world is an unfulfilled dream of America. We know that American perception about ruling over the world has always been in doldrums owing to some miscalculations on the part of American policy makers.

First, military can never install democracy in the world. It is a wild goose chase to establish democracy through uniformed men and with weapons of mass destruction. This will only earn hatred and enmity from the local people. Second 'megalothymia' (to consider itself superior from others) on the part of America has made it mad for ruling over the world without any moral norms. That is a big hurdle, America is facing today. Morality is the only mean to win hearts and to rule over the world. American failures in Granada, Panama, Vietnam, Afghanistan and now in Iraq are due to its immoral deeds. If current war stands for 'wisdom against radicalism,' it can be predicted that at the end of the twenty-first century American may start thinking rationally and logically as Islam is the fastest growing religion in America after 9/11. Therefore, I hope that this process of Islamisation will go on in America that can bring them home to think wisely rather wildly. May be one can believe that it is a height of optimism or living in fool's paradise. What I believe that it is better to live in fool's paradise than to live in a world where "war of all against all" is going on, recalling Thomas Hobbes' Leviathan, in which he wrote about three hundred years back that "quest for power after power that ceaseth only in death."

Therefore, we can say that so-called war against terrorism is in fact an American war for terrorism. American War for Terrorism and its Impact on South Asia American war for terrorism is a sorry state of affairs for international community. It will have serious impact in the world specifically upon Asia. Asian continent is the biggest continent and have different types of nations. These states are dominant with sub-state actors and some consociational groups those are very much involved in fighting against American interests in these nations. As America is fighting for its so called national interests and intend to live in the region through its vassal states. American base in the North of Afghanistan is serving American purpose to an extent. Afghanistan is at the junction of Middle East, Central Asia and South Asia and share a very small border with China. Therefore, strategically Afghanistan is the best country for America to linger on its stay in the region. Politically, economically and militarily war-ridden country suits best to America and its allies to control Asian powers.

The presence of foreign troops in Afghanistan under the umbrella of North Atlantic Treaty Organization's forces gives a justification to American troops that they are not intervening in the internal affairs of Afghanistan but fighting in Afghanistan against Taliban for installing real democracy and sustaining its staggering economy. This presence consequently, will have a big blow to the political and economic systems of Asian and especially South Asian countries as countries in this region are very weak that have certain vertical and horizontal cleavages. Consequently, American troop's presence in the region will enhance political and economic instability in Asia and South Asia and ultimately it will deteriorate cultural and environmental concerns.

War for terrorism is in fact another name of monopolization of resources, labour, and capital of the world by traditional societies with the assistance of Multinational Corporations, International Financial Institutions, and World Trade Organization. America has become a puppet in the hands of Jewish lobby that is holding the strings of American government. American economy and politics is categorically dominated by Jewish lobby and it always uses the superpower according to its objective of profit maximization. America does have its vital interests in waging war for terrorism to sustain its economic development for future generations that is a right of any sovereign state but it should be observed with morality not with selective morality.

7

Terrorism and Tourism Situation

In 2002, apart from the unstable global situation that affected tourism in many aspects including the economy, world oil prices, and terrorism in various destinations, etc., Thailand's inbound tourism grew reversely. The number of foreign tourists visited Thailand expanded towards a good direction, exceeding the expected rate as we received a total number of 10.79 million tourists, which is a growth rate of 7% from the previous year (the expected number was10.50 million tourists, an expansion rate of 4%). The mentioned growth rate is almost the same with the expansion rate of 7.9% of the Asian Pacific tourism. However, it is higher compared to world tourism, whose growth rate was estimated by the World Tourism Organization (WTO) to be 3%. It can be said that this year, Thailand succeeded its tourism promotion.

There was a good expansion rate in almost every region except Oceania and South Africa. Australia, the major market in Oceania, was affected by its aviation problem as Qantas and British Airways have changed the transit stop from Thailand to Singapore plus the terrorism in Bali in October; therefore, a direct impact occurred to Australian tourists and their confidence in the security system in attractions in Asia was also reduced. As for South Africa, the tourism trend within the market has changed. Nevertheless, the tourism still expanded in other markets. This is a result of the continuous sales promotion and marketing, which supported Thailand's tourism in a prospective direction.

Furthermore, when we look at each market, we can see tourists from major markets, which the Tourism Authority of Thailand (TAT) set as high potential markets and applied aggressive marketing strategies, received a larger number of tourists than expected. These markets include Malaysia, Korea, China, Russia, East Europe, the United Kingdom, Scandinavia, India, New Zealand, and the United Arab Emirates. Likewise, Thailand was successful in capturing more tourists from the high expenditure market segment of the top–end and middle markets, family, and seniors. This reflected that Thailand's policy to attract the top–end market was very successful.

The tourism situation in 2003 is expected to continually grow despite the fact that it is likely that war will happen between the US and Iraq. This is because the war might not affect tourism in East Asia, Thailand's main market. Moreover, medium and long-haul markets like Oceania, the Middle East, and some countries in Europe would prefer traveling to Asia, which is further away from the war scene. These markets will grow at a moderate level. Thailand has a policy to stay neutral and welcome tourists of all nationalities plus its value for money while the rest of the world is at a halt; these factors will benefit Thailand in maintaining its position of an interesting destination. However, the growth in the number of tourists might not be that high because of the unstable situation of the war and the world's economy to follow.

East Asia

The East Asian market had a growth rate of 7.71%, totaling 6,531,546 tourists. Markets that contained good expansion rates were Malaysia, China, Korea, and Japan. China, in particular, grew satisfactorily. Major supportive factors include tourism promotional atmosphere within China and Korea together with Thailand's tourism promotion all year round. Moreover, the Chinese market also gained an advantage from an increasing of flights at the end of the year. The increased flights covered 3 flights/week for Bangkok– Xia Men and Bangkok – Beijing by Thai Airways International Public Company Limited and 2 flights/week for Beijing – Phuket by Air China. As for Malaysia, there was a reduction in international arrivals to international airports excluding Bangkok International Airport.

However, considering the tourism trend via the southern border, it was found that the growth rate was still satisfactory resulting in a good expansion rate of this market. Meanwhile, some markets retained their growth rate; for example, Singapore and Hong Kong. Some markets such as Taiwan faced a reduction in its growth rate. The reduction was caused by the inactive economic situation which resulted in careful expenditure of people, especially for tourism. However, the overall tourism situation of this region was not effected.

The incident in Bali and the Philippines did not have an impact on these markets. In contrast, these created positive factors to Thailand's coastal destinations as they are competitors of Bali. The tourism situation of this region is expected to continually grow although it is foretold that the war between the U.S. and Iraq might occur. In case war breaks out, tourists from this region are likely to prefer traveling within the region to crossing regions. Therefore, it is predicted that the war would have a low impact on tourists from the region.

Europe

Thailand received a total number of 2,450,878 tourists from Europe with a growth rate of 6.35%. Generally, the number of tourists from this region consistently grew all year. Important markets with good expansion include the United Kingdom, France, Italy, Switzerland, Russia, Denmark, Finland, and East Europe. Some large markets like Germany and Sweden faced a dramatic slow down since the beginning of the year and had a growth rate of 1.31% and 0.97%, respectively. Main factors to this halt are a decreasing of flights from Frankfurt – Bangkok by Qantas and British Airways as well as a halt of the economy in both countries plus the current news on insecurity in these countries as a result of the incident in Bali. The mentioned factors caused a dramatic slow down in 2002 to Germany and Sweden, which are large markets with a good rate of expansion. In 2003, the tourism situation of Europe might not largely expand. It will probably retain the same or experience a little lower growth rate compared to 2002.

This is because Europe is still concerned about the global situation together with terrorism, which targets various countries in Europe, and the war between the U.S. and Iraq is trying to involve Europe into the controversy. The world oil prices fluctuate depending on the disagreement between the U.S. and Iraq. The unstable world oil prices have a direct impact on the tourism capital of European tourists in traveling a far distance. The stronger value of the Euro currency will affect the export of this region. This will further affect the economy of Germany, Sweden, France, and Italy. In conclusion, in 2003, major European markets that Thailand should be concerned about are Germany, Italy, Sweden, France, the Netherlands, and Norway while the United Kingdom, Russia, Switzerland, and East Europe will still expand.

Americas

The overall situation of the Americas grew moderately with an expansion rate of 5.98%, an equivalent of 640,143 tourists. This expansion rate is consistent with that of the major market of the U.S., whose growth rate is 5.06%, totaling 485,276 tourists. There is still an impact of terrorism in the U.S. that resulted in a reduction of tourism growth in this region, especially from the U.S. in the first half of the year. Later, the market recovered gradually especially in the beginning. In the third quarter, the market began to experience a dramatic increase in the growth rate replacing the reduction of the same period of the previous year. This is a result of the U.S. economy that gradually improved assuring the American people to spend more. The panic of terrorism reduced its psychological effect of American tourist behaviour.

We can see that although the U.S. regularly announced a warning for Americans all over the world to be more careful about terrorist attacks and to avoid traveling to risky areas of South Asia, the Middle East, Africa, and Southeast Asia including Thailand, the announcement did not affect international arrivals of Americans. This is partly because Thailand still maintains its neutral image as a peaceful destination with value of money. These are like magnets that attract more tourists from this region to choose Thailand as a destination.

The economic recovery of the U.S. also has a positive impact towards other markets within the region, especially Canada and Latin America that have economic relations with the U.S. Clear evidence can be observed in Brazil and Canada, who came back on track with a strong positive movement and a continuous satisfactory improvement all year. Canada gained an additional supportive factor by joint Toronto – Bangkok flights of Air Canada and Thai Airways International Public Company Limited. It is predicted that this market will moderately grow or achieve a rather low growth rate in 2003. An outside factor that might affect the market is the risk of terrorist attacks and the concern about the war between the U.S. and Iraq.

South Asia

There was a rather high expansion rate of 17.25% in the overall international arrivals from the region. In other words, Thailand received 309,745 tourists within South Asia. We received an increasing number of visitors from almost every market within the region except Pakistan that faced a dramatic slow down. Apart from the impact of the U.S. attack in Afghanistan, which resulted in an unstable political situation all over the region and an uncertain internal social status caused by groups of people in various countries, the crisis affected the market only for a short period of time. This is because South Asian people are familiar with the unstable situations within their own countries; therefore, the panic or psychological effect on the people was not tense. The market started to recover rapidly since the second quarter of 2002.

India, the major market that TAT applied an aggressive marketing strategy with, experienced an increasing growth rate of 22.79% totaling 253,110 tourists especially an outstanding expansion of group tours and visitors for medical check – ups and treatments as well as visitors on business trips, which is very popular in the market. As the U.S. and the U.K. as well as other destinations in the Middle East, Africa, and some countries in Southeast Asia, is at risk for security issues, Thailand became a destination with high advantages.

It is expected that the market will continue to grow strongly until the beginning of 2003. However, tourism promotion among markets in Southeast Asia must be processed with care, as there has been a group of people imitating documents for entrance to the kingdom. These groups have been proven to be Indian, Pakistani, Sri Lanka, and Nepalese nationals.

Oceania

International arrivals of tourists from this region totaled

423,501, which is a decrease of 0.98% from the previous year. The reduction occurred continually since the second quarter as a result of the changing of the transit destination from Thailand to Singapore of the Australia–Europe route by Qantas and British Airways. This created an obstacle in traveling from Australia to Thailand. At the end of last year, Thailand also received an impact from the rumor about terrorism in various attractions of Thailand; for example, Phuket and Pattaya as a result of the incident in Bali plus the Australian economy was giving a sign of entering a halt during the second half of 2002. The mentioned factors resulted in a reduction of the growth rate in Oceania. Although the minor market like New Zealand still continued to expand from last year, it cannot accelerate the overall expansion of this region as New Zealand is a small market.

It is predicted that in 2003, the unstable global situation will still have a psychological effect on tourist behaviour. Tourists are concerned about being a target of a terrorist attack, as the region expressed its stand point of being an ally to the U.S. in the war against Iraq. The positive factor for the region in 2003 is that Thai Airways International Public Company Limited is planning to increase the number of flights from Australia–Thailand. This is expected to help alleviate the decreasing of flights last year. In conclusion, it is hoped that the tourism situation of Oceania will still be retained, and if the global situation is not worse, only a small number of tourists from Oceania is likely to increase.

Middle East

The Middle East enjoyed a satisfactory movement with an increasing expansion rate of 14.98% or 272,805 tourists. Every market within this region contained a positive direction of growth regardless of the unsatisfactory condition at the end of 2001, as a result of the terrorism attack in the U.S. and the U.S. attack in Afghanistan, which caused an effect only for a short period. The tourism trend of visitors in this market returned to normal at the beginning of 2002, especially Israel and the minor markets of the United Arab Emirates and Kuwait. These countries adapted quickly and resumed an outstanding expansion. Part of the indirect factor to this is that various countries in Europe and the Americas as well as some Asian countries increased strict measures on visa approval specifically for people of Arab nationality causing inconvenience in tourism for visitors from this market.

Meanwhile, Thailand still maintained its image of a neutral destination, welcomed tourist of all nationalities, and offered fair tourism prices, the Arabs were, therefore, interested in the country. Since the second quarter, Arab tourists changed their plan to travel more to Asia, especially Thailand rather than Europe and America. Thailand's sales promotion in the markets of the Middle East in May, which presented new tourism products such as health, spa, and medical treatments, responded greatly to the demand of the market and is a popular new tendency. Since the third quarter of 2002, the market was affected by the incident of the U.S. weapons inspection in Iraq and preparation to attack the country. This has caused panic to the people of the Middle East for fear of a second Gulf War that is expected to be more violent than the first one.

The tourism of this market is not much affected by this factor, as we can see that Thailand still continuously received an increasing number of tourists from this region. Connecting flights from major cities in the region including Abu Dhabi, Bahrain, and Dubai, to Bangkok were increased in the winter flight schedule of 2002/3 in order to respond to the expanding demand of visitors from this market. In 2003, it is predicted that the market will still retain its positive movement although it will not achieve a very high growth rate as a result of the U.S. military operation in Iraq as well as the violent solution for Israel and Palestine in settling their disagreement, which began to have more influence on the reduction of the market expansion.

Africa

The overall growth rate of this market reduced 1.66%, a total of 89,449 tourists. South Africa, the major market, experienced a slow down with a growth rate of 10.24% or 37,721 tourists. The African market did not receive much impact from the incident in the U.S., as we can see from the consistent increasing number of tourists from South Africa to Thailand until the end of last year. However, as we entered 2002, the tourism trend of tourists from this market continually decreased although a positive factor was the sales promotion of South African Airlines; passengers who purchased 2 business class air tickets for the route Bangkok–Johannesburg received another ticket for free. The promotion was aimed to attract businesspeople and the top–end market. Unfortunately, it did not receive the expected response. The inconsistency of rapid change is a characteristic of this market; therefore, it is hard to predict whether or not tourists from this market will continue to increase. As Thailand is a far destination, it is impossible to avoid dramatic changes of the situation. In conclusion, it is expected that Africa will retain its negative movement in 2003.

Outbound Tourism Situation

In 2002, the number of Thailand's outbound tourists totaled 2,249,639, which was an increase of 11.89%. This is considered a rather high expansion compared to the growth rate of the previous year, which equaled 5.33%. This is a result of the improved economy of Thailand, which caused a psychological effect to Thai tourists. They were encouraged to spend more money on overseas trips. Regional trips to Malaysia, Singapore, and China, respectively, were the most popular among the Thai tourists. Various countries in East Asia adopted a tourism promotional policy for the economic improvement in each country; therefore, there was huge marketing and public relations in Thailand especially by our neighbouring countries such as Malaysia and Singapore. China is a very attractive destination for the world's tourists, as it is a new opening country that is abundant with things to be discovered and is also Asia's giant economic country. These factors encouraged more Thai tourists to travel to the mentioned destinations.

Details on Tourists

Despite the unstable situation of the global tourism industry, the year 2002 continued to experience an expansion in the number of international arrivals to the country at a rate of 7.33 percent, attracting 10.8 million visitors. Almost all markets enjoyed certain rates of growth except for Oceania and Africa. East Asia still maintained the largest market share with 6.53 million tourists. The average length of stay was 7.98 days, a slight increase from the previous year which was at 7.93 days. The length of stay was mostly due to the expansion of stay by tourists from the Americas, Oceania and the Middle East, resulting in a total stay of 86.14 million tourist nights, an increase of 7.95 percent.

More than half of the international tourist arrivals to Thailand in 2002 were first-time visitors, which was the group that experienced quite a rapid expansion in almost every market except for Africa, whereas the growth rate was not as high for the Revisits although there was still uninterrupted traffic by this group. Package tour travelling with a travel agency experienced a high expansion rate in almost all regions except for Africa. As a consequence, the market share increased slightly from 42.14 percent in 2001 to 45.66 percent in 2002. This was consistent with the tourist behaviour that was mostly first-time visitors.

The expansion rates of male and female tourist arrivals to Thailand were slightly different. Male tourists still had a higher market share than females, at a proportion of 60:40 percent or 6.43:4.37 million and there was also a slight difference of the two highest market shares of Tourist Arrivals by Age, which belonged to the 25-34-year-old group and the 35-44-year-old one, resulting in an average age of 39.61 years. The main Purpose of Visit was still for holiday with a proportion of 89.26 percent or an increase of 8.59 percent. Most of the international tourist arrivals to the country as classified by occupation were commercial personnel and labourers and tourists arrivals to Thailand in 2002 mostly stayed in hotel accommodation.

8

Living and Believing in an Unstable World

When people in the future look back on the decades that surrounded the turn of the twenty-first century and of the third millennium, what are they likely to notice most? Surely one thing will be the contrast between the beginning of the 1990s and the beginning of the subsequent decade. In the early 1990s, the world was still celebrating the astonishing collapse of Communism in Europe and the dramatic end of the Cold War period. No one could really imagine what would take the place of the bipolar relations that had marked the second half of the twentieth century, after the cataclysm of two world wars in the first half. Some, like Francis Fukuyama, opined that this meant the ultimate triumph of democratic capitalism, and perhaps the ushering in of what Immanuel Kant had dreamt of at the end of a century two hundred years earlier—a "perpetual peace." Others along the same line hoped that worldwide disorder might finally be coming to an end. It did not take long, however, for a very different picture to emerge. The Cold War standoff had kept many local conflicts under control; only those that served as proxies for the Big Power struggles were permitted to come to the surface.

Within a few years, Samuel Huntington was predicting a "clash of civilizations," with a key fault line between the

Christian West and the world of Islam. Today, those voices that heralded the world as being a place of such harmony and peace for the foreseeable future are silent. Hardly anyone sees the beginnings now of a perpetual peace. Rather, observers point to factors that portend badly for a peaceable future. To mention but one: the high birth rates in many countries in the world are providing a supply of unemployed young males for at least the next thirty years. This is the group most likely to cause unrest and civil disorder. But rather than engaging in a generalized apocalyptic doom, it is important to try to look closely and carefully at what is happening today. The intent of these lectures is to do that: to look at where we are in the world today, to find adequate ways of interpreting what is happening, and to see what resources in Christian faith and heritage might contribute to making this world a better place to be, for ourselves and for those generations that we hope will follow us.

In order to do this, I would like to devote this first lecture to the task of describing where are some of the neuralgic points in our world today—those points that cause us concern or even outright distress. Responding to this distress will then set the scene for the second and third lectures, which will take up themes of new ways of looking at these challenges, and the resources of Christian faith to respond to them. In order to fulfill that first aspiration, of looking at the world today, I want to point to four major movements that have largely (but not exclusively) begun in the last decade and a half that together are making the world a turbulent and unstable place. I would like to treat them in more or less in the order that they have come to our attention. They are: globalization, increased migration, the resurgence of religion, and threats of global terrorism. Having done that, I will turn to two of the principal frameworks available for accounting for the phenomena, and at times the consequences, of these movements. These frameworks are post-modernity and multiculturalism, respectively. I will argue that both of these have become increasingly unhelpful as analytic tools for reading the signs of our times.

Globalization

The first is globalization. This movement was already under way in 1990, but it took the end of state socialism in 1989 and 1991 to see how far it had already progressed. New movements of globalization are initiated by changes in communication and transportation. The information technology developments that began in the 1980s became widely accessible in the 1990s as first personal computers, and then the development of the World Wide Web changed the way people were connected and communicated. The consistent drop in air transportation costs did for space what information technologies were doing for time. Hence, both space and time have shrunk. When these were wedded to the economic forces of capitalism, a single, worldwide set of interconnected markets came into existence.

For those who were inside this network, there was an opportunity to make significant financial gain. But those on its fringes or outside the network, however, often fell even further behind, losing the little gain that had been made in the 1960s and 1970s. This has been affecting not only the historically poor countries, but also the working poor in the societies most directly benefiting from globalization. To be sure, at a macro-level, globalization was lifting the giant populations in India and especially China statistically to new levels of prosperity, but it is often those losing out within those societies who have felt the keenest pinch. Globalization creates a great deal of turbulence and instability. It is a rough ride for many, struggling to hold on as market forces and competition force us all to continue to lurch ahead. In the early 1990s, globalization's virtues were being sung in many quarters. Today, there is a great deal more caution. The language of its inevitability is fading, and parallels to other periods of globalization—and especially among the Great Powers in Europe leading up to the 1914 War—is beginning to emerge.

A crisis could arise that would make trading partners pull back within their borders, and send the dizzying juggernaut into a tailspin. A second voice being raised in recent years about globalization is that of the World Social Forum, with its slogan "Another world is possible." First seen as an anarchic alternative to the Davos Forum and the World Trade Organization, it is gradually taking on more contours of trying to imagine alternative and more humane approaches to the worse depredations of globalization. For those who are caught up in its thrall, however, the breakneck pace that staying up with globalization demands has been taking a greater human toll on personal relationships, societies, and the institutions within those societies. In a recent study done in the United States, arguably the epicenters of the globalization frenzy, Dr. Peter Whybrow of the University of California at Los Angeles describes what he calls the "American mania," of people caught up in the globalization whirlwind, constantly striving for more possessions and higher status even as it ruins their personal relationships and their happiness.

Migration

The second movement is migration. Migration is, of course, as old as human history. But the migration of the last two decades or so has brought some distinctive features into the mix. The nineteenth-century migrations to North America, Australia and New Zealand were largely out of Europe. The relative inexpensive possibilities of air transportation have now created migration from Asia, Africa, and Latin America, as well as inner migration from Eastern Europe to countries in the West. Migration is no longer solely to the Western world; internal migration in all of the continents is currently underway. The combination of "push" factors such as poverty and war, and the "pull" factors of opportunities for a better life have created a pluralisation of our societies such as we have never before seen.

The United Nations Development Programme's 2004 report on migration estimates that at this point in history one out of every thirty-five persons on the planet is a migrant. The number goes up to one out of twelve in Europe. London claims to be the most multicultural city in the world now—at least in terms of sheer numbers of immigrants and asylum seekers. Arguably, however, Toronto and Vancouver have the highest percentages and variety of ethnic backgrounds. Australia is the most multicultural country in the world (again, based on percentage and its relatively low population level), followed by Canada and the United States. Because of the relatively inexpensive means of communication and transportation now available, migrants do not break their times with their homeland as they once had to do. Telephone cards, the Internet, and cheap air tickets make it possible to send cash remittances home and to stay in touch with loved ones.

This has had an effect on how people are viewing citizenship, something studied especially by Canadian sociologist Will Kymlicka, and how they choose to align their allegiances between their country of birth and chosen country of employment. These highly pluralized societies today are experiencing some destabilizing tensions. For countries that have not seen themselves as end points for migration (such as most of the countries of Europe), xenophobic reactions have been taking place. Politicians in Denmark, The Netherlands, Belgium, France, Germany, and Austria are beginning to claim that their countries are "full," that is, cannot accept any more new faces. Great Britain—traditionally friendlier to immigration—has seen a turn in recent months against asylum seekers and other foreigners. Countries once known for their tolerance (such as the Netherlands) are drafting draconian legislation to deal with what they see as a growing "problem." At the same time, economists and demographers are pointing out in many of those countries that they will have to continue to import even more foreigners if they wish to maintain the national standard of living.

The settled population's birthrate is so low that the working population is not being replaced. Consequently, future welfare (if kept to its current level) cannot be paid for. Recent political assassinations of public figures critical of immigration in the Netherlands, and the increasingly shrill rhetoric of politicians and advocates for greater immigration control have reached a harsh level in some places. Two issues seem to underlie the debates. On the one hand, is there a limit to how much social diversity a country can manage? There are differing opinions about if there is such a threshold and where it might lie. In the views of many, democracy is the best form of social ordering found thus far to accommodate high levels of diversity and plurality. But does even democracy have limits? Second, a model of tolerance in which each ethnic group keeps to itself is not providing any cohesion for the total society. The disengaged tolerance of the Netherlands and Belgium is now coming apart. If tensions arise elsewhere, especially in societies with less of a history of tolerance, what will happen to those societies? These are serious questions to be pondered, and as of yet no one has found convincing answers to them.

The Resurgence of Religion

The third movement that is creating turbulence in the world is the resurgence of religion. Up into the 1990s, western sociologists followed the secularization hypothesis with which Max Weber had begun the twentieth century. In this view, the Western Enlightenment was leading to a desacralization of worldviews and of the world itself. First religion would become a private matter, and then it would gradually disappear altogether. That may still true for some societies (especially in the North Atlantic region, and for Australia and New Zealand), but some of those same sociologists who had predicted the forward march of secularization are now noting that there has been a resurgence of interest in religion across the world today. It manifests itself in a variety of different ways. Among the poor and the lower middle classes of Latin America and Africa, Pentecostalism is sweeping through the landscape like wildfire. A third of Guatemala is now Pentecostal. The single largest Christian congregation in the world is in Seoul: Yoido Full Square Gospel Church has more than six hundred thousand members, who fill its twenty-five thousand seat sanctuary six times on Sundays.

Some estimate that there will be more Pentecostals and Charismatics in the world by 2025 than all the Orthodox and mainline Protestants combined. Already there are an estimated 350-500 million of them. What is fuelling this rapid growth cannot be reduced to a single cause. The move from the countryside into urban megalopolises, the empowerment of women, the search for personal power in the midst of being tossed to and fro by globalization, the quest for quick money—all of these contribute to this phenomenon. It has been especially since 1970 that this rapid expansion has been seen. Whether it will continue at this rapid pace through the next decades is anyone's guess, but at the moment it shows no sign of abating. It is rapidly changing the face of Christianity around the world today. In Islam, the second largest religious body in the world after Christianity, there has been a resurgence of faith as well. It, too, is fuelled by diverse factors. Some point to the growing resentment of being humiliated by the Christian West. The invasion and occupation of Afghanistan and Iraq have been the most recent causes for resentment, of Christian forces humiliating Muslims in their own heartland.

The support of Israel by the United States to the neglect of the Palestinian people only confirms such resentment in the minds of many. But there are other factors as well. Many young, educated males in Muslim lands cannot find jobs. Since Western technology has failed them, they turn to their faith. The sheer pace of globalisation, and the migration of Muslims out of majority-Muslim countries into a Muslim diasporas have created an alienation that makes people cling more to their faith. Movements of revival have been moving through the Muslim world since the 1930s, but the recent developments of globalization and migration have brought them to the attention of the rest of the world. As recently as the early 1990s, French scholar Olivier Roy saw worldwide Islam as too decentralized and too disorganized to make much social difference. Today, he speaks more carefully about what he sees happening. It has not been uncommon for Westerners to label all these revival movements as Fundamentalism.

There are, to be sure, fundamentalist movements in Islam, but to paint all the movements with the same brush is surely a misperception, since many Muslims view these movements as a revival of faith in unstable times. There is the radicalization of some young Muslims, particularly those who find themselves marginalized in their own societies and in those countries of immigration where they are viewed with suspicion. The case of the young Muslim, who murdered Theo van Gogh in Amsterdam in November, 2004 is a case in point. Born in the Netherlands of Moroccan parents, he did well in school. But he took a yet unexplained radical turn in the last two years before the event, aligning himself with an extremist understanding of Islam. There are two things about this religious resurgence that intersect especially with the first two movements, namely, globalization and migration. Religion and religious belief —however construed—now is a major player on the stage of international relations. It can no longer be discounted as merely the intrusion of private faith into the public forum.

It is one of the factors that must be calculated into relations between and within states. The problem facing political figures is that all the currently available models for understanding international relations are secular. The only place for religion has been in humanitarian intervention—by religious aid agencies or the pleas of figures like Pope John Paul II. Political theorists are scrambling to move beyond their secular bias to include what has been called "the missing dimension of statecraft." That religion is now implicated so often in political violence has likewise given religion a prominent, if unwelcomed, place at the table. For secular agnostics, religion's role in violence simply confirms the oppressive quality of religion in public life outlined by Feuerbach and Marx in the 19th century. How to account for the attraction of religious legitimation for political violence—as well as how to account for religion's role in peace- building and reconciliation—is still a matter of lively debate, something to which we shall return in the final lecture.

The point is that religion's prominent role in public and international life is now so salient that it cannot be ignored—and to this point, has not been adequately accounted for by either its supporters or its opponents. Because of its great intellectual and emotive power, religion can add to both the stability of the world in the decades ahead, and well as to its instability. The other feature is the relation of this resurgence of religion to migration. Migrants are frequently more explicitly religious in their practice in their new countries than they were in their homelands. When their new country is a largely secularized one, their practice of religion may add another level of tension and conflict between the newcomers and the settled population. This is being seen especially in Europe. African immigrants are bringing with them their African Instituted Churches (AICs), marked by enthusiastic worship, lively singing, focus on healing and the powers of the Spirit. There are now six such congregations in Copenhagen whose Sunday attendance is higher than the rest of the attendance combined in the entire country.

Such African-led congregations are also the largest such congregations in Amsterdam, London, and Birmingham. They are attracting non- immigrants as well. What this will mean for the face of Christianity in a dechristianised Europe in a decade or two remains to be seen. The migration of clergy from India, Nigeria, and the Philippines to the United States is creating a situation where soon a third of all the Roman Catholic clergy in that country will be foreign born. That appears already to be the case among diocesan seminarians. The other intersection between religion and migration is seen also in Europe, where many of the newcomers are Muslims. Even as churches are being closed, torn down, or converted to other uses, mosques and madrasas are being built in the cities and towns of that continent. The opening of a large mosque just north of Vatican City in Rome a few years ago has become emblematic of that change in European society. In parts of secular Europe, where there is even hostility toward religion, this is likely to make things even more volatile, as the sharp contrast between the agnosticism of the larger population and the religiosity of the newcomers portends potential conflict.

The fourth and final movement causing instability in the world is global terrorism. The attacks in New York, on Bali, and in Madrid, as well as the ongoing acts of terrorist violence in the Middle East, have introduced new actors into international politics. Terrorists are not like the nation-states who have been the principal actors on the world stage in war up to this time. That is why a "war on terrorism" seems a bit of a misnomer. It is hard to make war on a concept, and it is harder still to see if one is winning or losing, and especially to see when such a war might be over. We are all aware, however, of how it has been changing our lives. It adds costs and time to air travel. It has had an impact on the flow of foreigners into our countries and universities. It creates periodic patterns of social anxiety as terrorist alerts are raised. It is most noticeable in societies that heretofore have felt them to be internally secure. Now they share the chronic anxiety of societies beset by violence and civil conflict.

Terrorist actions have multiple causes, stemming from resentment, humiliation, hatred, and desperation. It is an unwelcome fact of the twenty-first century, but unlikely to go away any time soon. Globalization, migration, and religious resurgence all contribute to the environment that spawns and sustains terror—and we hope that these three movements, too, will contribute to its resolution. Global terrorism, in a word, is emblematic of the instability with which we live in our world today. Other factors could be named that are adding—or will be adding soon—to this instability. A range of looming environmental crises is at the top of the list. As disputes about whether there will be an impending environmental disaster dwindle in the face of mounting evidence, this challenge will be coming more and more to the fore.

Its dynamics are somewhat different from the four already mentioned, and it is for that reason I will not be going into its implications in these lectures. It certainly deserves attention, but best attention in its own right, not as part of a longer list. So I will be concentrating on these four, since they are quite visible and—at least in the case of three of them—religious faith has something to say about them. This very long introduction to these lectures has been intended to set the stage for looking at how we are responding to these challenges and how we may have to change our frame of mind in order to do so more effectively. So it is not simply a matter of economics (globalization) or demographics (migration) or motivations for violence. Faith, I believe, has to account for itself in the midst of what is happening in the world, as well as begin to offer some contributions to resolving the dilemmas that lie ahead.

In this second part of this first lecture, I want to look at two of the principal frameworks that have been put forward to interpret this world of globalization, migration, religious resurgence and global terrorism —all of which are contributing to shaping a different world and—at least for the time being—creating a good deal of instability. The two frameworks I want to examine here are that of post-modernity and of multiculturalism. They have both developed as ways to help us deal with the dynamics of diversity and difference we encounter in our environments. And I would like to say at the outset that I think neither of them is serving us very well in these matters any more.

Post-modernity

Post-modernity is a slippery concept. As the word itself connotes, it is somehow after the "modern." It was first used in the art world as early as the 1920s. It came to be used in philosophy, the social sciences, literature and finally theology in the last third of the twentieth century. Within the wider domain of knowledge, Jean-François Lyotard's report on knowledge to the government of Quebec in 1979 has served as a kind of benchmark for the postmodern as an intellectual framework. Lyotard paints a picture of the increasing complexification and differentiation of high modernity, an outgrowth of the European Enlightenment. In that process of complexification, one discovers an increasing plurality of phenomena and types of knowledge, with a concomitant sense of the radically historical and the local.

The Universalist pretensions of the French and German Enlightenments seem to be slipping further and further away. One is struck in this complexity by the fact that difference seems to press itself as a priority over similarity and sameness. One is faced with unavoidable and irreducible difference. Metaphysics—on uncertain legs since the time of Immanuel Kant—becomes an untenable assertion. Indeed, as Lyotard pointed out most famously, the "grand narratives" (*grands reçits*), those shared narrative that are the basis of social cohesion and identity, slip further and further away. What we are left with is fragments, disruptions, and discontinuities. Even the sense of the self turns out to be illusory. The work of French deconstruction in literature, led by figures such as Paul De Man and Jacques Derrida, used these same insights to show instabilities in what has been otherwise perceived as coherent texts. Paul Lakeland has been one of the most thoughtful figures in seeing how post modernity has worked itself out in theology.

He has suggested that "postmodern" can refer to an intellectual theory, a set of social values, or even a subculture where these values are lived out. In theology itself, the postmodern turn has manifested itself in three principal ways. First of all, it is an anti- or counter modern turn, questioning modernity as a sound basis for doing theology at all. This is most evident in the Radical Orthodoxy group around John Milbank and Catherine Pickstock, a largely Anglo-American movement. Second, there is a belief that the postmodern is something radically new and thus separate and distinct from high modern theology. The "Death of God" theologians in the United States in the 1960s and the work of figures such as Mark C. Taylor would fit into this category. A third group would say that modernity is only failing us because it has not been thoroughly implemented enough.

Theologians following the German philosopher and sociologist Jürgen Habermas would be in this movement. Post-modernity for them (although some of this third category would not use the term) would entail a more radical delving into modernity. One can see how the postmodern framework might be compatible with the four movements contributing instability to our world today. Globalization has been a fragmenting, destabilizing force for many. Among the majority poor of the world it often wrests away from them any control they may have over their lives and livelihood. Among the wealthy, people are inundated with choices, so that it is hard to think in any other terms than small discrete elements—sound bytes—and to prefer the short-term gain over the long-term haul and development.

Migration heightens our sense of difference. Difference in language and custom, especially in urban areas where more than a hundred different ethnicities may be rubbing up against each other, seems to be the very height of the postmodern. The resurgence of religion has also meant the proliferation of new types of religiosity—either independent forms of Pentecostal and Charismatic faith, or New Age syncretism between Asian traditions and the West, homemade forms of witchcraft in the West, and Neo-Hindu and Neo-Buddhist forms of religion at home in Asian countries but in the West as well. Even within established traditions of Christianity such as Roman Catholicism and Anglicanism we see the fragmentation caused by different ideologies or changing social conceptions of things such as the ordination of gay persons and the legitimating of gay marriage. Contending parties within churches can seem as heterogeneous as those without. And finally, terrorism itself is about the strange, the other, the different, and the dangerous. When seen even cursorily in this light, an inclination might be to say that the postmodern framework is the most suitable one for understanding these changing, often turbulent movements in our kinds of societies.

Many people self-consciously describe themselves as "postmodern," as living in this fragmented, heterogeneous world where difference is prized in its very difference. It is most common among elites who are able to survey the difference around them. But it is also common among young adults who have grown up in this blooming, buzzing reality and see it as the way to survive and to thrive in an open-ending, ever-accelerating, always-changing society. But it is not a useful term for the poor of the world, who do not have the luxury of choice that post-modernity seems to provide, and for whom further fragmentation may threaten their very survival. Put succinctly, post-modernity is a useful way of describing the difference, discontinuity, and fragmentation we are experiencing provided that this difference, discontinuity, and fragmentation does not undermine a basic sense of security and safety.

It may be experienced as swirling around us, but we still have our feet planted firmly on the ground. If that ground beneath our feet is sensed as itself unstable, we are likely no longer to want to exult in difference and discontinuity. This is what happens when one finds oneself living amidst a war, in a failed state, and under direct threat of global terrorism. Then difference and discontinuity is not seen as providing more possibilities for choice, but rather as a threat to our survival. My contention is that many people in wealthier parts of the world who once saw post-modernity as enhancing their choices are now beginning to experience post-modernity's consequences as threatening their existence.

Multiculturalism

"Multiculturalism"—like its counterpart, post-modernity—carries multiple meanings. In the study of populations, it refers to people of many different cultural backgrounds occupying the same space. Within that space, they contend for recognition and respect, for goods and services, for power, and for access to the meaning-making resources of society. This has been—up to the last few years—a common meaning of the term. It is an acknowledgement of the fact that globalization and migration have changed our neighbourhoods and our cities.

It has another meaning, especially from the mid-1990s, a meaning used in a pejorative manner. It refers to the attempts to broaden the general education curriculum in universities to include non-Western texts. At times it has been used to decenter the educational syllabus altogether.

To be reading "dead white European males" was to be "Eurocentric" and hence not "multicultural." Because of those "culture wars" fought in the 1990s, multicultural has become a dirty word for those who wish to preserve the European heritage. The Nobel laureate in Literature Saul Bellow summed it up in these words: "When the Zulu produce a Tolstoy, I will read him." These discussions and debates have subsided somewhat in academe, but the miasma around the term "multicultural" lingers on. Most recently, another pejorative use of the term has appeared. "Multicultural" refers to failed government policies regarding the integration of newcomers into (predominantly Western) societies. Societies that welcomed newcomers with great tolerance, provided support for maintaining cultural heritage (as does the Canadian government), and generally encouraged cultural distinctiveness are now blamed for these same newcomers not being integrated into the larger society.

What "integrated" means varies from place to place? In some instances, it means that newcomers still do not speak the national language. In other instances, it refers to their rejection of dominant culture values regarding equality of women, freedom of choice, freedom of religion, and autonomy of individuals within families. In yet other instances, it means the failure of newcomers to take on citizenship in their adopted lands. In all of these instances, those pointing to what they see as failure are now announcing "multiculturalism is dead!"

By that they mean that such cultural tolerance is a failed policy that threatens the cohesion of the nation. Thus, when multiculturalism operates in stable circumstances, it can be seen as enhancing the variety in our experience of life. In unstable situations, on the other hand, the plurality of cultures bumping up against one another becomes a sign for the unknown, even the dangerous unknown. Toleration of difference becomes strained. If a genuine crisis emerges, then the channels of communication between the different groups may not be sufficient to bear the weight of information and feeling needed, because those channels are not familiar and trusted pathways.

The End of Multiculturalism

As can be seen from even this brief overview of uses of the terms post-modernity and multiculturalism, they both have captured important aspects of the world we are now living in. The diversity, the fragmentation, and the acceleration of life all are given some meaning by appeal to post-modernity. They are all factors that square uneasily with the optimism of the high modern period. Multiculturalism was an attempt to name the increasing plurality of our societies, without perhaps giving much further description of the complex interplay. Some have tried to overcome the limitations of multiculturalism by speaking of polyculturalism. I do not know if switching from a Latin-based to a Greek-based prefix really moves the debate along much. In these lectures I am trying to suggest that, while postmodern and multicultural may be useful descriptive terms for our experience when things are stable and can go relatively unquestioned, they do very little to interpret those experiences or to engage them constructively when we are perceived to be moving into a crisis.

The convergence of globalization, migration, the resurgence of religion, and now the threat of global terrorism have, together, given us a potent brew that makes the world seem at great deal more unstable than has been the case in the recent past. The Cold War certainly carried with its risk and uncertainty. But the lines of demarcation between East and West, between communist and capitalist, were more sharply drawn. The postmodern, by definition, lacks such clarity. The sheer multiplication of cultures in a given place complicates the matter further. I think that terms such as the postmodern and multicultural served us reasonably well in a time of relative stability—or at least perceived stability. That stability could be heard in the euphoric rhetoric after the fall of the Berlin Wall and announcements of the "end of history." We are now in a much more unstable time, especially in view of the threat of global terrorism and ecological collapse. Ulrich Beck, the German sociologist who first wrote about technological and ecological risk in the mid-1980s, has returned again to that theme.

The sense of indeterminate but real and uncontrollable risk now pervades social consciousness. One of the consequences of this is much less tolerance of ambiguity. The language of multiculturalism collapsed in the weeks about September 11, 2001. Instead of celebrating diversity, the clarion cry was: "United we stand." People of ethnic groups that looked to be Middle Eastern had to go out of their way to prove their loyalty to the American ideals. In some instances, Muslim institutions were attacked just because they were Muslim. Similarly, the language of tolerance—so long prized in Dutch society— has disappeared in the Netherlands since the political murders of Pim Fortuyn and Theo van Gogh. In times of risk, an openness to the different and the unknown becomes simply too dangerous. In the face of such threats to our security, the temptation is to move toward a kind of default position (to use the language of information technology) of self-defense. That is, an unexamined way of interpreting things takes over, reshaping our thinking and reorienting our action.

This frame may represent our genuine feelings and fears, heretofore papered over with the rhetoric of post-modernity and multiculturalism. Such unexamined thinking does not serve us well. It attempts to shield us from uncertain and unwanted intrusions into our world, but it does not engage them in any significant way. That is what is happening, I believe, in Western societies today, in the anxiety over the long-term effects of globalization, continuing migration, resurgent religion, and global terrorism. We know that, historically, societies who perceive themselves to be under such threat are willing to sacrifice their liberty to more authoritarian rule. If the perception of threat becomes interwoven with a sense of being wronged or humiliated, it can lead to forms of fascism and willingness to sacrifice those "others" in our midst at any cost.

The question then becomes: can we find a more adequate framework for interpreting this unstable world that will lead to a better way of living together on our planet, that will guide us in overcoming the challenges facing us (rather than ignoring, denying or repressing them)? These are the questions that animate this presentation and these lectures. In the second of these lectures, I want to take up the question of such frameworks. Can we find our way forward into a different kind of modernity that will account for what we are experiencing in terms of plurality, difference, contingency, and instability without engaging in violence toward one another or creating fortress-like havens of safety where people may survive for a time, but will not flourish? It is with this question that we turn to the second lecture.

Fundamentalism to a Cosmopolitan Worldview

The previous lecture looked at four factors that have made the world an increasingly unstable place in the last decade and a half. Globalization, migration, the resurgence of religion, and global terrorism has all contributed to creating a very different kind of environment for human life today. It was noted that two of the frameworks that were most frequently used to interpret much of this were invocations of post-modernity and multiculturalism. While these both had descriptive value, authenticating in some way the sense of diversity, difference, fragmentation, and instability, they did not of themselves have much explanatory power to help us interpret the world we live in, especially when that world became fundamentally unstable.

Nor did they suggest much by way of action to address that instability, other than affirmation of those same experiences they were intended to describe. And given the fact that the instability they herald provokes anxiety, the response we do give may grow out of our worst instincts rather than our best lights. We may well find ourselves falling back into a "default" position that will not permit us to deal with these realities in a creative fashion. In this lecture, I would like to propose an interpretive framework that will attempt to move us beyond relying on post-modernity and multiculturalism as modes of response. This is, needless to say, a first and tentative effort. The reality we are addressing here is complex. Nor can it be worked out in sufficient detail within the short compass of these lectures. My hope, however, is to give a first glimpse of a direction that might be taken to move along the discussion of how we are to live in the world that is taking shape around us.

My basic hypothesis is this: although Lyotard and others aligned with some form of postmodernism have declared the "death of the grand narrative" and even the "death of the subject," I think their claim is overdrawn. To be sure, their consigning to the dustbin of history socially shared narratives of whole societies that make overstretched claims is probably well taken. The claims of the utter universality and triumph of Western values over those of other societies does look like imperial overreach. The confidence that reason can lead to socially engineered utopias probably deserves the same fate.

If the twentieth century was the acme of high modernity, its far-reaching claims have much to answer for: two world wars, genocides on new and terrifying scales, nuclear destruction, and perhaps irreversible environmental degradation cannot be claimed as triumphs for humankind. Certainly such grand narratives need to be exposed for what they are. But to move from there and say that no grand narrative is any more possible goes a bit too far. If anything, global communications has made commonly shared narrative more possible now than in the past. Think of the rolling celebration of the millennium in the year 2000 from Kiribati around the world to the mid-Pacific on our televisions.

The mobilization of sentiment through those same media, be it at the death of Diana, Princess of Wales; the views on the Middle East from Al-Jezeera; or the devastating effects of the 2004 tsunami in the Indian Ocean have created shared narratives that were not possible before the information era. To be sure, viewers of these spectacles and reportage are not passive agents; they can construct meaning at local levels that elude the control of the meaning makers. One should more properly speak here of narrative flows, that is, chains of locally constructed and transmitted narratives that are at once mutually intelligible, yet reflect concrete circumstances in local communities. Such flows have been in evidence in the social forces of globalization since the mid-1990s, and are becoming more prevalent today.

These flows may well represent as close as we may come to an explicitly "universal"—be it socially or in our theology—in our complex and interconnected times. Similarly, how well people are able to adjust to constant and thoroughgoing difference —especially when it threatens identity and safety—cannot stand as an assumed and unexamined premise. Especially when the transition is very rapid, most of us are likely to need help through this period.

Unlimited difference may work when other aspects of society are secure, but when society itself appears under threat, our actions need to be more deliberate, and we need a place to stand from which we can see the bigger picture. I would suggest, then, that in an unstable world, the response to the heterogeneity, the difference, and the fragmentation of the postmodern and to the relativist juxtaposition of the multicultural is not more of the same—becoming more postmodern and more relativist.

To advocate this strategy is not to take into account how people act under threat. To write people off as being overly anxious or pathologically afraid is not a recipe for an ordered society. That is precisely not a celebration of difference: it is, rather, excluding people from the conversation. I think a more fruitful approach is to posit that, we as human beings, are involved in a constant searching for the whole, that is, an ongoing quest to take these disparate experiences, sensations and idea, and craft them into patterns of intelligibility. That intelligibility may be cognitive, moral, social, or aesthetic —or all of the above. The point is that we do not live in an utterly unordered world. To do so would condemn us all to solipsism and silence. Unless we can discern and delineate some of the patterning that is going on in this bewildering variety of data, we give ourselves over to a Hobbesian world where the strongest and those with most access to power will prevail. The first reaction to such a proposal may be one of extreme caution.

Because we know what kind of unities or wholes were crafted out of the chaos of the immediate past century. Varieties of totalitarian rule—be it fascist, communist, revanchist or what have you—have been imposed by strongmen upon a helpless population. To suggest such stirs resistance even in those who are the most critical of the Enlightenment. This is a set of dangers for which we must remain vigilant. But fear, uncertainty and the lack of security will drive even the most rational into postures they would not have accepted of themselves in calmer times. Recent legislation regarding immigrants and potential terrorists in different countries in Europe, the United States, and Australia are evidence of this.

To simply turn our heads away, saying that we must do this because the world has become too dangerous will not eliminate the danger. As human beings, we are symbol-makers, and we do not make them in isolation from one another. It seems to me better to pay close attention as to how we try to construct a sense of the whole rather than see it as a slippery slope that leads to totalitarianism. If we are able to learn from history and from previous reflection on great human failures, we have a better chance of constructing something that will indeed serve the well-being of the human community. In this lecture, then, I would like to begin by examining four such attempts at seeking the whole that go astray. They are all modes that have been engaged in by societies in recent times.

To simply dismiss them as pathologies fails to understand their attraction. To overcome them requires comprehending the needs they address and the questions they answer. As will be clear, I am not recommending any of them. But I recognize the kind of lure they have had for some people. Having done that, I will turn to an emerging model that is being discussed principally in Great Britain and Germany today that goes by different names: reflexive modernity, new modernity, second modernity. Here is where I think we have the best chance to overcome the misfires that turn quests for the whole into new oppressive forms of totalitarianism. In order to begin, however, there must be a few words about modernity itself. Like post-modernity it is a slippery concept, one that cannot be resolved here. What is offered is no more than a benchmark against which to measure what will come after.

One View of Modernity

A good way to get some perspective on the elusive concept of modernity is to step outside the North Atlantic, and in Western ambit, where modernity was born and where its flame is kept most brightly burning. As with secularization, there was once the view that the rest of the world would follow in the path blazed by Europe, especially with the French and the Scottish Enlightenments. Today, it is more common to speak of modernities in the plural. They bear family resemblances and can communicate with one another, but are not carbon copies or (perhaps now the more apposite metaphor) clones of one another. For such a view, I turn here to the Mexican critic Néstor García Canclini, in his study of hybridity, modernity, and mixing. 26 In looking at modernization from a Latin American perspective, he describes modernity as the result of four interlocking projects.

The first he calls an 'emancipating' project, wherein all aspects of life are secularized, i.e., emancipated from ecclesiastical or political control. Social life is rationalized and individualism becomes the norm, especially in urban areas. The second is an 'expansive' project, whereby society tries to gain power over nature as well as over the production and circulation of goods and knowledge. Extending scientific knowledge and enhancement of profit give this expansion an open horizon. The third is a 'renovating' project, that insists on constant innovation to elude sacred prescriptions and control, as well as constant renewal of the sign value of things in society as their value and meaning is eroded by a consumer mentality.

And finally, there is a 'democratizing' project that constantly tries to extend all these other projects across all sectors of society for greater participation and reinforcement of the modernizing enterprise as a whole. This combination of emancipation, expansion, renovation, and democratization can provide a general framework for how modernity has operated heretofore, in a variety of cultural contexts, as well as give us a point of departure for how to think about a different kind of modernity in the second half of this lecture. Before leaving this brief consideration, however, it is important to note that, for most of the world, modernity does not occupy a uniform space.

Particularly in urban conglomerations outside the Western world, people may be passing daily from premodern to modern into postmodern settings. In the squatter settlements around Lagos, the *favelas* of Rio or São Paulo, the *barrios* of Mexico City, those arriving from the countryside try to reproduce their premodern villages in their new locale, but go off to work (especially the women) in the modern or postmodern sites of the city—as domestic help or cleaning personnel, or doing the delicate work of computer board construction. More could be said about this different faces of modernity, but that is not our principal purpose here. Let us turn to some of the attempts to find the whole that are currently practiced, but fall short of the idea.

Detours and Dead Ends

I would now like to sketch very briefly four such quests for the whole that ends short of the goal, and often very badly. They are: fundamentalism, romanticism, universalism, and what I shall call "splitting." These last attempts are presented as bulwarks against anomie. Each will be described and, to the extent, possible, their allure identified and their point of weakness examined.

Fundamentalism

Certainly the most talked about of these quests for the whole today is fundamentalism. The term originates from struggles within conservative Protestantism in Britain and the United States at the turn of the twentieth century. At that time, a series of pamphlets circulated in the United

States, describing the "fundamentals" of Christian belief; hence the name. Today, the term is used somewhat indiscriminately, especially by non- conservatives, for any kind of conservative faith with which they disagree. It is extended also beyond Christianity to include a wide range of Muslim revival and reform movements, some forms of Judaism, and Hindu communalism. Despite numerous extended efforts to define and to map out the forms of fundamentalism (notably the University of Chicago Project conducted jointly with the American Academy of Arts and Sciences in the early 1990s), there is still not any agreed upon definition of fundamentalism. The definition I have found most useful was developed by Bruce Lawrence.

He sees fundamentalism first of all as a modern phenomenon. It arises in modernity as a reaction against modernity. It establishes its sense of the whole by lifting up elements from a religious tradition that are specifically anti-modern in character, and then making them a boundary of identity that separates off the true believer from the apostate and the infidel. Thus, in early twentieth century Christianity, the five "fundamentals" were the literal interpretation of Scripture, the virginal conception, the substitutionary atonement of Christ's death, his bodily resurrection, and his physical return at the end of time—all beliefs hard to reconcile with modernity. Other Christian dogmas like the Trinity, for instance, are not included here. Similarly, in contemporary Islam, the prescription for literal application of the sharia and the sequestering of women from the public sphere have nothing to do with what have long been considered the five pillars of Islam: the oneness of God, the duty to pray five times a day, giving alms, maintaining the fast during the month of Ramadan, and making the pilgrimage to Mecca.

Again, in asserting sharia and the sequestration of women, one sees a reaching for distinctively anti-modern elements to bolster an anti-modern outlook, thereby striving to create a community that will stand over against the corrosive acids of modernity. The fundamentalist quest for the whole sees modernity as incapable of ever fulfilling that dream, either because of the hybris of its claims for science and technology, the immorality of its rank individualism, or its lack of normative behaviour because of its being driven by consumption. Only by creating a sectarian group, clearly bounded by anti-modern markers, can one hope to live in integrity and wholeness within a tradition. Fundamentalism comes in degrees, of course. But it is its adherence to the explicitly anti- modern, and privileging those anti-modern elements of a tradition over what might be considered the principal elements in other settings that gives it its attraction. In the confusion of a pluralist world, it provides clarity, if not truth.

Romanticism

It was the late Sir Isaiah Berlin's studies in the early German and French Romantics who proposed a Counter-Enlightenment view of the world, that first alerted us to the power— and destructive potential—of this worldview. Starting with Johann Georg Hamann in Germany, a powerful reaction grew against the universalizing tendencies of the Enlightenment. Rather than stressing the general, the universal and the rational, Romanticism emphasized the genius of the solitary individual who had special insight into the nature of reality. Only by following uncompromisingly the true genius could one arrive at beauty and the true—which was not generalizable but particular. The power of the unconscious to reveal this reality ultimately supersedes what conscious rationality can attain. It is the Dionysian, not the Apollonian path that leads to true reality. Recently Richard Wolin has traced how this late eighteenth century and nineteenth century strand of quest for the whole leads through Nietzsche to right-wing movements in the twentieth century: the cult around the analytic psychologist Carl Gustav Jung, and the German and French New Right—including some of the scions of postmodernism.

Other strands flowing out of this cult of the personal and the irrational, and drawing in different ways upon Nietzsche, are to be found in the philosophy of Martin Heidegger and in National Socialism. To be sure, these are not direct genealogies; but the family resemblances are there. The irrational and the poetic, the singular and the particular, the solitary genius are seen to triumph over the pedestrian ministrations of the bureaucratic, the universal, and the rational. It goes without saying that this Romanticist strain in Western thought has tried to create its senses of the whole, either in esoteric readings not open to less discerning minds, or even in outright fascism, where violence is seen as purgative of the banal and the impure. It creates its own kinds of purity over against the hybridities of modernity. In emphasizing the ineluctable, the pure, the particular, it develops an especially aesthetic reading of the truth, which at times is counterintuitive to what otherwise would be held as moral truth.

Universalism

If Romanticism, in its search for the whole, counters the central tenets of the Enlightenment, and with it, modernity, then universalism is an attempt to find the whole precisely in the very tenets of the Enlightenment. The Western Enlightenment arose, as Stephen Toulmin has reminded us, out of an effort to overcome the sectarian feuding of the churches in the seventeenth century. The murderous outcome of holding in uncompromising fashion of each to one's own dogma, thereby not allowing any common ground where all parties could stand, but by insisting rather on the irreducibility of one's own position to any other, can only lead to the most powerful winning the day. Only when all accede to the rules of reason, common to all human beings, can such tribalism be overcome? These powerful ideas did much to shape a new sense of the whole in their French forms of rationality, and in their Scottish forms of polity and economy.

They appeared to free Europe from the rivalries of the churches and the unchallenged authority of their hierarchs. Science, not religion, would hold the day. The confidence (some would say the hybris) of such a confidence in rationality helped free the powers of scientific and technological innovation that religious authorities had to some extent held in check. It made the technological and political progress of Western society possible. It also helped move it into colonizing much of the rest of the world, where the "benefits" of this Enlightenment civilization would then raise the benighted peoples of the rest of the world from their darkness. In as much as any rational person could participate in this process, made this universalism in principle open to all, not merely to those who by birth or rank would control the levers of power.

Much can be said for this quest for the whole. It dwells especially on cognitive, scientific understandings of the truth that are, in principle, accessible to all reasonable people. But it, too, has had its overreach, notably in three areas. First of all, it posits a single and sole rationality, without retrieving the nuances of cultural difference. In its cruder nineteenth century forms (echoed in Kant's and Hegel's comments about the irrationality of Africans), it fails to understand that there are fundamentally different ways of organizing the whole. This fact continues to plague Christian theology today at a time when the majority of Christians live outside the Western sphere, yet their own theology and efforts at enculturation are largely ignored by the West. Second, and in the most tragic instance, "sciences of society" were devised in the nineteenth and twentieth centuries that have utterly crushed individuals and cultural life ways.

The depredation of Marxism in its various forms—be it Stalinism, Maoism, or Maoism's offshoots in Peru, Cambodia, and Nepal—can hardly be seen by most as a new whole in which human life flourishes. Third, and perhaps less obviously (at least to some), the negative dimensions of globalization—its relentless innovation, its brutal competition, its utter restlessness—go hand in hand with this universalism and continue, in Habermas' words, to colonize the life world. Habermas himself has not always been clear about the universalism of his ideal communicative situation, in which all will be resolved by rational argument, might have cultural and class biases itself even in these idea societies.

Given that, one cannot foreclose a judgment on just where all of that will end up. But it is noteworthy that even the most rational of quests for the whole does not automatically yield the desired human flourishing. While such universalism might seem to be the single best candidate for seeking the whole—because of its democratic access, its universalized rules, its shared criteria for evaluation of outcomes—it too potentially falls short in a complex, pluralistic world. Nonetheless, its distinctive advantages should not be underestimated.

Splitting

A fourth way of seeking the whole I would call splitting. This entails splitting off the problematic parts of the perceived reality, and trying to construct the whole out of what is left. The construction is then regarded as a bulwark against the anomie that threatens a society because of its complexity, pluralism, and conflicted situation. Muslim scholar Bassam Tibi gives a useful example of how this is done by some Muslims who face Western modernity, but find parts of that modernity incompatible with their sense of Islam. He distinguishes between 'institutional modernity' and 'cultural modernity.' Institutional modernity is the modernity evident in the achievements of science and of technology. It is based on a mathematicization of nature.

This kind of modernity Muslims can accept, as is evident by the number of Muslim immigrants to North

America who are engineers, physicians, chemists, and workers in the natural sciences. This is the modernity created by the scientific worldview. Cultural modernity, on the other hand, is problematic; for this is grows of the results of accepting values such as individual free will, the freedom to change one's social or cultural environment, the acceptance of relativism as a principle for dealing with pluralism. Such cultural modernity is rejected by some Muslims. In other words, they live in the modern West as workers in institutional modernity, but try to continue their life world as opposed to cultural modernity.

This is not something that besets only Muslims. One finds it among other religionists as well, including among Christians. The point here is the attempt to wall off part of modernity and to live in a way that accepts only parts of it. This is different from taking a critical stance toward aspects of modernity; here we see an attempt to simply ignore or suppress a dimension of it altogether. Splitting happens in many other ways. One sees it in politics where one is willing to ignore unpleasant aspects of a political programme in order to embrace other, cherished values. This has been pointed out in a recent study in the United States, where it was shown that some of the poorest sectors of the United States consistently voted for the Republican Party because of that party's commitment to "family values," even though that same party's economic policies toward poor families actually harms them. Yet another way is found in atavist reassertions. Samuel Huntington did this in 2004 with his controversial book, *Who Are We? The Challenge to America's National Identity*.

In that book, Huntington asserted that the United States' identity is based in White Anglo-Saxon Protestant values, and the influx of Latinos from the various countries of Central and South America (especially Mexico), constituted a threat to the nation. Similar voices can be heard today in Germany, with the assertion of a national *Leitkultur* or guiding culture that is under threat because of immigration. "Germany is not a land of immigration (*Zuwanderungsland*)" is frequently heard there. In these instances, reasserting a reified version of the national culture is seen as a hedge against the complexity emerging because of the entry of people whose cultures are fundamentally different. Perhaps given the complexity of the world we live in, some such splitting is difficult to avoid. Difficult choices have to be made. But to simply cordon off attitudes or policies, rather than critically engage them, seems to be short-circuiting, in the long run, the search for the whole.

A New Modernity

Given the fact that people are likely to continue to seek the whole—that this is something inherent to the meaning-making, symbolizing process that makes us human beings—are there strategies for creating a way of living in the complex, plural realities we live in that can take into account the shifting factors in our existence, that can deal with the instabilities that are created without giving in to ways of seeking the whole that may be deeply flawed, either morally or socially? What I would like to sketch out here are some attempts that are being made in that direction, that going beyond simply revelling in plurality (what Canadian sociologist Reginald Bibby designated a number of years ago as "mosaic madness") or a kind of Balkanized multiculturalism that collapses at the first sign of stress. It goes by a number of names, and is being constructed especially by thinkers in Great Britain and in Germany. It was initially called "reflexive modernity." Somewhat later, Scott Lash called it a "second modernity." Most recently, Ulrich Beck has been calling it a "new cosmopolitanism." experiencing the limits of progress and innovation as values that can be accepted uncritically.

This is most evident in debates about the environment. Is drilling for oil in wildlife reserves to be accepted because of the West's insatiable hunger for petroleum, even if it is a potential danger to the environment? The threat of global terrorism likewise compels us not take our security for granted any longer. Our sense of risk in general has been heightened, be it for reasons of ecology, the volatility of financial markets, the spread of communicable diseases such as SARS or avian flue. Reflexive modernity, then, means that we experience reality increasingly at one remove. We now question what we once took for granted. "Second modernity" is an attempt to seek the whole, using the framework of reflexive modernity. It reflects the fact that we have moved beyond the first modernity, but are not mired in a fragmented post-modernity.

One of the features of a second modernity is a sense that many of the boundaries that defined the first modernity have been shifted. These shifts are sometimes experienced as a deterritorialisation, that is, boundaries which once defined and even protected us are no longer fulfilling these functions. This is most evident in the experience of the pluralization of our societies through migration. Not only are dominant culture people confronted with a multiplicity of ethnic identities, the situation has become such in some places that there is no ethnic majority any more. That, for instance, is the case in Los Angeles, and becoming increasingly so in other urban centres of immigration. Ecological threats in the atmosphere—be they the hole in the ozone layer or the cloud of smog hanging over South Asia from the cooking fires—know no national boundaries. Thus boundaries that define identities are found to be shifting as are those we thought once protected us.

The United States thought it was largely safe from global terrorism because of the expanse of two oceans on its eastern and western frontiers. September 11 changed all of that. Deterritorialisation is experienced also in the fact that boundaries that once defined purity are being replaced by concepts of mixing and hybridity. As people migrate, mix, and marry racial identities become blurred. Jacques Audinet has called this "the human face of globalization." To be of mixed race was through much of the nineteenth and twentieth century a sign of being impure, even of weaker stock. But things are changing rapidly in this regard. The golfer Tiger Woods has become an icon of this new hybridity: not only drawing his identity from African and Asian resources, but also by being the very opposite of a scion of a debilitated stock. He is the number one golfer in the world. *Mestizaje, métissage,* creolization—whatever it is called—represents now a new and positive way of being in the world. The second modernity not only forces us to rethink boundaries; it calls forth new decisions.

The debate about genetically modified crops, and the divide between North America and Europe on this matter, represents one set of such decisions to be made. The capacities of biotechnology to prolong life have created another. The line between medicinal supplements and doping in professional sports raises yet another. This second modernity raises, therefore, a whole set of questions that must be addressed now in a way that was not the case even in the immediate past. Finally, the most recent term introduced for this new modernity is cosmopolitanism. This is of course an older term, usually intended to convey the sense of being (as its etymology implies) a world citizen. It was typically used of elite populations, who had the means to travel frequently, and who as a result of this felt at home in many places in the world. In this newer usage that older meaning is not denied, but has been supplemented in two key ways.

First of all, the new cosmopolitans are not so much an elite as they are the mass of migrants moving around the world today. Some are professionals and middle class, but the great majority of them are working class people. They are cosmopolitan in their capacity to negotiate multiple cultures, both in their current place of residence, their workplace, and their country of origin, and in their use of communications media to hold all of this together. Cultural critic Paul Gilroy sees them creating a new sense of *convivência,* or capacity to live together and interact with the great deal of difference that surrounds them. They do not experience cosmopolitan life as tourists or sometime visitors, but as those who must encounter and interact with difference every day of their lives. They do not have the luxury of experiencing the different as exotic or romantic; it is part of their ongoing struggle for survival.

The other dimension of this new cosmopolitanism is that it's thinking and decision- making is increasingly characterized by a "both-and" rather than an "either-or" approach. Modernity was marked by its capacity to differentiate and make distinctions. That is, after all, a key aspect of critical thinking. Confronted as it is with increasing plurality and complexity, the new cosmopolitanism is more keenly aware of the need to capture that sense of complexity in its decision-making. A simple differentiation is less useful to explain phenomena in the world today. For example, the early stages of globalization were often characterized as a homogenization of the world: global flows from the media would gradually erase differences and we would all come to be more and more alike.

Experience has shown, however, that such is not entirely the case. While some things have become more the same, the reaction against this homogenization has been new emphases on the local. English may be becoming the universal language of commerce and education in Europe, but this has also led to a revival of many local languages—such as Breton, Frisian, and Ladino—that once were considered doomed to extinction. Globalization has become, in the words of Roland Robertson, "glocalization," a mixture of the global and the local. It is this "both-and" attitude that is most characteristic of the new cosmopolitanism. Ways need to be found to incorporate the plurality we experience into our decision- making, our policies, and our ways of life, and taking an inclusive, rather than an exclusive, attitude is a major way of doing this.

A Second Modernity

What I have tried to outline in this lecture is how terms like post-modernity and multiculturalism have become less useful, especially for any analysis of the world we live in today. They both pointed to important dimensions of contemporary experience: a sense of pluralisation, of fragmentation, of irreducible difference. Both terms did describe for a time these aspects of our existence. But we can now see they were best suited to a relatively stable set of social conditions. One can revel in plurality and fragmentation when one feels secure that the larger world will hold together without any great effort on our part. One can celebrate cultural diversity when encounter with those cultures is a choice or an exotic excursion to an ethnic restaurant. But the instability of the last years has shown that these concepts are not resilient when put to the test. People quickly seek a new whole when they cannot presume that the erstwhile arrangements are going to stay in place.

The rhetoric of multiculturalism has collapsed under social stress in a number of countries today. People need some sense of the whole in order to know how to navigate a crowded and confused world. In the words of Reginald Bibby, they need frameworks for moral and social judgements. I examined briefly four such quests for the whole that mark the current landscape of our world. Fundamentalism, Romanticism, Universalism, and Splitting present a series of options for such quests for the whole. Each has certain advantages, but often also glaring disadvantages that do not address the complexities of our time. Because of those shortcomings, I suggested a look at a new viewing of modernity, which is increasingly being called a second or new modernity. It is marked first of all by a reflexivity that has tried to learn from the shortcomings of high modernity, with its sometimes overweening self-confidence, its unexamined belief in innovation and progress, its tendency to believe in the efficacy of its utopian social engineering.

Secondly, it is aware that boundaries that had provided relatively stable identities and becoming more porous and are being redrawn. Some boundaries that we thought would protect us are disappearing altogether and creating new senses of risk. Thirdly, as a result of these shifting, porous and disappearing boundaries, older concepts of purity are being replaced by sense of mixing and hybridity. Where once multiracial identity was seen as debilitating (especially by Europeans), such hybridity today means resilience and capacity to survive and even flourish in pluralistic and difficult circumstances.

The capacity to see the positive dimensions in such mixing creates also the possibility of a new *convivência*, a capacity for an engaged living together amidst, and indeed with, people and identities that are quite different. Fourth, these aspects of reflexivity, shifting boundaries, and hybridity call forth a new cosmopolitan view of the world that tries to encompass and interconnect the various dimensions of this complex world. This view recognizes that, if left to itself, a pluralized, complex world will seek the whole in ways that might become pathological and detrimental to the well-being of society. It realizes that decisions will have to be made, that moral and social judgements cannot be suspended or postponed indefinitely. Let me conclude by returning to the four major features that have been creating instability in the world, and look at them briefly through the lens of a second modernity.

Globalization

The interconnectedness of communication and the global flows that such communication creates will continue to be with us, barring a political cataclysm that pulls countries back, fortress-like, behind high walls. But a second modernity realizes that there is no "invisible hand" guiding globalization and making it socially responsive. More and more in the coming years, multilateral ways will have to be found to see that globalization does not collapse under its own excesses. Recent concerns about Africa among some of the developed countries is a heartening example of this.

Migration

Migration is likely to continue as long as there is economic inequity and political instability in the world. It is creating multicultural societies that will have to find more explicit ways of negotiating difference, of promoting cultural interaction, and of continuing to seek what will bind all of this together in some kind of a whole. The crisis now surfacing in a number of European countries (and also in Australia) is indicative of this need. A second modernity realizes that the question is not whether we will be multicultural; it is, rather, how we will be multicultural. Here new patterns of engagement, and a logic of "both-and" will likely be part of the response.

Resurgence of Religion

The resurgence of religion has called into question secularization as the sole paradigm for dealing with diversity, or at least is prompting a critical review. That religion is resurgent at a time of instability is itself evidence of one of the quests of searching for the whole—either as fundamentalism or in revival movements. Simply to try to re-privatize religion is not an option. The question is rather how to encourage the positive dimensions of religion for the sake of a second modernity, and how to curb those totalizing tendencies that threaten the well-being of others. I will be returning to this in the third lecture.

Global terrorism is not likely to go away any time soon. Large groups of unemployed, disaffected males will provide a steady demographic stream into its ranks for at least the next thirty years. Reducing the conditions that feed and sustain the turn to terrorism—poverty, humiliation, a sense of powerlessness—will reduce its attractiveness. The "both-and" thinking of a second modernity is likely to provide better intermediate resolutions than ever greater disjunctive policies and discriminating practices against certain populations. The prospect of a second modernity is only now being sketched out. But it seems likely to provide some direction in dealing with the complexity and the instability of the world as we are experiencing it. The question now comes: how do we as Christian believers direct the resources of our faith to this kind of world? That will be the subject of the final lecture.

The New Catholicity

The first two lectures have dealt with what it means to live in the unstable world we are now experiencing. It has tried to locate some of the principal sources of that instability, and to look at the possible critical and analytical frameworks that might be used to address them. In this final lecture, I want to turn to the resources of faith, especially Christian faith, to engage and address these challenges that lie ahead. I have suggested that the framework that might best describe our situation and direct our response is what is being called a "second modernity."

This second modernity has a reflexive or critical relationship with the first modernity, and recognizes how things have become more complex, how boundaries and identities are changing, how we have to consider plurality in make-up of identities, and how a more cosmopolitan worldview will serve us better in the years ahead. How might our faith provide an adequate and engaged response to the new modernity? If the Second Vatican Council, whose fortieth anniversary we are celebrating this year, helped give contour to living in the first modernity, how might we seek out our responses for living in a second modernity?

The Role of Religion

The Second Vatican Council, especially in its Pastoral Constitution on the Church in the Modern World, *Gaudium et spes*, charted out a trajectory into modernity that has served us quite well. Its commitment to the fundamental goodness of the world, its recognition of the centrality of the concept of culture in shaping human and social life, and its valuing of human agency or activity for the sake of that world are ideas that will continue to guide us. At the same time, no doubt inevitably, the world has continued to change. Globalization was still an unknown concept for most people in the 1960s. No one would have imagined the urbanization and the extent of migration that we now experience nearly a half-century later, nor the profound pluralism of our societies as a consequence of this. The international religious issues at the time of the Council were atheism and secularization.

Today, as we have seen, there is a resurgence of religious feeling in the world. We have already talked about some of these features thus far in these lectures. I would like to take as a point of departure for this final lecture the role religion can play in the world as it is developing, and some of the potential things that religion can contribute on the international scene today. It was already noted that religion now intrudes into international politics and studies of international relations in a way unimagined only a short time ago, because of a renewed interest in religion, and its own resilience. Scholars working in these areas are struggling to come up with models that give an appropriate place to religion in these settings. Richard Falk has been one of the leading figures in this regard. In a work on the role of religion in creating a more humane model of governance on the international scene, he has made some brief suggestions about a number of potential contributions religion can make to this important area. Let me enumerate them here as a way of beginning this reflection:

- An appreciation of suffering, and a commitment to lift up people in society who are suffering.
- The mobilizing potential of religion and its resonance with the deep roots of a society.
- An ethos of solidarity, especially when religion shows its inclusivist face.
- Normative horizons that affirm humanity even in the midst of fragmentation and diversity.
- The transformative nature of faith and ideals, particularly as they are related to struggle and self-sacrifice.
- A sense of limits, growing out of an awareness of finitude and the capacity of human beings for evil.
- A sense of identity that is not achieved by subjection to the state, but rather in reference to a spiritual journey, making of the "citizen" a "citizen pilgrim."
- A sense of reconciliation that recognizes human limits and the need for forgiveness and the beginning of life again after conflict and catastrophe.

These eight points stake out a considerable agenda for faith as it faces a second modernity. I would like to combine them somewhat and focus on four areas where Christian faith might make a contribution to living in the second modernity, of believing in an unstable world.

Suffering

Suffering is theological category that does not get much attention in the developed world. It is a reminder of the finitude and shortcomings of human existence, and of the oppression and injustice that the developed world either imposes on the poor two-thirds world or acquiesces to in order not to be disturbed. Yet suffering is the lot of much of the world's population today, either suffering caused by poverty, malnutrition, and disease, or the suffering caused by civil conflict, political oppression, and a variety of forms of racism and xenophobia. The theologian Edward Schillebeeckx speaks of the "ecumene of suffering," the widespread, pervasive character of suffering that marks the world today. Suffering can be reduced, but not entirely eradicated. Its causes are at times too complex to admit of simple solution. The fact that it cannot be completely eradicated reminds us of the *hybris* that haunts some of our enterprises.

It recalls to our minds that margin that we cannot control. But more importantly, suffering calls to respond to the things we can indeed change, the suffering that is propped up and sustained by human sinfulness, by greed and injustice, by pride and by power. The call to justice has again echoed loudly in Catholic Social Teaching, especially since the Bishops' Synod on Justice in 1970. The quest for justice will continue to be central to the Christian agenda. Within the context of the second modernity, we are called upon to refocus our sense of justice, in order to create workable goals for eradication of certain kinds of suffering. There are forms of suffering, such as malnutrition and disease that can be directly and effectively addressed by more effective food production and medical distribution systems.

There are other forms, such as racism and xenophobia that will require education especially to combat. Advocacy, using international forums and the means of modern communication, are already finding new avenues of effectiveness. Reflecting on the meaning of suffering in no way legitimates it. But we need to come to understand better how it is that so many people who suffer manage not to lose their humanity in the process. What resources of the human spirit are called forth in the best of human beings that can take even the destructive trajectories of suffering and turn them into a source of an expanding and even transcending human spirit? What happened to someone like Nelson Mandela in all those years of imprisonment on Robben Island that produced not a man bent on revenge and retaliation, but one of the great statesmen of the close of the twentieth century?

What lessons can be learned from his life to help oppressed people elsewhere? What did Mother Teresa learn from living among those dying people who had been abandoned by society, what did she learn about faithfulness, abiding presence, and care that has gone on to inspire so many people around the world? Spiritual guides have often spoken of the "school of suffering," a trying discipline that strips us of our illusions, makes us adhere to what is central and fundamental, and steadies our hand in unstable, unsteady times. To learn from suffering is not to condone it; it is, rather, an attempt to harness its awesome power to a nobler calling and broader spiritual horizon.

Christian faith in the second modernity must face the reality of suffering more squarely. It must not avert its eyes from suffering's searching gaze. It must bring to it the wisdom of the cross, that central symbol in Christian faith that makes us rethink power and recipes for success. Indeed, all the great religious traditions of the world have reflections on suffering. How can these be brought to bear on the suffering people experience today, not as a palliative, but as a means of strengthening the human spirit in its struggle to overcome suffering, and for the sake of recognizing the nobility that sometimes emerges in suffering rather than seeking ways for ourselves to insulate our lives from it?

Mobilization and Solidarity

One of the features that mark the resurgence of religion in the world is its capacity to mobilize energies and to create bonds of solidarity. Pope John Paul II, in his many trips to different parts of the world, has exhibited again and again this mobilizing power of faith. Because faith makes an appeal not only to transcendent realities but also has what Richard Falk calls "civilizational resonance," it can draw the different strands of narrative in a society together into a greater sense of the whole. In the recent debates about whether to make inclusion of references to God and to Christianity in the European Union Constitution, EU leaders worked studiously to avoid recourse to religious references. At the same time, as the sense of multiculturalism was collapsing in those same countries, the possibility of a religious "grand narrative" was unavoidable: the religious face of Islam and of many of the African immigrants to those countries reminded an older Europe of its religious heritage.

Reference to religion can be divisive, but it can also mobilize solidarity. When Bosnia and Herzegovina were invaded by the Serbs in the early 1990s, the leaders of the three major religious traditions all spoke out against the invasion and the war. Yet none of the voices was strong enough to be heard outside its own community, and sometimes was feeble even within them. After the war, those leaders committed themselves to forming an interreligious council. In the last years of the 1990s, they met publicly, sometimes as often as biweekly, in order to impress upon the public consciousness that they were acting together. In this way, they hope to be prepared should another war come to their country.

The centennial celebration of the 1893 Parliament of the World's Religions, held again in Chicago in 1993, has created an ongoing organization—the Council for a Parliament of the World's Religions—that has sponsored parliaments in Capetown in 1998 and in Barcelona in 2004. Besides bringing religionists of all kinds together, each of these parliaments has provided a forum for religious leaders to address together some of the world's most pressing problems. These landmark events of religious cooperation show the potential of religion for making the world a better place. Much is being written about religion's collusion—wittingly or unwittingly—with violence, and for the sake of a better world those collusions need to be uncovered and eradicated. But perhaps the best long-term antidote to such conspiracy is linking the religions together for the sake of good.

In so doing, the potential for creating new bonds of solidarity for the sake of the betterment of human kind can help point the rest of the world toward ways of redefining the boundaries that separate rich and poor, the powerful from the powerless, and the races of humankind. The term "solidarity" first arose in the trade union movements of the nineteenth century. Pope John Paul II has made it very much part of the vocabulary of Catholic Social Teaching. In a second modernity, as boundaries shift and are redefined, we must find new ways to bring people together as well. The affective bonds of faith are certainly among the strongest that may be able to do that.

Forming Identities in a Second Modernity

The complexity created by globalization and migration has put identities under greater stress. One of the things that a second modernity stresses about identities is similar to its understanding of the concept of culture. In modernity, culture was often seen as a reified, definable entity that was relative stable and enduring through time. It had its roots in Johann Gottfried Herder's definition of culture from the eighteenth century: that culture was a union of three things: language, custom, and territory. Migration and globalization has deterritorialised culture. The media have undermined any defining custom, and have creolized language. Culture is much more a negotiated reality now, having a certain historical core, but constantly in conversation with forces all around it. What happens to a migrant's culture over the span of the first two to three generations in a new setting has been the object of much study.

Culture is now seen more as a kind of force field in which identities are negotiated. To say this does not make culture or any constructed identity utterly pliable or arbitrary. It is, however, to recognize that culture and identity are never utterly stable. They are living entities that react to and change in the midst of all kinds of stimuli. For that reason, it may not be useful to think of identity as an entity or reified lump of stuff. It might better be seen as the intersection point of multiple relationships. Rather than thinking of identity as an isolate or independent entity, it might better be viewed as an interdependent reality that is greater than the sum of all its parts. An identity is not dependent upon a single relationship; rather, it gets its resilience from its capacity to identify with a whole range of relationships.

One of the basic principles of *convivência* is to have people in many different sets of relationships, so as to avoid identifying solely with one single such set. Identities today have to be capable of functioning amid many cultural realities. Religion plays a significant role in this. It has already been noted that religion is one of the most salient strands of identity in a migrant's life: migrants often become more religiously attuned in their new country than they were in their homeland. This seems to be so because religion provides a connecting and familiar bond in an otherwise strange world. The great religious traditions such as Islam, Christianity, Buddhism and others have the additional quality of creating solidarity among peoples who are otherwise so different.

The experience of a papal audience in St. Peter's Square in Rome, or of the *hajj* in Mecca can give one of the sensations of being one with a greater humanity. Those transethnic, transnational identities are important building blocks for creating a different kind of human community for the future. The calling on those principles to create genuine *communio* (as Roman Catholics would call it) or a worldwide *ummah* (as Muslims would call it) would be a powerful antidote to the xenophobia, the racism, and the forms of prejudice that still mark the human family. To see identity as a series of relationships, to see religion as providing both face-to- face community, as well as a transcendental allegiance, is an example of the cosmopolitan "both-and" that is a hallmark of the second modernity. As Falk pointed out, in that transcendental allegiance, life and human community can also be seen as a pilgrimage or spiritual journey.

This helps create a critical distance from kinds of nationalist loyalties that harden boundaries between people and create obstacles in communication. "We have here no lasting city," as the Letter to the Hebrews reminds us (13:14). While this can be viewed as playing down citizenship and the commitments that flow from it, it should be read rather as not engaging in idolatrous behaviour—ascribing divine meaning to a human institution. Religion, it seems to me, can help balance the quest for identity between a static, immobile sense of self and an arbitrary, unstable anomie. It can help maintain flexibility but within the context of direction, moral grounding, and normative horizons.

Reconciliation and Forgiveness

Since the time of the fall of the Berlin Wall in 1989, there has been a dramatic growth in interest in reconciliation and the possibilities of forgiveness. Some of this has come from a heightened awareness of the amount of destructive conflict that has happened in the last decade and a half. But it has also arisen from an admission of the profound damage that colonialism has done to indigenous peoples around the world, and how their cultures and personal lives were often wrecked by the advance of European settlers. The upheavals and social conflicts that have uprooted more than a hundred million people worldwide to create ongoing camps of displaced persons and flows of refugees into other countries has made people yearn for peace and repair from such disastrous occurrences.

The idea of reconciliation has been at the forefront especially of Christianity and increasingly Islam during this period. Caritas Internationalis, the umbrella organization for 164 relief and development agencies in the Roman Catholic Church, has been working since 1995 to build and implement training programmes in reconciliation in its member organizations. To date thousands of people have been trained on all six continents to engage in this work. In its current phase, it is working especially with its counterparts in the Muslim world to collaborate in this work of reconstruction and peace. It has been noted that these religions dare to believe in reconciliation *and* forgiveness, in justice *and* living together. My own involvement in this work has convinced me that it helps to have a religious, even eschatological vision of reconciliation. Reconciliation is not an extrapolation from cessation of conflict to some point of living together.

To create the conditions for reconciliation, one has to have what John Paul Lederach, a leading practitioner in the transformation of conflict, calls a "moral imagination." Reconciliation is more than finding the right strategies or techniques to end conflict. It is built on a sense of humanity as a peaceable existence, sensitivity to securing and sustaining justice, and a capacity to imagine those rituals and other practices that will ground such peace and celebrate it regularly. As Desmond Tutu put it so eloquently in his memoir of South Africa's Truth and Reconciliation Commission, there is "no future without forgiveness." Without embarking on forgiveness, we remember too much and forget too little.

As the narratives of a society are reconstructed in the forgiveness process, there has to be a capacity to see wrongdoers in a new light—not just as malevolent beings bent on our destruction, but as vulnerable, finite, even broken human beings acting out of a jumble of emotions and motivations. Forgiveness is the creation of a space for a different kind of future. The religious capacity to envision both reconciliation and forgiveness creates the conditions for the development of a genuinely new and renewed society. This possibility is crucial for a second modernity, as it tries to negotiate its way between destructive pasts and complex present situations.

The Two Pillars for a Theological Vision

In order to bring especially Christian faith into engagement with the second modernity, two areas of theology will need closer attention. One is the area of theological anthropology. The other is our sense of Christian faith itself—what I have called a "new Catholicity." It could be argued that Christology was the key area for systematic theology in the last quarter of the twentieth century. This period coincided with what has been called the "third quest of the historical Jesus." During that period the social study of the New Testament, with its use of contemporary sociological and anthropological methods, helped bring to life the Gospel stories about the life and ministry of Jesus in a new way. It was also the period when an emerging question—the relation of Christian claims about Jesus to the other great world religions—reached a new height of attention.

It has been my contention that the major area for theological reflection for the first quarter of the twenty-first century will be theological anthropology, our theological understanding of what it means to be human. In doing so, theological anthropology will need to move beyond the "anthropocentric turn" that marked theology at the turn of the twentieth century, as cosmocentric views of creation made way for anthropocentric ones. Certainly the looming ecological crisis has made a solely anthropocentric view of the world obsolete and even dangerous. But there are a number of other reasons that have made a return to a theological anthropology more urgent. One of these is the presence of biomedical technologies that have complicated the boundary between human and non-human life. The prospects of cloning, of continuance of life by technological means, and advances in cognitive science have all raised questions about the human that were not even thinkable a few decades ago.

Here in the second modernity, boundaries are being redefined with great rapidity. We must constantly be thinking about how these affect our sense of the human. Second, the development of concerns about human rights, the forms of racism that globalization have created alongside the intractable historical forms we have inherited from colonialism, the slave trade, and the racist ideologies of the nineteenth century all call us to expand what is included in the topic of theological anthropology. How identities are formed and how we will live together with all our difference yet find means of social cohesion constitute challenges to theological anthropology. Third, our capacity to move beyond the anthropocentrism that shaped much of twentieth century theological anthropology is crucial.

To be sure, this anthropocentrism was experienced at the time as liberating from ecclesiastical and social strictures, but our continued survival is based on learning our proper place within the world and all its systems. As ecological theologies move into greater maturity—beyond lists of desiderata into carefully constructed new anthropologies—theological anthropology as a whole will benefit from this. Fourth, the ways that new social cohesion, through solidarity and *convivência,* is theologically grounded will be an important part of how we talk about human community. As has been noted, the second modernity will have to find ways for greater engagement and cohesion between groups that are different. To invoke simply the beauty of difference when societies are under stress will not be effective. An intercultural hermeneutics is an important dimension of interpreting these communities to one another. The other theological concept that will be important to the Christian theological interpretation of this vision is what I have called elsewhere a "new Catholicity."

Let me remind us here of the three dimensions that I saw as central to this new Catholicity. The first two have long been seen as constitutive of catholicity as a descriptor of the Church. The first was the universal extension of the Church throughout the world (catholicity in its etymological sense). While such worldwide extension is even more true today, in the twenty-first century, than it was through much of the Church's history, that "seeking of the whole" of the Church today will have to include aspects that have been discussed here as part of the second modernity: a cosmopolitan, rather than an ethnocentric view of humanity and human cultures; ways of including a sense of the "both-and" view of reality rather than the more familiar "either-or" attitude that has shaped much of our history; and ways to extend our sense of *communio* to include a *convivência* of peoples, where difference is not only recognized, but engaged. The second was the fullness of faith.

Not only must the faith handed down to us from the apostles be maintained in all its integrity, we may wish to emphasize within that faith elements that will keep us attuned to the fullness of humanity that must receive this fullness of faith. I would suggest two themes here. The first is to bring together more closely the long Catholic tradition of natural law with the newer worldwide emphasis on human rights. In many ways this is what efforts at the global ethic are trying to do across religious lines. How these might be brought together should be high on the theological agenda. The second is to continue to explore the theme of reconciliation, both for its Christian theological resources, and also for how it can link with those theological resources from other religious traditions. Here is one of the places where religious traditions can collaborate most fruitfully.

The third dimension of the new Catholicity is communication. It should be clear from what has been said in these lectures that communication—efficacious speech, constructive listening, and creating the speech environment where all of this can happen —is going to be essential for the well being of the human family in all of its complexity. For the constructive engagement of cultural communities, patterns of communication and interpretation will have to be strengthened. Ways to keep all the groups in the conversation will need to be found in order to do this. An effective pedagogy of listening within the Church itself will be one of the important ways of modelling this for the larger society. The Roman Catholic Church is the largest transnational, multicultural organization in the world. If it can translate its theology of catholicity into ways of creating this engagement, it will be doing incomparable service to humanity.

The possibility of embarking on a new or second modernity is the challenge before us. We must find more effective ways of analyzing our world if we are to be able to live together in the shrunken space and time of globalization, in the convergence of peoples in migration, amid new ways of living and believing in an unstable world. I would like to conclude here with a passage from the Letter to the Ephesians, since it embodies to my mind the vision that can animate this quest for a new way of seeking the whole: So you are no longer aliens or foreign visitors; you are fellow-citizens with the holy people of God and part of God's household.

You are built upon the foundations of the apostles and prophets, and Jesus Christ himself is the cornerstone. Every structure knit together in him grows into a holy temple in the Lord; and you too, in him, are being built up into a dwelling place of God in the Spirit. No longer aliens and strangers; citizens in a common household of God; built upon firm foundations; anchored by Christ as the cornerstone; knit together as a holy temple, a dwelling place of God in the Spirit: that strikes me as the visionary agenda for the Church in a second, a new modernity.

9

New World Disorder

The world's lone superpower, fearful of being attacked by one of many real or perceived enemies, sets out to solve the problem by increasing weapon sales and military aid to the world. But the sales and aid aren't just made available to existing allies; indeed in the wake of Sept. 11th, the race is on to arm governments formerly considered unstable or otherwise "off-limits" due to gross human rights violations, on grounds that these nations are assisting in the sweeping "war against terrorism."

If that sounds illogical, then perhaps you're beginning to understand the perverse logic that pervades the U.S. arms industry. After Sept 11th, the industry has—with the support of the Bush Administration—stepped up its efforts to further reduce oversight and regulation of arms sales and military aid. This, despite a clear track record of providing weapons to the very forces now portrayed to a frightened public as threats.

In the process, the administration is apparently jettisoning efforts to use military aid as a carrot to encourage the advancement of human rights. In the past year, restrictions on military aid and arms sales to formerly off-limits regimes have largely been eliminated. Of the 67 countries which have received or are set to receive U.S. military aid, 32 have been identified by the State

Department as having "poor" or worse human rights records.

"Two key [FY2002] Defense Department funding allocations—$390 million to reimburse nations providing support to U.S. operations in the war on terror and $120 million 'for certain classified activities,'" according to a report in the *Arms Sales Monitor* (Aug. 2002), can now be delivered "notwithstanding any other provision of the law."

In other words, Congress has approved a staggeringly large sum of military aid for regimes fighting an ill-defined "war on terror," and is working to ensure that there will be little or no public scrutiny of how such aid is spent. The central question is: does this make the world a safer place for anyone but arms manufacturers and the politicians who love them?

Conflicts of Interest

From 1991 to 2000, the U.S. delivered $74 billion worth of military equipment, services and training to countries in the Middle East, according to a Sept. 2002 General Accounting Office (GAO) report. You might expect that a majority of that military aid went to our staunch ally in the region, Israel, which has been cited repeatedly by the U.N. and Amnesty International for human rights abuses. However, military aid to Saudi Arabia—where a majority of the terrorists reported to be involved in the Sept. 11 attacks were from—topped $33 billion for the period, outpacing aid to Israel by a more than 5-to-1 margin.

What's more, there is ample evidence that arms sales to the Middle East are, in fact, destabilizing and dangerous. "Foreign [military] assistance to the Middle East," noted West Virginia Democratic Senator Robert Byrd in 2001, "virtually ignores the spiraling violence in the region."

In a November 9, 2001 interview with Pakistan's *Ausaf* newspaper, none other than Osama bin Laden justified the

Sept. 11 attacks by noting that the U.S. sells advanced weaponry to Israel, which is in turn used in the military occupation of Palestinian territories. Bin Laden was specifically discussing the sale of Lockheed Martin's F-16 fighter planes. It's worth noting that Lynne Cheney, the wife of Vice-President Dick Cheney, was on the board of Lockheed Martin from 1994 until 2001, and would have been involved in overseeing this sale.

On July 13, 2002, the *New York Times* also reported that Vice President Dick Cheney's former employer, the Halliburton Company, is "benefiting very directly from the United States' effort to combat terrorism." From building cells for detainees at Guantanamo Bay ($300 million) to feeding American troops in Uzbekistan, the *Times* reported, "the Pentagon is increasingly relying on a unit of Halliburton called KBR, sometimes referred to as Kellogg Brown & Root." KBR is the "exclusive logistics supplier for both the Navy and the Army, providing services like cooking, construction, power generation and fuel transportation."

And then there's the Carlyle Group, described by the *The Industry Standard* as "the world's largest private equity firm," with more than $12 billion in assets. A Washington merchant bank specializing in buyouts of defense and aerospace companies, the Carlyle Group stands to make a substantial sum of money from a global "war on terror." Former U.S. President George Bush, Sr.—whom current President Bush is known to consult about policy matters almost daily—works for the firm. According to the Baltimore Sun, so do former Secretary of State James Baker III and former Bush Sr. campaign manager Fred Malek. Former Republican Defense Secretary Frank Carlucci (a college roommate of Defense Secretary Donald Rumsfeld), is the Carlyle Group's chairman and managing director.

The bin Laden family, hailing from Saudi Arabia, is also heavily invested in the Carlyle Group. On Sept. 27,

2001, the Wall Sreet Journal published an article entitled "Bin Laden Family Could Profit from Jump in Defense Spending Due to Ties to U.S. Bank." The "bank" in question? You guessed it: the Carlyle Group.

Cold War Communism vs. New World Terrorism

One of the more disturbing aspects of post-9/11 arms sales is the wanton redefinition of various dissident groups around the world as "terrorists." Even longstanding conflicts such as the 38-year-old civil war in Colombia have been re-cast as a war between our Colombian allies and "terrorists." In the Phillipines, "counter-terrorism aid" has been released to fight a band of Islamic militants, the Abu Sayyaf Group (ASG), despite the fact that even government analysts admit the ASG poses no credible threat to the U.S. In Nepal, counter-terrorism aid has been allocated to help the Nepalese military quell Maoist dissent, despite State Department testimony that there's no evidence that these dissidents are connected to al-Qaeda.

Military aid flowing to Central Asia under the auspices of fighting terrorism seems equally ill-justified, with virtually every country in the region receiving increases in U.S. military aid despite connections to the war on terrorism that are, at best, tenuous. What seems clear from a close look at military aid policy over the past year is that the U.S. military is using the threat of terrorism to garner support for its ambitious goals for extending its reach around the world, and that it doesn't mind arming unstable or anti-democratic regimes in the process.

The "weapons against terror" rationale is strained even further by a 2001 report released by the Centre for Defense Information, an independent non-profit research group. The report, entitled "US Arms Exports to Countries Where Terror Thrives," found the following:

"There are 28 terrorist groups currently operating in 18

countries, according to the State Department's bi-annual list of active foreign terrorist organizations...In the period of 1990-1999, the United States supplied 16 of the 18 countries on the State Department list with arms....In addition, the U.S. military (and CIA) has trained the forces of many of these 18 countries in U.S. war fighting tactics, in some cases including individuals now involved in terrorism."

In sum, the U.S. has sold weapons or training to almost 90% of the countries it has identified as harboring terrorists. A severe restructuring of U.S. arms export policy is in order, but little or nothing is being done to ensure a safer future.

Guns and History in the Middle East

Perhaps nowhere is the correlation between arms sales and violence more apparent than in the Middle East, where the U.S. sells an enormous amount of weapons. According to an August 6, 2002 congressional report on arms sales to developing countries, "The Persian Gulf War....played a major role in further stimulating already high levels of arms transfer agreements with nations in the Near East region. The war created new demands by key purchasers such as Saudi Arabia, Kuwait, the United Arab Emirates, and other members of the Gulf Cooperation Council (GCC) for a variety of advanced weapons systems."

"The Gulf States' arms purchase demands," the report continued, "were not only a response to Iraq's aggression against Kuwait, but a reflection of concerns regarding perceived threats from a potentially hostile Iran." The U.S. dominated the arms market in the region from 1994-2001, selling more than $13 billion worth of weapons to Bahrain, Egypt, Israel, Jordan, Kuwait, Lebanon, Saudi Arabia and the United Arab Emirates. Russia and China also sold $8 billion worth of weapons to Iran, Algeria, Syria, Yemen, and Libya. Judging by numbers alone, it's hard to miss the parallels to Cold War-era geopolitical strategy.

Also hard to miss is the profit motive. 2001 marked a slump for arms dealers, as sales to developing nations dropped 43%, according to a Congressional Research Service (CRS) report. Peace, obviously, is not good business for the "defense" industry. Why would countries siphon money from all manner of social programs in order to purchase expensive weapons systems if they didn't feel threatened?

The reason has more to do with insecurity than fiscal logic, as evidenced by the fact that Israel, despite a declining economy, was the number one U.S. arms importer in 2001, purchasing, among other weapons, 52 F-16 fighter jets and six Apache helicopters. Given that Israel has repeatedly violated international humanitarian law with its advanced U.S. weapons systems, it's clear that profits—and geopolitical advantage—trump human rights when it comes to selling weapons.

Focusing on the War, Not the Battle

"Every gun that is made, every warship launched, every rocket fired signifies, in the final sense, a theft from those who hunger and are not fed, those who are cold and are not clothed," proclaimed former U.S. President Dwight Eisenhower. "The world in arms is not spending money alone. It is spending the sweat of its laborers, the genius of its scientists, and the hopes of its children... This is not a way of life at all, in any true sense. Under the cloud of threatening war, it is humanity hanging from a cross of iron."

Fifty years later, the figures seem to back Eisenhower up. The 2002 Federal Military Budget stands at a mind-boggling $343 billion. Consider that the same budget allocates a comparatively paltry $39 billion to children's health, $6 billion to the Headstart program, and $1 billion to combat world hunger. It's estimated that it would cost just $6 billion a year—or approximately 1/57th of the military budget—to provide healthcare for all uninsured children in the United States.

Given the broad bipartisan support for a war with Iraq, and considering the largely-abysmal quality of most mainstream coverage of the subject, even the encouragingly large number of spirited anti-war protests around the world may not be enough to prevent an attack. However, there are battles and there are wars: the battle to prevent an attack on Iraq might fail, but the war to end a global arms race and U.S. militarism can still be won.

The U.S. military-industrial complex is a giant enterprise, employing hundreds of thousands of people, raking in billions of dollars in profits every year, and utilizing a veritable army of lobbyists and Washington insiders to maintain its dominant position in the U.S. economy. As such, the struggle to wean the country from its dependence on the defense industry has been—and will continue to be—a difficult one. The good news is that the defense industry is not a monolith, and that opposition to U.S. arms sales is actually a popular, majoritarian stance. The problem is not so much one of educating the public on why arming the world to the teeth is a bad idea, but what can be done about it.

We can start by supporting efforts to end export subsidies on U.S. arms sales. Every year, defense contractors receive billions of dollars in subsidies: that's taxpayer money poured right into the pockets of arms dealers, and it needs to stop. Defense industry types claim they need these subsidies in order to remain competitive around the globe, but at a time when U.S. military spending dwarfs our nearest competitor—Russia—by a margin of more than 9-to-1, this argument simply demonstrates the greed and lack of restraint that defines the defense industry.

The Bush Administration has been working, with relative success, to end all export controls on weapons in the name of fighting terrorism. Rebuffed in their efforts to completely do away with weapons controls, they have turned to a strategy of incrementalism, successfully weakening or circumventing a host of weapons export controls, including the Export Administration Act. All efforts to weaken the control, oversight, and regulation of arms exports should be challenged vigorously. Most importantly, the defense industry must not be allowed the secrecy it seeks. Public servants of both major parties must be scrutinized for conflicts of interest, and barred from public office if such conflicts come to light. This should include virtually everyone in the Bush Administration.

The agency once called the Bureau of Export Administration, which controls weapons exports, recently changed its name to the Bureau of Industry and Security (BIS). The BIS is part of the Commerce Department, and although lip service is paid to the office's responsibility for controlling arms exports, the BIS is also charged with promoting arms exports. Politicians cannot simultaneously serve the interests of peace and war, nor can an office like the BIS serve two masters well. This office must be restructured or split in two if the concept of arms "control" is to be taken seriously.

Instead of crowing on its website about its Defense Trade Advocacy Program generating "high-level, government-to-government advocacy on behalf of U.S. firms," helping them "succeed in today's highly competitive global defense market," and supporting "$22 billion in U.S. [weapons] exports since 1994," the BIS might instead make it its business to actually help stem the flow of arms to the rest of the world.

In 1925, President Calvin Coolidge uttered the famous line, "The business of America is business." However repugnant a truth that may be, fighting over the long haul against U.S. arms exports to the world—and diminishing the political influence of the defense industry—is important if we, as a nation wish to avoid the continuation of an even uglier truth: that the business of America is the business of war.

10

The Roots of Terrorism in Strategic Approaches to Global Insecurity

It is very common to talk about the "roots" of terrorism, but this conference is unusual because these roots are not so typically addressed with rigorous social science. I am very glad, therefore, to be part of this. However, it's also worthwhile to think about why we use this metaphor in a rigorous social science conference. It is appealing to use this imagery because we realize that, as with a dandelion, if one only chops off what is apparent to the eye, one will only have the dandelion grow back by the next time you cut that lawn next. This is indeed a powerful image, but it is not at all apparent that this metaphor is useful when we don't make common our sense about what roots mean, and why they are not apparent to the eye. And this variation in vision is not a disciplinary difference most of all, but a reflection of the political and strategic approaches we take in that definition of roots.

If we are going to develop a scholarly approach that takes this diversity of roots' interpretations not as a political obstacle, but as an intellectual asset, we must be clear about how we view these roots and how they are located in various strategic approaches themselves. Let me start, however, with some apology. I have no real place in a conference of experts about terrorism, for I am no such expert. I have not studied the traits that make people violent. I have not studied peoples assigned a violent role in this story. I have not studied policies that are designed to address violence. I have studied the relationship between intellectual and social change, and especially those cultural formations that structure the relationship between knowledge and power. My last book, for example, was about how the transition from plan to market set up a series of problematics that focused research, but simultaneously distracted scholars from critical problems that were at the heart of the social transformations accompanying communism's collapse and post-communism's alternatives.

Perhaps for that very reason I do have a place here when you are trying to figure out how to study something so apparently concrete as the roots of terrorism. And that may be why Cambridge University invited me to their conference, involving faculty, private sector experts, and other professionals, with an occasional foreign consultant or NGO official, to think "outside the box" about root causes for human insecurity. My summary of that conference, originally prepared for another publication, follows this introductory comment. That summary should be useful, especially if we are to consider how we might cumulate research across very different traditions of academic inquiry, and across very different presumptions about the character of global affairs. And that requires that we begin our discussion of root causes with such intellectual plurality in mind.

Root Causes of Human Insecurity

Invoking Alex Haley's Roots, we considered causes embedded in the past, as long enduring, like genealogies. We also thought of root causes as embedded in systems, whether they are economic, social, cultural, kinship or other enduring patterns of human behaviour. Finally, we should also think about root causes in terms that seminar participant Anton Obholzer helped us imagine, as those causes that might be difficult to recognize, acknowledge, or articulate. In this sense, root causes are beneath the surface, hard to see, and hard to describe. Our organizers didn't tell us what kinds of human insecurity to address. Terrorism was the obvious concern of many, but we also had sessions devoted to other manifestations of insecurity, including how a networked polity of informal economic flows is substituting for conventional forms of development aid. For its resonance with root causes, our focus groups settled relatively easily into terrorism as the main problem. But this provisional consensus only enabled much greater disagreement on how to address its causes.

Of course participants generally recognized that it was important to understand better those value sets and cultural models that motivate terrorists to destroy them and others. At the next level, we discussed the values of the communities in which terrorists are embedded – what leads these communities to allow or support terrorists? But it was not clear how we should think of these communities. Are these communities formed around inequalities they perceive to be unjust? What makes inequalities appear particularly unjust? Do the media exaggerate the problem, or just make the inequalities more apparent?

While evocative, this discussion was also manageable, especially compared to our discussion around religion. One participant identified religion *per se* as the root cause of terrorism. Of course, he quickly corrected himself; religion itself is not a problem. Someone helped him out and offered that dogmatism or inflexibility found in religions, especially when they are traveling across the world imposing their ideas on others, is the real problem. But which religions are so problematic? Certainly he didn't consider the Dalai Lama part of the terrorist wave. Nor did he consider Christian missionaries who traveled the world over the last five centuries to be part of the problem.

The problem may not be religion, but rather our difficulty in discussing religion, and its diverse expressions, in secular company. Britain may, in some ways, be more able to carry out this conversation than we are. That, at least, is one impression we might take from Ellen Laipson's report that the authors of "Global Trends 2015" shied away from making predictions about rising religiosity and its political implications because they feared such judgments would be controversial and would be misunderstood. The British were not so cautious. Their Joint Doctrine and Concepts Centre strategic trend project noted religion as a key element, identifying not only fundamentalist reaction to Western (particularly U.S.) power and culture but also ever increasing tensions between Islam and the West as likely developments of the future.

Of course this forthright approach is careful too, and it exposes many anxieties buried beneath the surface. One participant demonstrated just that disposition when he expressed frustration at my innocent questions about which religions were the problem. He finally said that "they won't be satisfied until there is an Islamic Republic of Great Britain." This was not politically correct, but it was helpful, for it reflected a broader inexperience in dealing with the challenge of Islam in Britain. But inequality and religion are not the only problems that deserve wider analysis and discussion, for a new, less confident, imperialism looms large, at least from some British viewpoints. One observer found the USA's hegemony more fragile than older imperialisms. British imperialism knew the world's future, and Britain was to be at the core. They may have been wrong, but they were, at least, confident.

He doesn't find that confidence in the U.S. today. He thought this new world led by the U.S. is based on a profound doubt, worried that the secular, capitalist and liberal order organized around American values could itself be at risk. I hadn't considered this uncertainty seriously before, but when one group of respondents argued that imposing democracy was making the world unstable, and another group argued that the failure to impose democracy was at the root of terrorism's existence, I saw the problem. It may not be uncertainty about America, but it is certainly an uncertainty about America's model for and relationship to the rest of the world that some believe to be a root cause for human insecurity, if not terrorism. And the American problem goes beyond its example. The conference participants were certainly divided about how to interpret America's power in the world.

While some celebrated the closeness of American and British intelligence, and others expressed a wish that more Americans could be present at the conference, others openly doubted the commonality of U.S. and UK interest. Isn't it the UK's interest to constrain American unilateralism? What about the apparently contradictory interests of the U.S. and the U.K. on genetically modified foods, on the international criminal court, and even on the European Union's place in the larger world order? Here, among the academic and policy intellectuals of America's closest ally we find a great ambivalence, characterized by a "Yes, but..." attitude toward the alliance. Ultimately, however, this uncertainty redounds to the British homeland itself and not only with anxiety over immigrants' place in the British way. Some openly worried that foreign policy had become too democratic. Indeed, some troubles, one person suggested, rested in the requirement that leaders be *absolutely* certain that Saddam Hussein had weapons of mass destruction; they couldn't be just reasonably sure, and the public could not simply trust them. Some were prepared to conclude expecting infallibility and certainty of one's political leaders is a recipe for political failure, and a symptom of democracy's overextension.

The root causes of terrorism and human insecurity can therefore run very deep – not only from the motivations of terrorists and their communities' support for their path, but into much broader and systematic features of the world in which we live. Are these root causes additionally found in religion's awkward place in a secular globalization, or might they be rooted in the global information infrastructure's broadcast of the wealth of some communities in the face of others' poverty? Perhaps the problem rests in American imperialism itself, or in America's lack of confidence, or in the uncertainty about whether democracy is good for everyone, or even good for making foreign policy. As the list indicates, we don't have good answers for what the root causes really are, and we don't have adequate methods for even addressing the question. Many would prefer, therefore, to focus only on the terrorists themselves, but given the anxieties and uncertainties facing the world and the consequences of violence in shaping global trajectories, it hardly seems wise to focus only on what is apparent and relatively simple.

Academic Cultural Formations Studying Terrorism

The previous summary reflects one major conference, although there are others now in the planning stages in Britain and in this country modeled on this British example. Each conference may suggest a different route to understanding terrorism's root causes, but I would propose that before we go off and consider our particular special interests within this larger problematic, that we answer a couple key questions first. First, while terrorism is clearly a major problem, is it the right problem on which to focus if you are developing any nation's foreign policy? For domestic political reasons, America must have terrorism as its principal foreign policy focus, but it may not be the biggest problem.

As more than one international relations expert has pointed out, nuclear proliferation and real war between India and Pakistan, or North Korea and other states, may be far more of a threat to American national security than terrorism is. Nevertheless, given the significance of this problem in American politics, and in the politics of certain other nations, notably in Israel, India, Spain and Great Britain, it is significant regardless of its relative threat to national security. Nevertheless, just as the 9/11 bi-partisan commission interrogates why the Bush administration failed to attend sufficiently to Osama bin Laden and Al Qaeda before 9/11/01; we must also ask what we miss when terrorism becomes the principal lens through which foreign policy is conducted. Secondly, as we focus on terrorism, fully aware of why it deserves the focus that it does, we must also consider how the framing of that problem shapes its engagement, especially when we search for its roots. Interestingly, we often hesitate to dig too deep, for our focus on the causes of terrorism typically stops at the motivations of terrorists.

This is not to say, of course, that we should not focus on motivations, even if they are not root causes. These are proximate causes, and of terrific interest to all security agencies concerned for terrorism. The front lines of Britain's homeland security were clearly focused on this issue, as are most research agencies associated with security. This is clearly an important issue to address, but it should not be confused with being a "root cause" in any of the senses with which I began this paper. However, if one is to understand motivations, one must also understand them in context, and that means in communities whether organized in place or in networks. Here, however, you face a challenging problem: through what lens does one interpret the community in which terrorists are embedded? Do you interpret them as the victims of terrorism view terrorists, as pathological and beyond explanation? Or do you interpret these communities in ways that lend dignity to the communities themselves?

It is politically impossible to assign dignity to terrorists, but how does one recognize dignity in the communities that shelter them? As one scholar put it from the British conference, most military strategists cannot afford to interpret their enemy with the lenses that are most comfortable; they must use the cultural lens with which their opponent mobilizes their forces. Shouldn't the terrorists' communities be understood in these terms too, even if they are the communities that legitimize terrorists? While we should interpret these communities in network terms, we also must consider how they articulate with the dominant perspectives shaping the explanation of these networks, around inequality and around religion. There is, of course, a small cottage industry saying that this is not about inequality – look at Osama's wealth is the most frequent refrain.

There is another cottage industry that says this is not about religion, but about a religion hijacked. But neither of these convenient explanations gets to the question of why terrorists in the name of Islam capture the appreciation of so many people beyond the terrorists' immediate communities. For this reason, I don't believe one can focus on the motivations of terrorists to understand root causes of terrorism – one must move instead ask what makes terrorists legitimate to so many otherwise very decent people, in varying degrees of affinity, from personal to imagined communities. That is a key question, and denying the fact of terrorism's legitimacy in these ever widening circles only reinforces the problem we face in recognizing terrorism's root causes. I therefore appreciate very much what Madeleine Albright suggested in the conference's opening: that the assault on dignity, on the one hand, and the lack of hope for the future, on the other, moves people to the desperation that is associated with terrorism. I also think she is quite right, and here she resonates with Mark Juergensmeyer's work.

Some religious worldviews can give much the confidence that they may sacrifice all for a cause that is greater than anything in this world. If this world offers no hope and dignity, religiously motivated terrorism becomes even more compelling for the hope and dignity it affords based on that viewpoint's construction of a world beyond. It is, of course, absolutely wrong to assume that such terrorism is embedded in the doctrine of any religion, but it is important to see how religion can become implicated in terrorism. But that also is a subject that is terribly difficult to write about, or to discuss as the British conference itself suggested. This is due, in large part, to the ignorance that typically goes into those who purport to explain how someone else's religion is implicated in the violence that offends. Perhaps, then, we should shift focus when we discuss religion. Instead of focusing only on a question about whether any particular religion is itself implicated in terrorism's spread, might we ask how any particular religion might become implicated in the production of dignity and hope in this world?

For instance, shouldn't we consider how we might explain the presence in Iraq of the coalition of the willing in the terms that assign dignity and morality in everyday life, and not only in the terms most comfortable for those who occupy? Might this, itself, be part of the problem, a root cause so to speak? If dignity's assault and hopelessness is the key to explaining the communities from which terrorists come and are given shelter, then the answer to terrorism's root causes cannot be found alone, or even primarily, in the communities of the terrorists themselves. They can be held partially responsible, as Tom Friedman does when he assaults Arab leaders for their poor leadership of their peoples. However, by seeing this only as a matter of will, and not as part of a dynamic system that moves leaders and others to the choices they make for short term gains if long term costs, we practice a very poor social science and that poor social science may be, however, politically necessary.

There is not much political space in a war on terrorism to wonder whether the war in Iraq or the violence used to confront violence itself creates more terrorists. But that is precisely the question that must be asked. And here, then, we must ask the question then about how the policies of states are formulated not necessarily to deal with terrorism as such, but to deal with the anxieties of people about being potentially victims of terrorism, or to carry out other agendas that are poorly, if at all, connected with the war on terrorism. For this reason, I especially appreciate Scott Atran's assessment of current policy. I especially look forward to the debate about it, for if it is assaulted on ideological grounds, then I will only see another root cause for terrorism's spread at work. If, instead, it leads to innovative out of the box thinking, then there may be some good reason for hope, not only for the world, but for the productive connection between a free academy and the multilateral search for global security.

The Impact of International Terrorism on Market Entry and Expansion

The global marketplace is volatile. Cast against the backdrop of promising emerging consumer and industrial markets, U.S.-based firms continually confront the perils of economic, political and social instability. Consider how the recent global economic crisis B marked by significant fluctuations in currencies and financial markets, the demise of long-standing political regimes and the veritable stagnation of consumer spending B required multinationals (MNCs) to re-evaluate their market entry and expansion strategies. Marketers assay various signaling cues to weigh market opportunities and challenges in the global marketplace. Researchers have proposed a surfeit of predictive models aimed at calculating the risks associated with market entry and expansion in emerging and newly industrialized markets. However, some variables are difficult to predict, and (once forecasted) the variables may be difficult to quantify.

One variable that has received a paucity of attention in the marketing literature is terrorism. Why should marketers be concerned with terrorism? By some estimates, U.S. businesses spend more than $200 million each year to protect their top executives. From bullet proof vests to armored cars, companies expend resources to protect key personnel. Sales and marketing professionals are often the firms first emissaries in new markets. They face jeopardy especially in markets characterized by high levels of instability. Terrorism may have both direct and indirect impacts on marketing plans and strategies. Consider the dramatic fall in U.S. tourism in the mid- and late1980s, impacting luxury hotels in Rome and other parts of Western Europe. The Cavalier Hilton and the Sheraton EUR had to employ aggressive pricing and promotional strategies to thwart occupancy declines after terrorist attacks in Rome and Vienna.

The hospitality industry increased sales and marketing expenditures to allay customer's fears regarding their safety. Rate reductions, intentional drops from five-star to four-star designations and increased advertising on electronic media helped to rebuild its market positioning. The objective of this paper is to provide a descriptive summary of terrorist behaviour in order to inform marketers of the dangers of market entry in unstable political economies. There has been a great deal of literature about the risks associated with market entry and internationalization. Likewise, there is an evolving research stream addressing the effect of catastrophes on shareholder value. Terrorism engenders many of the characteristics of risk management; but, it is increasingly difficult to calculate the outcomes of terrorist activities in a country or region.

Protection from the consequences of terrorism is multi-faceted; one might expect that an ounce of prevention is a panacea for dealing with market uncertainty. However, market uncertainty begets missed opportunity, and marketers are in search of new customers to fortify their global market positioning. Even relatively safe markets can be targets of unpredictable terrorist activities.

Real and Present Danger

Although often perceived as occurring in mostly poor nation, terrorist attacks may occur in industrialized markets less likely to be characterized as politically unstable. For example, Sainsburys of London was the target of a terrorist bomb threat (in both stores and the retailer's home office). While Johnson & Johnson distinguished leadership in the Tylenol tampering crisis transformed consumer product packaging in the U.S. and Canada, the same standards are not global. In fact, open packaging is a mainstay in most countries of the world.

Consumer-initiated terrorism has convinced MNCs to develop and implement crisis management teams. In 1998, the global marketplace has been replete with examples of terrorist activities aimed at MNCs. For example, on February 3, 1998, bombs were detonated at two McDonald restaurants in the Halandri and Vrilissia suburbs of Athens, Greece, causing extensive damage. Authorities suspected anarchists carried out the attacks in retaliation for the arrest of an alleged leader of the Fighting Guerrilla Formation (MAS). McDonald had no public declaration of political affinity toward any party or Contra-party. Just one month later, Revolutionary Armed Forces of Colombia (FARC) guerrillas kidnapped two French businessmen. The hostages were brothers who ran a hotel in the Meta Department. One hostage was released shortly after his abduction with a huge ransom demand by the rebels for his release.

By March 23, FARC rebels killed three persons, wounded 14 and kidnapped at least 27 others at a roadblock near Bogota. Four U.S. citizens and one Italian were among those kidnapped, as well as the acting president of the National Electoral Council (CNE) and his wife. While all of the hostages eventually were released (or escaped), the Colombian marketplace remains on high alert for all U.S. businesses. In late April 1998, militants thought to be from the National Union for the Total Independence of Angola (UNITA) abducted a Portuguese couple involved in trading. An administrative source told the Angolan Press Agency that the abduction occurred after 150 armed men occupied the commune of Ebanga. UNITA did not have a record of kidnapping foreigners, so there were no indications of danger.

The motive for the abduction remains unclear. Many U.S.-based marketers have successfully marketed products and services in Portugal, and most of these firms continue their market presence. The aforementioned examples were only a subset of nearly 170 significant terrorist attacks occurring in 1998. Eleven U.S. citizens were injured, and about three-fifths of the total terrorist attacks were bombings. While there are discordant post hoc explanations for the terrorist attacks, there is one fundamental accord: these terrorist activities were business-related.

Terrorism is defined by Phillip Wilcox, U.S. Coordinator for Counter Terrorism, as politically motivated violence against a non-combatant." Another more explicit definition is given by Devost, Houghton, and Pollard, who define terrorism as systematic use of actual or threatened physical violence in the pursuit of a political objective, to create a general climate of public fear and destabilize a society, and thus influence the population or government policy!

Basically, terrorism is an international crime, and it certainly poses a great threat to any country and to any firm operating within that country's marketplace. The openness precipitated by democracy in the U.S. makes American businesses a particular target for terrorist activities. Accordingly, the democratic political structure implicitly heightens the potential threat for U.S.-based firms abroad. Terrorism is difficult to counter without destroying the very framework of that democracy.

Organizational Bases of Terrorism

Nearly two decades have passed since the seminal classification of terrorists was introduced to the business literature. It posited three delineation's of terrorist profiles, namely: the criminal terrorist, the mentally deranged terrorist, and the political terrorist. This classification was largely based on the mental states of the terrorists. However, terrorist's mental state offers little normative insight into the selection of and penetration of markets outside the U.S. Although there are a variety of terrorists, with different motivations, structures and governance norms, one tripartite framework B concordant with motivational theory B is offered by The Terrorism Research Center.

While these groups are not mutually exclusive, there are core differences in the cognitive processes that effectuate their *modus operandi.* The Terrorism Research Center divides terrorists into individuals who are rationally, psychologically or are culturally motivated.

Rational Motivation

The leaders who may deal in rational terrorism use terrorism as only one possibility in searching to fulfill their goals. They tend to be cost-conscious to the extent to which terrorism seems to work. Rationally motivated leaders use terrorist activities to fulfill (at least in part) their goals or long-term mission. When that terroristic action becomes too expensive, they will seek other goal-satisfying activities.

Psychological Motivation

In this context, the terrorists find their satisfaction in the degree of alienation from the system or situation within which they operate, and the deviation from societal norms essentially intensifies their commitment to non-normative behaviours. They do not consider that they are doing anything wrong or immoral; instead, they believe that their terrorist activities are righting a wrong in society, diminishing or eliminating evil in the political economy. They polarize themselves as a real moral believer against a very immoral society. Hence, they tend to often dehumanize their victims as unworthy and since they are morally pure, they can do no wrong in their quest to right the wrongs of society. Very likely, the end justifies the means.

Cultural Motivation

In many ways, cultural motives, most especially those tied to a religious belief, are the most difficult to deal with. Culturally motivated terrorists stubbornly resist attempts to reconcile differences through a peaceful negotiation tactics. Excellent examples today are the troubles in Northern Ireland and the Middle East. Most Americans and ardent sojourners find cultural terrorism the most inexplicable type, and they are inclined to judge these actions quite harshly. Yet, in many societies of the world, vendettas, martyrdom, and other self-destructive behaviour are often tolerated, sometimes admired, and certainly understood.

In some countries of the world, there is no non-violent means for changes of government power, the terrorist, if successful, is considered a freedom fighter and may be welcomed by the populace in general, at least initially. This is not to excuse the excesses of modem terrorism, especially in an age of the possibility of mass destruction of large segments of a population by weapons of mass destruction. Nor does it excuse a destruction of the sophisticated computerized society that many countries have developed. The absence of electronic civilization would cause not only inconvenience but also actual suffering to large populations of people. The Y2K scare associated with possible breakdowns of our computerized economies exemplifies the effectual linkage between technology and human welfare.

Level of Threat

The Terrorism Research Center has identified five levels of threat, ranging from critical to negligible. One may view this along a continuum analogous to most likely to least likely to encounter terrorism. In this way, these five levels of threat can be used as one indicator for marketing managers to consider in their market entry and expansion strategies. A critical threat is one in which a group enters a country or region with the capacity to attack specified targets. Even though the intentions of the attack may not be known, the propensity for terrorist activity is high. Today, one may view Colombia to be a critical threat-marketing environment. High threat terrorist environments indicate that such groups exist, and that terrorists have the ability and intention to attack. In these cases, there have generally been one or more incidents where the identified group has attacked before in the country or region.

Here, their intentions are known; in the medium or moderate level of threat, terrorist intentions are not necessarily identified. While low terrorist groups exist and have the ability to attack, their histories may or may not be known and their intentions are unclear. The least likely terrorist environment is characterized by negligible threat and suggests that there is no information on the existence of terrorist activities in the market areas. These same designations are likely to be used by the U.S. Government and its agencies to issue warnings American travelers who might be visiting different countries of the world. When the situation is critical, warnings are likely to be issued to

Americans in the area to either avoid that country or region or to keep a low profile while there.

Dealing in Practical Terms with Terrorism

A brief mention here might be some dos and don'ts which marketers can use in dealing with terrorism overseas.

This list is not exhaustive but only intended to be suggestive.

1. Get all information possible about your area of operation from the nearest U. S. Embassy.
2. Keep a relatively low profile if possible, so as to reduce your "target" status.
3. Reference employees as much as possible as to their feelings about your company specifically and the United States generally.
4. Be careful about wearing expensive jewelry or other "target" items.
5. Vary your route to and from work so as to avoid "traps" as much as possible.
6. Keep some of any necessary medicine on your person at all times in case of kidnapping or other unavoidable delay.
7. Be suspicious of any "unusual" letter, package or other item from an unknown source.
8. Use television surveillance cameras either openly or covertly.
9. Have an area designate as a "safe" room in case of emergencies.

Implications for Marketing Operations

The instability of Eastern Europe, the ongoing military maneuvers in the Persian Gulf, the civil chaos in the former Yugoslavia, the Russian intrusion in Chechnya, and precarious socioeconomic conditions in Asia may instill fear in marketing managers with a bent toward globalization. Although terrorism is a long-standing political tool, international terrorism is at all-time high. So, marketing firms (and those with manufacturing and distribution operations abroad) need to increasingly consider terrorism as a signaling cue in their environmental scanning efforts. The whole area of logistics is especially vulnerable, as goods tend to be at their greatest risk when being moved from one place to another or when being stored in regions where there are factions with disdain for American policy. Just-in-time distributive practices may cause disruption in sales to both industrial users and final consumers if such goods are logistically disrupted.

American marketers working or traveling overseas may also be at some risk. The amount of exposure depends on the level of danger as noted above. Certainly, any American traveling frequently to conduct overseas sales and marketing must be aware of the economic, political and socio-cultural climate, monitoring and heeding American Embassies, and Consulates warnings. One of the basic problems in dealing with terrorism today is that everything done of a startling nature is immediately and even instantaneously reported by the worlds press media. This gives the terrorist instantaneous publicity a fundamental mission of nearly all terrorist- type activities. In the last decade, what Thomas Friedman called super-empowered angry men like Hitler and Stalin first controlled a state and then directed their desires onto other populations and/or countries.

Today, nearly anyone who is a computer hacker can develop terrorist activities and the cancerous spread of their ideas or political aims is almost immediately and globally accessible. In short, as the world gets increasing numbers of people and as they become more and more interconnected through the use of increasingly sophisticated electronic communication systems, the cultural differences of peoples worldwide as well as their prejudices, will become much more apparent, Individuals and social groups will, in turn, likely conflict with each other, sometimes violently.

With instant and voluminous news coverage worldwide, small incidents of a local nature can become world crises overnight. Business and marketing people worldwide will need to develop new strategies to confront the fragility of the political economies in emerging, newly industrialized and (especially) transitional economies.

11

Terrorism and Weapons of Mass Destruction

The potential use of nuclear, biological, or chemical weapons by a terrorist group remains the nightmare scenario of our times. The fear that the use of any of these weapons in an urban environment might be catastrophic is probably well founded, particularly given the demonstrated willingness of some groups, such as Al Qaeda, to sacrifice its members in performing violence against civilian populations. This paper will examine the potential use of non conventional weapons by terrorists that are not surrogates of a state. Some States that have sponsored or supported terrorism in the past have current programs to develop weapons of mass destruction (WMD). Though the number of these terrorist sponsors has diminished since the collapse of the Soviet Union, there are serious concerns about the WMD programs and the suspected intentions of Iraq, Iran and North Korea to actually use these weapons.

The possibility that any of these states might provide non-conventional weapons to terrorists that are not adjuncts of the state will also be considered. In the past, most terrorist groups have had a political objective in wielding their violence, seeking to obtain a desired outcome through force. The employment of WMD would appear at first look to be inimical to the political agendas of such groups, whether that agenda was territorial concessions, the reversal of a state policy or another goal. Usually, the appeal of the group carrying out dramatic violence was to a broader audience beyond the immediate target. Traditional terrorists sought to benefit politically from their violence, drawing sympathy from the wider audience. This set of objectives argued against the use of WMD by the group, even when such weapons were available.

Groups in the past that attempted to use of variety of WMD, e.g. Aum Shinrikyo in Tokyo, not only failed in causing mass casualties (only 12 people were killed in the subway attack) but discredited themselves internationally and failed to achieve any political objective whatsoever. To be sure, conventional attacks in the past could have catastrophic effects and often undercut the stated political goals of the perpetrators. The killing of 168 persons in the Oklahoma City bombing by Timothy McVeigh is an example. McVeigh, influenced by ethnic supremacists and radical groups such as Christian Identity, seriously miscalculated the effect of his violence on the wider audience, thereby diminishing support for white supremacists and his political objectives. And Al Qaeda itself, which has defined specific political goals for its actions, carried out the attacks on the American Embassies in Kenya and Tanzania in August 1998 which killed 224 and injured nearly 5000, mostly Africans.

We can see that inflicting mass casualties using conventional weapons is a feature of the past several years. This era of trying to achieve mass casualties is characterized by Hezbollah's use of suicide bombers in Lebanon to attack the French and American military barracks and the American Embassy. Osama bin Laden articulated the political goals for his terrorism on several occasions. His public issuance of a "Fatwa" or declaration of struggle, on 12 October 1996, stated:

"The people of Islam have suffered from aggression, iniquity and injustice imposed by the Zionist-Crusader alliance and their collaborators . . . It is the duty now on every tribe in the Arabian Peninsula to fight jihad and cleanse the land from these Crusader occupiers. Their wealth is booty to those who kill them. My Muslim brothers: your brothers in Palestine and in the land of the two Holy Places are calling upon your help and asking you to take part in fighting against the enemy – the Americans and the Israelis. They are asking you to do whatever you can to expel the enemies out of the sanctities of Islam."

Later in the same year Bin Laden said that "terrorizing the American occupiers [of Islamic Holy Places] is a religious and logical obligation."

In February 1998 bin Laden issued and signed another Fatwa which included a decree to all Muslims:

"...the killing of Americans and their civilian and military allies is a religious duty for each and every Muslim to be carried out in whichever country they are until Al Aqsa mosque has been liberated from their grasp and until their armies have left Muslim lands." In the same 'fatwa' he called on Muslim scholars and their leaders and their youths to "launch an attack on the American soldiers of Satan."

He concluded, finally:

"We – with God's help – call on every Muslim who believes in God and wishes to be rewarded to comply with God's order to kill Americans and plunder their money whenever and wherever they find it. We also call on Muslims . . . to launch the raid on Satan's US troops and the devil's supporters allying with them, and to displace those who are behind them."

When asked, in 1998, about obtaining chemical or nuclear weapons, he said: "acquiring such weapons for the defense of Muslims [was] a religious duty."

We must understand not only the nature of the threat from religious extremes but its possible evolution. In America, in addition to the presence of some Islamic fanatics, we also have fundamentalists such as Christian Identity, and other religious extremists who kill or maim in the name of God, blowing up abortion clinics and gay bars. Comprehending the danger and the mind-set of these groups is a first step to deterring their violence. But it is also important to understand their willingness to employ so-called "doomsday" weapons if they believe they are carrying out the will of God. This is the common thread from Islamic fanatics, to Jewish extremists and Christian radicals: the belief they are carrying out divine instruction.

Terrorism has evolved significantly over the past twenty years to the point that most contemporary terrorism originates from these extremist religious groups and ethnic and sub-national elements. Whether the political goal is the expulsion of Western influence from the Middle East and the Persian Gulf, or the resistance to Israeli occupation in Palestine, extremist religious groups such as Hezbollah, Hamas, Palestinian Islamic Jihad and Al Qaeda are in the forefront. Radical, secular groups' pursuit of violent means to achieve ends is, of course, very much present in today's world but overall these secularists are in a long decline dating back to the collapse of the Soviet Union. Here we can cite groups such as the Red Army faction, the Brigate Rosse, and even the 17 November group in Greece.

There are, of course, ethnic and regional conflicts fueled by political violence that have flared with varying intensity. Groups with a non-religious perspective formed the base of the Chechen resistance although the Chechens are slowly being influenced by religious extremists who provided the only real international support to the struggle against Russia. There are also the secular elements of the Palestinian resistance (in partnership with religiously based parties) that pursue the use of terrorism as a political tactic. And the major conflicts in Sri Lanka and Northern Ireland have had a non-religious character. In general, the major threat facing Western democracies today comes from fundamentalist religious groups.

Religious extremism includes Hindu, Muslim, and Jewish groups as well as Christian Identity and similar White Supremacy groups derived from fundamentalist Christian origins. Al Qaeda, Hezbollah, Hamas and the Palestinian Islamic Jihad are examples of religious militants that have used suicide bombings regularly as a political weapon. Hamas and the Jihad, which has become increasingly sophisticated in its capabilities recently, use violence to demoralize the Israeli people to the point that the groups hope they will achieve their proximate goals of ending Israeli occupation. They have not, until now, considered the use of WMD because of the congested geography in which both Israelis and Palestinians live but the possibility that their calculus will change is growing especially as the frustration level of their constituencies rises. At some point, terrorist tactics will evolve and limited use of some kinds of WMD could be attempted within Israel.

Already these groups are experimenting with chemical additives to their explosive devices and it is not a leap to expect them to use other and more deadly forms of biological and chemical weaponry. Israeli weapons technology, advanced as it is, will provide little deterrence to the use by extremist religious groups willing to use WMD in suicide operations. A number of terrorist groups that have been active in the past several years have shown significant interest in acquiring weapons of mass destruction. In addition to the well known development of nerve gas by Aleph, the new name for Aum Shinrikyo, that was demonstrated in Japan to minimal effect, groups such as Al Qaeda have conducted active experiments with poison gases, as at the Darunta Camp in Afghanistan; they have also developed plans for the construction of a radioactive explosive device (the so-called dirty bomb) and pursued attempts to acquire weapons grade uranium.

While the efforts of non-state sponsored terrorist groups to independently develop WMD have been limited by lack of infrastructure and resources that are usually only available to nation states, there is among some groups a highly developed appreciation of the effect the use of WMD would have on the Western audience. During the war against the Taliban and Al Qaeda inside Afghanistan, a number of Al Qaeda training camps yielded information on the group's experiments with WMD and its exploration of various operations using some elements of WMD designed not only to cause mass casualties, but to inflict a significant psychological blow on its Western audience. Documents recovered from Al Qaeda facilities in Afghanistan show that Bin Laden was pursuing a sophisticated biological weapons research programme.

Terrorist groups worldwide have ready access to information on chemical, biological, and even nuclear weapons via the Internet, and we know that Al Qaeda was working to acquire some of the most dangerous chemical agents and toxins. It has been speculated by U.S. government officials that Al Qaeda or other terrorist groups might try to launch conventional attacks against the chemical or nuclear industrial infrastructure of Western nations to cause widespread toxic or radiological damage. Complementary to this fear is the suspicion that terrorists might use cyber warfare attacks. September 11 demonstrated the western world's dependence on critical infrastructure systems that rely on electronic and computer networks.

Attacks of this nature will become an increasingly viable option for terrorists as they and other foreign adversaries become more familiar with these targets, and the technologies required to attack them. As noted, Al Qaeda, and most transnational groups that are not the surrogate of a state, lack necessary resources on their own to develop WMD. Ironically, the very lack of resource infrastructure has impelled Al Qaeda to consider new and imaginative uses of conventional weapons with elements of WMD that are more easily obtainable. The use of radioactive substances, such as found in medical equipment, can be used in a conventional explosive to disseminate low level radiation over the blast area. Another example is the possible use of the chemical Chlorine. Chlorine has a legitimate civilian use but it is also the raw material for the synthesis of precursor chemicals used to produce blister and nerve agents.

Chlorine can be employed in its gaseous state as a deadly poison and can be disseminated by crop duster aircraft and other techniques over a wide area. Although aerial dispersion is often an ineffective delivery system for a poison gas, it can generate hysteria when the gas in employed in a congested urban environment. The psychological effect would likely be many more times the actual physical damage, but this is often precisely what the terrorist group intends. Bin Laden, who has shown a strong interest in acquiring WMD, has had some of his operatives trained to conduct attacks with commonly available chemicals.

The use of a nuclear weapon is, of course, the most lethal tool that could be used by a terrorist group. The technology of building a nuclear weapon is understood by some terrorist groups, particularly including Al Qaeda, but also by some Pakistani radical Muslims. Yet the key to actually building a nuclear device is the availability of fissile material. This would mean the acquisition of plutonium or highly enriched uranium. Indicators of al Al Qaeda's interest in WMD and its pursuit of these capabilities include the following taking from Congressional testimony in the United States:

Well conceived schematics detailing the construction of a nuclear device were discovered in Afghanistan. Al

Qaeda so far has not succeeded in constructing such a weapon. Several attempts by the group to acquire nuclear materials since the 1990's have been documented. In September 1998, Mamdouh Mahmud Salim, an Al Qaeda operative, was arrested for attempting to purchase "enriched uranium" in Western Europe. Enriched uranium is defined in terms of its concentration of uranium-235 molecules. The more uranium-235 molecules that are in uranium, the more enriched is the unranium. Weapons grade uranium or HEU is enriched to over 90%. In February 2001, Jamal Ahmad al-Fadl, a bin Laden aid, testified that he participated in a deal to acquire uranium. Al Qaeda's bid for enriched uranium may indicate their interest in developing conventional nuclear weapons. Enriched uranium would probably be used in a gun-assembly device similar to the "Little Boy" device that was dropped on Hiroshima.

Approximately 25 Kg of highly enriched uranium (HEU) is needed to build a gun-assembly device, and there is no evidence that Al Qaeda ever acquired any highly enriched uranium or other radioactive substances that could be used to develop conventional nuclear weapons. Al Qaeda has also attempted to purchase spent nuclear fuel. In September 2001, a Bulgarian businessman claimed that aides to bin Laden approached him to purchase spent fuel from a local plant. The businessman said he first met with "the Saudi dissident," taken to mean Osama bin Laden, and the next day a young Arab chemical engineer contacted him to ask if he would serve as an intermediary for the transaction. According to the businessman, no deal ever took place. Spent fuel could be used to develop both conventional nuclear weapons and dirty bombs. If it were to be used in nuclear weapons, it would require reprocessing.

Spent fuel is reprocessed by separating neutron-absorbing fission products from unused fissile uranium 235 and plutonium 239, and fertile uranium 238. This task requires extensive knowledge of chemical processes and reactions, access to various chemicals not commonly available in industry, laboratories with hot cells, shielding to protect against radioactivity, and other equipment to complete the task. Al Qaeda does not appear to have any of these. Spent fuel could be more easily used in a dirty bomb. In this case, the substance would be combined with a conventional explosive that when set off would spread highly radioactive material over a wide area.

Evidence pointing to Al Qaeda's interest in developing dirty bombs can be found in the June 2002 arrest of suspected Al Qaeda associate Abdullah al Muhajir, also known as Jose Padilla. Muhajir was arrested by U.S. authorities for scheming to develop and use a dirty bomb in an American city. Another piece of evidence is a set of containers found in Afghanistan that were marked with skull and cross bones and filled with a liquid registering a slight radioactive signature. Investigators believe that Al Qaeda members were duped into thinking that this substance was actually highly radioactive material that could be used to develop a nuclear or radiological weapon.

In Pakistan, a number of nuclear scientists were arrested for allegedly assisting Al Qaeda with nuclear technologies. Media accounts do not detail the scientists' assistance to Al Qaeda, but they do cite one scientist, Sultan Bashiruddin Mahmood, admitting that he met with Al Qaeda and helped the organization through his non-profit "humanitarian" organization. Mahmood is believed to have been a senior member of Pakistan's nuclear weapons program, "with broad access to classified information." Western experts are concerned that he and others may have transferred nuclear knowledge, equipment, or materials to the Taliban, which in turn would have been passed to Al Qaeda.

Reports also claim that Al Qaeda attempted to purchase whole nuclear weapon assemblies. In 1998, the Paris-based

Arabic paper Al-Watan Al-Arabi ran a story about a "nuclear warhead deal," where Al Qaeda members and Chechen crime figures met to exchange two tons of opium and $30 million in cash for 20 nuclear warheads. There is no evidence that this exchange ever took place, nor is it likely that Al Qaeda has ever possessed nuclear warheads.

In reviewing the information publicly available, we can conclude that one of Al Qaeda's objectives is to develop a nuclear capability. However, to the present there is no evidence that the organization ever did not acquire enough nuclear material to develop a nuclear weapon, nor does it appear that they were able to acquire whole nuclear weapon assemblies. The more immediate risk is that Al Qaeda has succeeded in obtaining a limited amount of enriched uranium or other radioactive material from Central Asia or Russia and intends to employ it as the core of a conventional explosive device. It has been estimated that if such device were detonated in an urban environment, depending on the lethality of the core material, the blast area would be uninhabitable for several years until all of the soil was physically removed.

According to CIA public declarations, Al Qaeda has aggressively pursued a chemical and biological weapon (CBW) capability. The organization appears to have made more progress in these fields than in the nuclear realm. Although it is difficult to point to physical evidence of Al Qaeda's CBW capability, several hints suggest the likelihood that Al Qaeda has produced small amounts of some type of agent. One comes from the ten volumes "Encyclopedia of Afghanistan Resistance" which was found while coalition forces were inspecting a camp close to Jalalabad in Afghanistan. The encyclopedia contains precise formulas for manufacturing toxins, botullinum, and ricin.

The document also instructs would-be perpetrators in methods of disseminating the deadly materials. From the American investigation of the September 11 tragedy it was discovered that some Al Qaeda wanted to purchase crop dusters that analysts believe would have been used to disseminate anthrax and chemical or biologic agents. Another indicator of Al Qaeda's chemical weapons interest comes from a recently discovered videotape that records experiments involving dogs that were exposed to vapors from a "white liquid." In the tape, the dogs struggle, vomit, have trouble breathing, and finally die. Some experts speculate that the gas was a nerve agent such as sarin. The last hint of Al Qaeda's chemical weapons capability comes from Ahmed Ressam, the Algerian convicted of planning to bomb the Los Angeles airport during the Millennium celebrations.

Ressam testified that Al Qaeda taught him to poison people by putting toxins on door knobs, and that he engaged in experiments in which dogs were injected with a mixture containing cyanide and sulphuric acid. Although a stock of agents or their precursors has not been found, it is apparent that some quantity of an agent was obtained by Al Qaeda personnel. How did Al Qaeda acquire CBW materials in the first place? One possibility is outlined in a September 2001 British media report alleging that operatives may have acquired samples of anthrax, salmonella, and e-coli through Czech facilities. However, this has not been proven and Czech officials deny the allegations. What we can conclude from captured documents, media reports, and U.S. government statements is that Al Qaeda has obtained chemical agents, albeit probably in small quantities, and performed experiments on live subjects to determine the lethality of the substances.

Manuals and testimony also indicate that Al Qaeda has determined how to operationalise chemical and biological warfare. Notwithstanding the above, there are significant obstacles to terrorist groups in acquiring a WMD stockpile. For example, terrorists working outside a state-run laboratory would have to overcome extraordinary technical and operational challenges to effectively and successfully weaponize and deliver a biological agent to cause mass casualties. While many biological agents can be obtained or grown with relative ease, several significant steps remain on the way to weaponization and effective use of these agents. The main challenge is effective dissemination, which requires an aerosol form. The formulation of agents for airborne dispersal requires dissolving optimal amounts of weaponized agents in a specific combination of different chemicals (with each agent requiring a unique formulation).

This is possibly the major remaining secret of the former U.S. and Soviet BW programs. Moreover, aerosol disseminators need to be operated effectively and suitable meteorological conditions must be present to carry out a successful BW attack. Despite the fact that the Aum Shinrikyo sect had substantial resources, members who were trained chemists and bioscientists, motivation, and ample time for research, they failed to carry out an effective BW attack despite several attempts. Some experts in the field believe that less efficient aerosol techniques may be obtained by capable non-state groups, and that even a crude delivery system could still cause casualties or injuries in the thousands, especially if the attack is carried out against a large indoor population. Toxic industrial chemicals such as chlorine or phosgene, as noted above, are easily available and do not require great expertise to be adapted into chemical weapons.

Nerve agents are more difficult to produce, and require a synthesis of multiple precursor chemicals. They also require high-temperature processes and create dangerous byproducts, which makes their production unlikely outside of an advanced laboratory. Aerosol or vapor forms are the most effective for dissemination, which can be carried out by sprayers or an explosive device. However, agents are vulnerable to temperature, moisture and wind, and are unreliable in the open air. Their most effective use as a terrorist weapon would be on an indoor population.

If transnational terrorist groups have only a limited capability to develop and exploit WMD as tools for their violent acts, states that have sponsored terrorism in the past do have a marked capability in this area. These states include Iran, North Korea, Iraq and Libya. Among these countries, the CBW threat continues to grow for a variety of reasons but the dual-use nature of many CW and BW agents complicates any assessment of offensive programs. Many CW and BW production capabilities are hidden in plants that are virtually indistinguishable from genuine commercial facilities. There have been reports of dubious reliability indicating that Iraq has acquired Smallpox strains from a Russian laboratory that are impervious to inoculation. Iraq may have had access to some strains of common smallpox although there is no confirmation that such stocks exist in Iraqi inventories. Yet the possibility of a smallpox scourge unleashed on a world where inoculations against the disease no longer exist is terrifying to modern societies.

A repressive government such as the one headed by Saddam Hussein that has demonstrated a willingness to employ chemical weapons in the past against its own Kurdish population will probably be willing to use the most deadly chemical and biological agents at its disposal when the government is placed in extremist. But would Saddam Hussein or another leader with stockpiles of WMD release these weapons to a terrorist group such as Al Qaeda? Certainly we have no evidence that this is the case right now. We will consider the future possibilities.

Iraq is the poster child for states that have developed weapons of mass destruction, at least in the past, and which has also harbored terrorist groups such as the 15 May Group, the Abu Nidal Organization, and others. According to public dossiers issued by the United Kingdom and the

United States, Baghdad has been producing chemical warfare agents, including mustard, sarin, cyclosarin and VX. The Iraqis have experience in manufacturing CW bombs, artillery rockets and probably possess CW bulk fills for SRBM warheads, including warheads mounted on extended-range Scuds. Iraq has also developed incapacitating BW agents and has been able to weaponize such agents, including Anthrax, for delivery by bombs, missiles, aerial sprayers and covert operatives. Iraq has also used chemical weapons in the past. Some examples:

- August 1983, mustard gas used against Iranians and Kurds.
- February 1986, mustard/taban gas used against Iranians (8,000 casualties).
- October 1987, mustard gas and other nerve agents used against Iranians.

Western intelligence analysis assumes that Iraq is unlikely to produce enough weapons-grade material for a deliverable nuclear weapon until the end of this decade. Iraq could, in this analysis, produce a nuclear bomb if it were able to acquire weapons-grade fissile material abroad. But the question remains: If Iraq has a WMD capability, how likely would it be that it provides some of these weapons to terrorist groups for their own use? There is no precedent among the states that have sponsored or support terrorism to provide WMD materials to non-state groups. The Libyans, who for years provided safe haven and support to the Abu Nidal Group, never provided chemical or biological agents to the group.

Iran, which is the sponsor of the Lebanese Hezbollah, has provided that group with significant assistance, including rockets and other sophisticated conventional weaponry. But there is no record that Iran has not provided any components of WMD to the Hezbollah, nor does it appear likely to do so in the future. There are significant obstacles to states, which by and large are attempting to conceal their WMD programs, in providing these weapons to groups they do not entirely control. Once the weapons are ceded to such a terrorist group, the state loses operational control and has potentially incriminated its own clandestine WMD program. There are few incentives for states with a WMD capability to loosen control over weapons programs developed in great secrecy and considered an essential component of the nation's political and military strategy.

WMD programs are also becoming more advanced and effective as they mature, and as some countries become more aggressive in pursuing them. This is exacerbated by the diffusion of technology over time–which enables proliferators to draw on the experience of others and to develop more advanced weapons more quickly than they could otherwise. Proliferators are also becoming more self-sufficient. And they are establishing advanced production capabilities by taking advantage of both foreign assistance and the dual-use nature of WMD– and missile-related technologies. This also allows them to conduct WMD– and missile-related research under the guise of legitimate commercial or scientific activity.

Iran remains a serious concern because of its across-the-board pursuit of WMD and missile capabilities. Tehran may be able to indigenously produce enough fissile material for a nuclear weapon by late this decade. Iran may also flight-test an ICBM later this decade, using either Russian or North Korean assistance. It also continues to pursue dual-use equipment and expertise that could help to expand its BW arsenal, and to maintain a large CW stockpile. Syria has a longstanding chemical warfare program and is pursuing the development of biological weapons. It has signed but not ratified the BWC and is not a state party to the CWC. Damascus has a stockpile of the nerve agent sarin that can be delivered by aircraft or ballistic missiles.

It is trying to develop the more toxic and persistent nerve agent VX and will likely continue to improve its chemical agent production and delivery infrastructure. Iraq made extensive use of chemical weapons (CW) during the 1980s, both against Iranian troops and Kurdish civilians in Iraq. Iraq probably retained a stockpile of CW munitions in the form of aerial bombs, rockets, and artillery shells, as well as precursor chemicals and agents, including mustard gas, VX, and other nerve agents. Iraq may have built new agent and munitions production facilities since 1998. UN weapons inspectors are currently in the process of determining whether Iraq has retained CBW stockpiles. Iraq is not a signatory of the Chemical Weapons Convention.

Libya remains dependent on foreign suppliers for precursor chemicals and other key CW-related equipment, and may be re-establishing contacts with sources of expertise, equipment and precursors now that sanctions have been suspended. Tripoli has not given up its goal of establishing its own offensive CW capability and continues to pursue an indigenous production capability for the weapons. Libya also may use its new procurement opportunities to develop an indigenous BW capability.

Libya is not a signatory of the CWC and probably retains an inventory of nerve and blister agents. In 1987, Libya used small quantities of mustard gas munitions against Chadian troops. Because of its reliance on foreign suppliers for precursor chemicals, Libya's chemical weapons (CW) program was severely hampered by UN sanctions in the 1990s. It is important to note when considering the use of non-conventional weapons by terrorists that attacks using WMD need not be directed only at humans. Plant and animal pathogens may be used against agricultural targets, creating both potential economic devastation and the possibility that a criminal group might seek to exploit such an attack for economic advantage. As deadly as they now are, BW agents could become even more sophisticated.

Rapid advances in biotechnology present the prospect of a new array of toxins or live agents that require new detection methods, preventative measures, and treatments. Particularly with respect to chemical weapons, there is a growing risk that new and difficult-to-combat agents will become available to hostile countries or sub-national groups. Countries are taking advantage of denial and deception techniques, concealing and protecting BW and CW programs. BW in particular lends itself to concealment because of its overlap with legitimate research and commercial biotechnology. The technologies used to prolong our lives and improve our standard of living can quite easily be adapted to cause mass casualties.

The terrorist threat in the modern world goes well beyond Al Qaeda. The situation in the Middle East continues to fuel terrorism and anti-US sentiment worldwide, but other Western nations are not immune to the threat. Groups like the Palestine Islamic Jihad and Hamas have escalated their violence and have attracted support from radical secular Palestinian groups. There is increasingly a convergence of common interest among anti-Western and anti-democratic elements in striking at Europe and America. The war on terrorism may have crippled Al Qaeda and its leadership and the group seems no longer able to run large-scale training and recruitment programs in Afghanistan. Yet the group remains dispersed throughout the world, certainly entrenched in some societies, and retains the loyalty of a fanatical cadre.

This cadre is willing to use violence against those who do not share their religious fervor and it heeds what it believes to be the voice of God as interpreted by charismatic fanatics such as Bin Laden. Poverty, alienation, territorial occupation and ethnic and religious tensions are factors that terrorist groups exploit, and these conditions may grow more acute over the next decade. This will especially be the case in those parts of the world that have served as the most fertile recruiting grounds for Islamic extremist groups. We have already seen–in Afghanistan and elsewhere–that domestic unrest and conflict in weak states is one of the factors that create an environment conducive to terrorism.

Importantly, demographic trends suggest that the world's poorest and most politically unstable regions–which include parts of the Middle East and Sub-Saharan Africa–will, have the largest youth populations in the world over the next two decades and beyond. Most of these countries will lack the economic institutions or resources to effectively integrate these youth into society. One of the places where they converge that has the greatest long-term impact on any society is its educational system. Primary and secondary education in parts of the Muslim world is often dominated by an interpretation of Islam that teaches intolerance and hatred. The graduates of these schools–"Madrassas" –provide the foot soldiers for many of the Islamic militant groups that operate throughout the Muslim world.

The current conflict between Israel and the Palestinians has been raging for almost a year and a half and has been deteriorating. The peace seekers are difficult to find. The violence has hardened the public's positions on both sides and increased the longstanding animosity between Israeli Prime Minister Sharon and Palestinian leader Yasser Arafat. Moderates on both sides admit that ultimately the conflict can only be resolved through negotiations. But there is an absence of any meaningful security cooperation between Israel and the Palestinian Authority, there is escalating and uncontrolled militancy by the Islamic Jihad and Hamas, and there is an increasingly harsh and repressive occupation inflicted by the Israeli military over Palestinian territories. All this makes any meaningful progress extremely difficult. In this environment there are many opportunities for state sponsors of terrorism to escalate the violence and for terrorist groups to appeal for support from a wider audience.

It is a common trait among specialists in the field of counterterrorism to dwell on the worst case scenario. I have tried to be realistic in surveying the threat presented by terrorist use of non-conventional weapons, including WMD. But as I have pointed out, there are limitations to the acquisition of such weapons by non-state actors. Yet there is one hypothesis that mandates the use of the worst cast scenario- it is when the regime of a nation that has a well developed program of WMD is under threat of elimination. Where there are no restraints imposed by a democratic system, where the ruler, his family and his loyal retainers are all in jeopardy of total destruction, then the use of WMD either by the country's military or by its surrogates is not only possible but likely. Depending on the stockpiles available, and the dissemination tools at hand, the worst case scenario will become all too real.

12

Dealings with Nuclear Terrorism

Since 1945 the world has been confronted with three major fears associated with the existence and possible use of nuclear weapons: a potential clash of superpowers during the Cold War era; the political and military peril of nuclear proliferation; and the threat of catastrophic nuclear accidents. Derived from the attacks of 9/11, the latest nuclear anxiety is the danger that sub-state groups will integrate nuclear terrorism into their strategic repertoire by getting hold of unsafe fissile materials or ready-made, black-marketed nuclear weapons. Just like the nuclear countries, terrorists see the 'ultimate destructive power' of nuclear weapons as an instrument for the attainment of their goals.

Nuclear weapons are, in this sense, a realistic strategic option that these groups may recur to in order to push the US and its partners to accede to their demands which can range from the withdrawal of US support for Israel, the annexation of Kashmir by Pakistan, or the creation of Islamic governance systems (Shariah) around the world. William C. Potter of the Center for Non proliferation Studies and Charles D. Ferguson argue that a nuclear terrorist attack is more likely to happen now than in any other time in the past. The rationale behind this statement lies in two basic premises:

1. Non-state actors have emerged in the form of terrorist

networks/organisations, which have the urge to use nuclear weapons for furthering their agendas.

2. Crude but real nuclear weapons, as distinct from radiological dispersal devices, are well within the technical reach of some terrorist organisations.

It is due to these realistic and almost tangible threats that nuclear non-proliferation has become 'the pre-eminent national security issue for the US '. The most prominent policy goal of the US is therefore to keep nuclear weapons, the know-how required for their construction, and the fissile materials that make them dangerous, out of the hands of those who could inflict harm on the country or one of its allies.

Thus, the current US strategy of non-proliferation with regards to the terrorist threat could be categorised along the following dimensions:

1. Securing nuclear materials and warheads at the sites where they are stored, a matter that could be termed the 'first line of defence'.
2. Reducing the risk of proliferation or even of nuclear confrontations in South and Central Asia.
3. Securing vulnerable Russian nuclear weapons.
4. Improving protection of nuclear facilities within the US.
5. Improving border and cargo monitoring at the frontier crossings and embarkation points most likely to be used by smugglers.
6. Containing the spread of nuclear intelligence, defined as the know-how and material elements required to build a nuclear explosive device or even more cursory (yet sensitive) information that could give some group access to ready-made nuclear weapons.
7. Preventing more states from acquiring nuclear weapons.

Graham T. Allison has shown, in this sense, the inevitability of nuclear **terrorism**, arguing that this activity could pick up pace during the next decade. In order to prevent such inevitability, Allison has suggested that the 'thousands of unsecured weapons (soft ball size lumps of highly enriched uranium and weapons-grade plutonium) in Russia should be guarded from being stolen by criminals who could then sell them to terrorists deriving great economic gains'. The US has forged a network of alliances with many countries as a measure to ward off terrorism after the attacks of 9/11. In this respect, the basic strategic goal of the US is to deploy a policy which makes 'prevention the highest priority' in 'countries of concern'.

North Korea, Iran, Iraq, Pakistan and Russia could be labeled as 'countries of concern' because of their undemocratic governments, the anti-Americanism that exists in some subgroups of their societies, and the existence of unsecured nuclear weapons or fissile materials which are vulnerable to thefts and may be diverted for their use in nuclear terrorist attacks. The focus of this paper will be limited to the case of Pakistan, a strong partner of the US in its 'war against terrorism', that nevertheless poses, due to its unstable situation and precarious socioeconomic structure, a high risk of being the source of black-marketed nuclear weapons and/ or fissile materials. This paper will delve into the current US strategic cooperative efforts towards Pakistan in order to assess and fill any gaps that might exist in a foreign policy approach based on the US 's 'first line of defence' rationale.

Nuclear Terrorism

Nuclear terrorism is a term that is not restricted solely to the use by a terrorist organisation of an explosive nuclear device. According to Ferguson, nuclear terrorism in its broad definition includes actions such as

- The seizure and detonation of an intact nuclear weapon.
- The theft or purchase of highly enriched uranium (HEU) or plutonium, leading to the fabrication and detonation of a crude nuclear weapon, or an improvised nuclear device (IND).

- Attacks against, and sabotage of, nuclear facilities, such as nuclear power plants, to try to cause the release of large amounts of radioactivity.
- The unauthorised acquisition of radioactive materials contributing to the construction and detonation of a radiological dispersion device, popularly known as a 'dirty bomb,' or a radiation emission device.

Nuclear terrorism involving the detonation of an (albeit primitive) nuclear device is not to be deemed a technically unachievable scenario. The simplicity of a gun-type weapon design makes it easier for a terrorist, given access to HEU, to engage in nuclear terrorism. A terrorist group could use, for instance, a commercial explosive to shoot two sub-critical masses of HEU into one another to 'form [the] supercritical mass needed to sustain an explosive chain reaction'. Plutonium could likewise be used as a fissile element, though it implies a greater deal of technical challenges. Plutonium would have to be employed in the more technically sophisticated implosion-assembly method, which uses military-grade explosives and precision detonation electronics to squeeze the plutonium into a supercritical mass.

Al-Qaeda and the inevitability of nuclear terrorism

The probability of a nuclear terrorist attack has increased in the aftermath of 9/11. Security experts agree that although unlikely, a nuclear terrorist attack is possible. Several episodes in the contemporary history of nuclear proliferation unveil, in particular, al-Qaeda's clandestine efforts to get the bomb. As early as December 1998, Bin Laden showed great desires to acquire nuclear weapons for the mass killing of so-called 'infidels'. Bin Laden believes, it is said, that it is a religious duty to possess nuclear weapons and that were he not to follow this duty, he would be committing a sin. Bin Laden tried to acquire nuclear materials as far back as in 1992 when he sought to forge relations with South Africa. Bin Laden was also alleged to have sought a deal with Chechen rebels in Russia to buy a nuclear war head. The fact that, until now, Bin Laden's network has not recurred to a nuclear attack does not mean that such attack will not occur. Evidence shows that there is an important probability of a large-scale terrorist attack involving the use of nuclear weapons.

In the aftermath of 9/11, Osama Bin Laden was reported to have said in an interview with the Pakistani news paper Dawn that if the US uses nuclear weapons on Osama Bin Laden groups and affiliates, he would attack the US with nuclear and/or chemical/biological weapons. In the same interview, Bin Laden also assured that he possessed weapons of mass destruction. The statements issued by al-Qaeda before and after the 9/11 attacks are evidence of the intense hatred this network holds towards Americans. Graham Allison argues, in this sense, that al-Qaeda would not miss any chance to kill and injure millions of Americans, since they believe that America's collaboration with 'the Jewish' 'is the cause of corruption and is responsible for the breakdown of values: moral, ideological, political and economic'. The poor state of Muslims in the contemporary world, according to their view, is due to America.

The document Terrorist CBRN : Materials and Effects produced in 2003 reports, for instance, that Islamist extremists linked to al-Qaeda leader Osama bin Laden 'have a wide variety of potential agents and delivery means to choose from for chemical, biological and radiological or nuclear (CBRN) attacks.' The goal of these terrorists would thus be to use CBRN to cause mass causalities. 'Attacks would be small scale, incorporating relatively crude delivery means and easily produced or obtained chemicals, toxins or radiological substances'. However, many analysts and policy makers have argued that nuclear terrorism is not inevitable. Robin Frost argues that obtaining access to fissile material and consequently assembling an explosive device would prove to be a very difficult for a terrorist organisation.

Frost does not limit the definition of terrorist organisations to al-Qaeda; he includes many other such organisations.

These organisations draw their motivations from multifarious political, spiritual and historical events, like Aum Shinriko in Japan, the National Liberation Front of Nigeria, the Irish Republic Army, and other separatist organisations who could find 'hostage- taking, conventional bombings, shoot and run sniper attacks more feasible and cheaper to attain their terrorist motivations'. Despite these criticisms, the sheer danger posed by the possibility of a nuclear-armed al- Qaeda makes focus on this organisation highly relevant. Even Frost has contended that al- Qaeda stands today as the most dangerous religious terrorist organisation. Frost even concedes that al-Qaeda has attempted to acquire a nuclear weapon and is obsessed with killing American citizens.

Similarly, I argue that al-Qaeda believes in nuclear terrorism as an instrument that will allow this organisation to fulfil its goals (in particular, the assassination of Americans). Osama Bin Laden, leader of al-Qaeda, runs this organisation on the core beliefs of extremist political Islam, making it easier for these Sunni fundamentalists to renounce to their lives in the process of killing the 'infidels' in this world. After all, this belief contends, martyrs will be rewarded with 72 wives and a mansion of gold in the afterlife which, incidentally, is more important than earthly existence. For Bin Laden and his followers, praying, marrying twelve wives, living in caves, crossing the snow-clad mountains of northern Kashmir and Afghanistan without the basic amenities of survival, fasting in Ramadan, or killing 'infidels' are all on the same level, all mere acts to make Allah content.

The force of Imaan (belief in Arabic) could make them do anything. These extremist individuals, whether from Hizbollah or Jaish-e Mohammed, draw their motivations from the battles fought between Prophet Mohammed and the Jews of Medina in the 600 AD Battle of Badr, where Muslims were a small minority but overwhelmed their opponents. The battle of Karbala is also a mythical figure in the minds of Sunni fundamentalist terrorist groups, and although a defeat for Husyn, grandson of Prophet Mohammed, it is seen with reverence, extreme passion and devotion. Moreover, due to their beliefs in a Muslim brotherhood (based on the fear of Allah and giving one's life while pursuing jehad for saving Allah's religion), al-Qaeda deems it reasonable to use any means available, whether it be nuclear weapons or aeroplanes and buildings, for spreading Islam and killing the western 'Satan', i.e. the US Bin Laden wants to bring the 'rule of Allah' to the world and is not inspired by any 'cult' or driven by the need to make his 'personality special or gifted'.

Bin Laden said in one of his sermons:

All these crimes and sins committed by the Americans are a clear declaration of war on Allah, his messenger, and Muslims. And Ulema have throughout Islamic history unanimously agreed that the jihad is an individual duty if the enemy destroys the Muslim countries. This was revealed by Imam Bin-Qadamah in Al-Mughni, Imam al- Kisa'i in Al-Bada'i, al-Qurtubi in his interpretation, and the Shaykh of al-Islam in his books, where he said: 'As for the fighting to repulse [an enemy], it is aimed at defending sanctity and religion, and it is a duty as agreed [by the ulema]. Nothing is more sacred than belief except repulsing an enemy who is attacking religion and life'. The above mentioned evidence makes it clear that al-Qaeda is adamant to engage in nuclear terrorism.

Deterrence and Nuclear Terrorism

The traditional strategy that was used between states to prevent either the spread of nuclear weapons or their first use was that of deterrence. This concept, however, may fail in its applicability once it is extended to the domain of nuclear terrorism due to the mere fact that sub-state actors do not respond in the same way as a nation or a centralised bureaucratic system. Thus, in the literature, arguments have been made both for and against deterrence as a line of defence against nuclear terrorism. The main position in the literature argues that deterrence, defined as threatening an enemy with assured destruction, cannot work effectively against non-state actors, i.e. the terrorists. Deterrence, in this view, is only viable for enemies having a territorial reality.

However, Micheal A. Levi argues that 'with a little technological innovation, deterrence can become a useful strategy against terrorist use of nuclear weapons'. Given that nuclear terrorism depends on the existence of a state-based source of either active weapons or basic fissile materials, deterrence could work under the guarantee of massive retaliation against countries involved in the promotion and/or sponsorship of terrorism: 'those rogue states who are caught secretly or overtly providing nuclear materials and weapons to terrorists' and who could consequently be threatened with complete nuclear retaliation in the form of a inter-state confrontation (although the legality of this issue is left open to questioning). Levi thus argue that, building on scientific techniques developed during the Cold War, the United States stands a good chance of developing the tools needed to attribute terrorist nuclear attacks to their state sponsors. If it can put those tools in place and let its enemies know of their existence, deterrence could become one of the most valuable tools in the war on terror. I concur with Levi, insofar as deterrence can be used as a measure against nuclear terrorism.

Once the links of the rogue states with terrorists are unveiled, massive retaliation could be used destroy such links: focus should be on breaking the links of terrorist with any states/non state actors transferring fissile material. The US and Pakistan The history of the US-Pakistan relationship is chequered. Sometimes Pakistan has been the US's most favoured ally and sometimes a troublesome friend. Now, Pakistan represents three things to the US; 'a staunch ally', 'a threat' and a 'troublesome friend'. For instance, Pakistan is termed as the most favoured non-NATO ally by the US (specifically by the administration of President George W. Bush and in reference to its role in the war against nuclear terrorism.) This position has been cemented by the work of Pervez Musharraf, President of Pakistan; he is often referred to by anti-American elements within the country as 'Busharf' due to his strong pro-American leanings.

On the other hand, after the A. Q. Khan nuclear black market network was exposed in 2004, Pakistan also came to symbolise a 'hub of terrorists', remaining as a great concern for the international community. The doubtful ability to secure loose nuclear materials in Pakistan is, in this sense, one of the sources of anxiety. In particular, there is a fear that followers of al-Qaeda holding major posts in the Pakistani army and the Inter Services Intelligence Agencies might choose to divert nuclear weapons to their parent organisation. President Musharraf has reiterated that nuclear command and control in Pakistan is securely delegated and that nuclear materials are secure and protected from terrorist elements.

However, it has been argued that this false 'expressed belief' of Musharraf poses a major problem in securing nuclear material from the twisted ideologies of terrorists. Nuclear command and control in Pakistan Command, Control, Communication and Intelligence Systems (C 3 I) are the arrangements of facilities, personnel, procedures and means of information acquisition, processing and dissemination used by a commander in planning, directing and controlling military operations. Safe and reliable C 3 I systems are thus a prerequisite in preventing access to nuclear materials. There are many features of the existing

Command and Control (CC) system in Pakistan which deviate from the typical US - USSR model. Pakistani policy makers contend that 'the issues relating to the nuclear [CC] in the Indo-Pakistani context are different in nature from those of the Cold War Model.

The geographical proximity of the two countries, the asymmetry in conventional forces, and the low strategic warning times are factors that demand highly efficient and reliable CC executed by their respective decision making authorities. The absolute failsafe CC is not likely to be achieved by either side in near future; indeed, such an ideal was perhaps not even achieved by the US or the USSR. Thus, an 'always/never' dilemma will continue to be part of the risk calculus for accidental or unauthorised use of nuclear weapons on both sides'. Khalid Banuri of the Pakistani Strategic Plans Division elaborates that 'Pakistan has established an effective and reliable National Command Authority (NCA) that is at the apex of a decision-making body under the chairmanship of the President, with the Prime Minister as its Vice-Chairman.'

This system consists of an Employment Control Committee and Development Control Committee as well as of a Strategic Plans Division (SPD) which acts as its Secretariat, and a Strategic Force Commands with clearly defined functions. The operational The United States dealings with nuclear terrorism: cooperation from prevention control of all strategic assets in Pakistan rests directly with the NCA through the SPD which has, on ground, a very elaborate and layered security structure under a Director General Security, reporting directly to the Director of SPD Pakistan has also taken steps towards the evolution of its export-control legislation, now approved by the Cabinet and under revision within the Parliament.

This legislation lays down strict export-control measures and will take stringent actions for any attempt or violation of export-control laws. Pakistan furthermore has a rigorous screening for human reliability at various levels of access to nuclear materials. Likewise, Pakistan is open to outside assistance, the overarching principle being, however, non-intrusiveness. In particular, it is Pakistan's Strategic Plans Division which looks after the security of nuclear materials and facilities. Other measures taken by Pakistan to secure its nuclear materials include:

- The introduction of domestic legislation to tighten controls on nuclear-related exports
- The improvement of physical security at sensitive facilities
- The strengthening of the personnel reliability system
- The relocation of nuclear materials and weapons to more secure locations, and
- The removal of individuals involved in the nuclear black market from their posts within the nuclear establishment.

No to sanctions – yes to economic help Ferguson has argued that certain countries that have terrorist cells, like Pakistan, should be penalised. However, while refuting Ferguson, Touqir has argued that any kind of American sanctions towards Pakistan would not be a good tool to combat terrorism for they would have overall debilitating effects. Sanctions would 'squeeze Pakistan economically, giving rise to more extremist elements. Resource-starved sectors such as health care, education and correctional services should be stimulated so that more jobs, better education and health services are provided to the marginalised populations. In this sense, the focus of attention should not be on the sanctioning of a nation-state (i.e. Pakistan), but rather the recognition that unemployed youth facing severe economic challenges, for instance, are attracted by extremist organisations are therefore candidates to become suicide bombers.

The US has to forge a policy towards Pakistan which plucks out the root causes of terrorism following an approach different from that of sanctions and diplomatic retaliations. As in the past, the US should help Pakistan both economically and socially. The United States should not suffer from any political myopia while reviewing its economic policies towards Pakistan. The US has to commence its anti-terrorist fight by educating both the civilian and military populations: an implementation of social and educational reforms is essential. In addition, the US should help India and Pakistan to build peace and pursue complete disarmament, so that the ambitions of nuclear terrorists are nipped at their base.

The US and Pakistan have cooperated with each other to root out the menace of terrorism in the past, so actions of this type are not without some sort of precedence. For instance, within the three years that followed the 9/11 attacks, the US gave economic aid to Pakistan in the order of $1 billion, and wrote off $1 billion in debt. In June 2003, the US announced it would give a $3 billion aid package to Pakistan to be distributed over five years. This aid is aimed at assisting the (traditional) economic and security sectors. A framework agreement on trade and investment has also been signed between these two countries, including a $1.2 billion arms-sales package that includes the sale of P 3 Orion aircrafts. The United States has also reinstated a military-training programme through which some three hundred officers have received instruction at American military institutions since 2001.

Pakistan- US relations are not limited only to this kind of military intelligence relationship but extend further. Curtailing anti Americanism US economic assistance towards Pakistan could be used to curtail anti-Americanism. The traditional Pakistani army has been inculcated with doctrines imbedded with a deep hatred for Jews and Hindus. A strategic reorientation of the Pakistani army's thinking is needed to pave the way for the evolution of liberal-minded officers who are tilted more towards US interests than those of Osama Bin Laden. Broader reforms in Pakistan are central to combating terrorism all kinds. For many years, political parties and governments used the goad of anti-Americanism to win public support and to divert attention away from festering domestic issues.

Now the very same anti- Americanism is being used by extreme Islamists. Both the Pakistani and US governments should cooperate to root out hatred towards the US amongst Pakistani civil and political elites as well as within the larger population via, for instance, media campaigns and education.

India-Pakistan Rivalry and Nuclear Security

The rivalry between India and Pakistan enhances the risk of nuclear material from being diverted into terrorist activities. The 'new peace' between India and Pakistan could bolster this aspect of security in the region, in direct benefit to the US and its allies. Pakistan's first-use policy and inferiority in conventional weapons *vis à vis* India have given it strong incentives for the deployment of its nuclear arsenal, raising concerns in the US policy- making elite, and forcing them to work even harder to provide assistance on detection technologies to Pakistan So far India and Pakistan have participated in nuclear-threat reduction measures.

They have signed or acceded to regional cooperative agreements containing disarmament components; and have participated in IAEA nuclear safety and security training courses. 'Both countries are also required to provide the highest standards of security for fissile material under UN Resolution 1540, and as members of the Convention on Physical Protection of Nuclear Materials'. Although India and Pakistan have taken measures to secure their nuclear stockpiles, they have done so on their own terms and have not provided concrete evidence to the international community that their nuclear storage facilities are not vulnerable. Their national sovereignty overwhelms nuclear security measures. Both countries are suspicious about any intrusive act of the IAEA. The US could encourage Pakistan to become more cooperative and transparent about its nuclear programme, without compromising its national interests. Unlike Russia, Pakistan is not likely to allow any US nuclear experts or laboratory specialists in its nuclear facilities, even if it.

The United States dealings with nuclear terrorism: cooperation from prevention was part of an upgrade in security. In the future, Pakistan cannot be expected to dismantle its nuclear establishment, 'closing down facilities and blending down fissile materials'. While looking for a cooperative deal with Pakistan, the US should embark on the development of a 'not-so-hyper' intrusive tool to safeguard fissile material that keeps in view Pakistan's national security interests and sensitivities related to sovereignty. The US should pave the way for bilateral dialogue on the possible 'menu' of low-intrusive tools, for both civilian and military sites where nuclear material is stored, that could be further adopted and implemented by Pakistan unilaterally. Other cooperative measures could be as follows: training programs, exchanges of best practices, and steps to strengthen the security culture in all nuclear-related institutions.

Organisational links, such as lab-to-lab relations and scientific exchanges, could also be explored. Dialogue might need to begin by addressing the outsider threat (guard training, fences, cameras, equipment, et cetera) because the insider threat is more sensitive and touches on broader internal issues that will be more difficult to address without a certain level of trust. It may also be possible to provide uncontroversial and non intrusive up-to-date technology that is not nuclear specific, including surveillance monitoring and physical access controls.

Some more steps proposed in the literature go as follows: ensuring that personnel reliability systems are as up-to-date and efficient as possible updating physical security standards at all nuclear facilities and for weapons, weapon components and materials, including barriers and perimeters, surveillance, and access control techniques strengthening the security of radioactive material held by non-state agencies ensuring effective planning for dealing with emergencies and response procedures ensuring effective control and accounting for weapons, weapon components, and materials reviewing the most likely threats and designing protection that ensures a high level of security, and discussing stringent export control law implementation.

The 2001 visit by Secretary of State Collin Powel initiated a bilateral dialogue between the US and Pakistan to talk about nuclear security. They were called the 'non intrusive and non sensitive expert-level' discussions. The scope of the discussion extends from 'export and commodity controls to personnel reliability programs, nuclear material protection, control and accounting, transportation security, knowledge exchanges, and training'. Progress on these dialogues is successful. PAL assistance to Pakistan under cooperative threat reduction measures Permissive Action Links, or PALs, is a technology integrated into nuclear weapons to force any potential user to enter an authorisation code before the weapon can be armed.

The combined features in PAL mean that any group that were able to obtain one of Pakistan's weapons would encounter great difficulty in arming or using the device. PAL deals with securing nuclear weapons and not the underlying nuclear material. Securing nuclear material and nuclear weapons are two different things. Cooperative Threat Reduction Measures (CTRM), on the other hand, are a cooperative assistance program offered by the US to countries like Russia who are signatories of the Non-Proliferation Treaty (NPT) for securing nuclear materials and arsenal. There are various kinds of constraints faced by the US for the application of CTRM in Pakistan. For instance, international legal constraints make it difficult for the US to provide any kind of technology to Pakistan, which is (in the framework of the NPT) a non-nuclear state. US domestic laws have 'incorporated significant non proliferation requirements' which also make it difficult to cooperate with Pakistan.

For instance Atomic Energy Act requires that states Receiving US original nuclear material should not transfer it to anyone, putting this technology under tight security. The act also needs and Agreement of Cooperation before any technology is transferred, and currently, the US and Pakistan do not have such an agreement. There are also technical limitations for the US to provide nuclear securing technology to Pakistan, namely, because of its very secretly guarded nuclear weapons programme. Knowledge about Pakistani nuclear weapons is inadequate, posing a technical hurdle for the US since there is great uncertainty as to what they would be dealing with.

However, it is desirable that the United States 'offer security assistance [to Pakistan] that includes generic physical security procedures, unclassified military handbooks, portal control equipment, sophisticated vaults and access doors, and personnel reliability programs'. Conclusion Al-Qaeda's core philosophy is to bring mass deaths to Americans and to bring 'Allah's rule' around the world. Bin Laden's network believes they could only be successful if they 'bring death to the US'. This destructive goal requires powerful weapons and nuclear weapons seem a viable option to achieve their end. Concerted efforts are needed with the help of the US to secure nuclear materials and nuclear weapons around the globe particularly from countries of concern, thus denying al-Qaeda any access.

Pakistan's factional infighting within the Pakistani Army could put a dangerous question mark over the command and control of Islamabad's nuclear material and weapons. Similarly, a wider civil war in Pakistan could jeopardise the safety and security of its fissile material stocks and nuclear installations. A few assassination attempts on President Musharraf in 2003 and 2004 are examples of militants trying to oust him from the leadership of Pakistan. This reality has added more to the insecurity of Pakistani nuclear material.

Although the US has cooperated with Pakistan in some quarters for the security and safety of nuclear related issues, America's own domestic laws, the Nuclear Non-Proliferation Treaty, the sensitive nature of Pakistani nuclear arsenal, the India-Pakistan nuclear rivalry and the lack of confidence-building measures between these two nations, illiteracy and anti-Americanism in Pakistan, remain hurdles preventing the US to forge true cooperation for the security of nuclear weapons and materials in Pakistan. Cooperative Threat Reduction Measures, which are currently applicable to Russia, should be made globally accessible to prevent nuclear terrorism at its roots.

Joint Declaration of the Russian Federation and the People's Republic of China, the Kremlin, Moscow, May 27, 2003

At the invitation of the President of the Russian Federation, Vladimir Putin, the President of the People's Republic of China, Hu Jintao, made a state visit to the Russian Federation on May 26-28, 2003.

The heads of state of the two countries had a substantive and in-depth discussion on the development of bilateral relations in the last decade, their state and prospects, and agreed that no matter what changes take place in the world, the deepening of the good-neighborly relations, friendship, mutual advantageous cooperation, partnership and strategic interaction between Russia and China will remain a strategic priority in the foreign policies of the two countries. The parties are resolved to take the baton over from the previous generations and carry it into the future, exert joint efforts to discover new ways for the development of Russian-Chinese relations.

To this end, the heads of state of Russia and China state the following:

I. In the last decade Russian-Chinese relations have gone from constructive partnership to partnership and strategic interaction along the historical path of relations between friendly states. The two countries have jointly worked out an optimal model of cooperation that has taken relations between the two countries to the path of stable development. Political trust between the two countries is increasing, practical interaction is constantly expanding, and friendship and mutual understanding between the peoples of Russia and China are strengthening. The development of Russian-Chinese relations has brought real benefits to both states and peoples and has become an example of relations between neighboring countries and great powers.

Russia and China intend to continue to strengthen their partnership and strategic interaction and jointly solve practical questions of bilateral ties in the interests of national security of both states, the prosperity of the Russian and Chinese people, stability and calm in the neighboring regions.

The Treaty of Good-Neighborliness, Friendship and Cooperation Between the Russian Federation and the People's Republic of China of July 16, 2001 is a concentrated reflection of a number of achievements in the development of bilateral relations over the last years and has laid a solid legal groundwork for the steady and sustainable development of relations between the two countries in the new century. The treaty has become an inalienable part of the legal systems of the two countries.

The parties believe that both countries have all the necessary conditions to ensure the implementation of the treaty. The parties state their determination to adhere to the policy and principles set forth in the treaty, continue the implementation of all agreements on cooperation that have been reached between the parties, constantly fill the partnership and strategic interaction between the two countries with new substance, find new ways to encourage continuous movement forward in bilateral relations, and exert efforts to maintain the high dynamics of Russian-Chinese relations at all times.

II. Top-level contacts between Russia and China and bilateral intergovernmental and interagency commissions on cooperation are important mechanisms that secure the development of strategic interaction between the parties in all areas and serve as an effective conduit for the operational exchange of views and coordination of positions on bilateral issues and topical international problems. The parties stress that the mechanism of regular meetings between the heads of government of the two states is of great importance and appreciate its contribution to the long-term development of trade and economic cooperation between Russia and China. The parties will strengthen existing structures, while expanding other conduits for exchanges and consultations at all levels and in all spheres. To this end, the parties will continue to discuss ways to implement the agreement on the creation of a Russian-Chinese interstate mechanism of security consultations.

The parties confirm that they will find a final solution to border disputes between the two countries, which have been inherited from the past, in the shortest possible period of time on the basis of the principles of justice and equality, mutual understanding and mutual concessions, in order to strengthen the calm and stability on the Russian-Chinese border and ensure economic interests of the population in the border areas of both countries.

The parties will continue to resolutely support each other's efforts to protect state unity, sovereignty, independence and territorial integrity, which is an important element of the Russian-Chinese partnership and strategic interaction. The Russian side confirms the unchangeability of its position of principle with regard to Taiwan and Tibet.

III. With a view to strengthening and expanding the material base of Russian-Chinese relations, the parties have agreed to invigorate, on a mutually advantageous basis, practical cooperation between the two states in trade, economic, military-technical, and scientific-technical spheres, in the fields of energy, transport, atomic energy, finance, spaces, aviation, information technologies as well as cross-border and inter-regional cooperation.

The parties assess highly positive tendencies in bilateral trade and economic cooperation in the last years and state the need to expand trade, improve its structure by increasing the share of high-tech products, machinery, electronics, and other commodities with a big added value, and its balanced development; the creation of favorable conditions for mutual access of goods, services and investments of the two countries to each other's markets, the intensification of technical-economic and investment cooperation, including the creation of joint ventures, industrial cooperation, the transfer of technologies; the perfection of the trade servicing system, including the strengthening of cooperation in the sphere of bank settlements, credit guarantees, insurance, enhanced work of both countries in the field of legal and administrative regulation of trade and economic activities in order to bring the trade regime in compliance with international standards; the strengthening of cross-border and inter-regional cooperation, as well as contacts between small and medium-sized enterprises of the two countries.

The parties are determined to make a breakthrough in the development of the entire range of bilateral trade and economic relations and achieve a major increase in trade turnover. The parties believe that cooperation in the energy sphere is of great importance to both states. The implementation of large oil and gas projects, including the construction of the Russia-China oil pipeline, supplies of Russian natural gas to China, Russia's participation in the construction of the West-East gas pipeline with possible supplies of necessary Russian energy equipment for this project and cooperation between the oil companies of the two countries in oil prospecting and development in Russia should serve as the basis for strengthening energy cooperation.

China states its support for the Russian Federation's accession to the World Trade Organization. The parties believe that further active and constructive bilateral negotiations on the terms of Russia's admission to the WTO and an appropriate agreement based on respect for mutual interests will help strengthen Russian-Chinese trade and economic relations.

IV. Since its creation in December 2000, the Russian-Chinese Commission on Educational, Cultural, Health and Sport Cooperation has held three meetings, developed concrete plans aimed to expand and deepen humanitarian cooperation between the two countries, and successfully shown its coordinating and governing role in humanitarian cooperation between the two states. The parties will continue to tap the potential of this mechanism and enhance the exchange of cultural achievements of the two great nations.

Given the outbreak of a new illness in the world — the severe acute respiratory syndrome — the parties believe it necessary to invigorate contacts between health and medical authorities by using available mechanisms of interaction. The parties attach great significance to the joint fight of Russia and China against illegal migration and other forms of trans- border crime, and to assistance to cooperation in the law-enforcement field. In a follow-up to the existing agreements, the parties will create a joint Russian-Chinese working group on migration that will become operational in the very new future.

V. The Russian-Chinese Committee on Friendship, Peace and Development is a bilateral non-governmental friendship organization that has been created at the initiative of the heads of state of the two countries. Over the six years of its existence, the committee has contributed heavily to the development of bilateral non-governmental exchanges, the deepening of understanding between the two nations, the strengthening of traditional friendship and the social framework of Russian-Chinese relations.

The holding of the fifth plenary session of the committee in Beijing will become an important event in Russian-Chinese relations this year. The parties will cooperate closely in preparing the plenary session in order to ensure its success and will take energetic efforts to encourage contacts between young people, education and cultural figures, and businesses, and cooperation in the field of tourism.

VI. The modern world is undergoing complex and deep changes. Peace and development remain our era's priorities, peace-loving aspirations; hope for stability and progress are common objectives of people in all countries. However the international situation is still unstable, some old contradictions have not been resolved over a long period of time. Traditional and unorthodox security threats get mixed; the logic of force and the policy of unilateral actions introduce new factors of instability in the already unstable world. International terrorism has become a global threat and common evil.

Experience and reality show that in order to solve global problems affecting international security, stability and the future of universal development, and to counter common challenges, it is necessary for all states and nations to act jointly and strengthen international cooperation. Russia and China advocate a multi-polar, just and democratic world order based on the mutually recognized principles of international law, harmonious and rational relations, and co-existence of different states.

All countries, as they seek joint prosperity, should build their relations by respecting and taking into account mutual interests, encouraging and developing economic ties and interaction, assisting cultural exchanges and communication, exercising mutual trust in the sphere of security and readiness to interact, helping develop new approaches in this field that are based on equality, solidarity and mutual respect for each other's concerns. It is necessary to resolve disputes through dialogue and cooperation, strengthen and improve the system of international relations, ensure the central role of the United Nations in the modern world, and facilitate the implementation of different models of development. The tendency toward a multi-polar world is a dominating one. At the same time it's a difficult process that requires joint international effort.

The parties note a broad coincidence of interests of Russia and China in international and regional affairs. The relations of partnership and strategic interaction between the two countries are of key importance as a major factor of international relations for the future of world politics, preservation of peace, maintenance of global security and stability. The Russian-Chinese partnership, including interaction of Russia and China within the UN and other multilateral forums is making a substantial contribution to the strengthening of international peace and security.

Coordination of foreign policy efforts of the two countries on a broad range of questions of international life, pursued on a regular basis through different channels and at different levels, makes it possible to effectively contribute to solving global and regional problems of contemporary world. The sides are declaring their readiness to continue holding consultations and interacting in international affairs, jointly with other interested states to make tireless efforts to establish a lasting peace and stability, to contribute to democratizing international relations.

VII. The parties stressed the priority of using peaceful methods of resolving disputes and crises on the basis of generally recognized principles of international law with the aim of settling global and regional questions on a multilateral basis. The UN plays an irreplaceable role in the matter of maintaining peace in the whole world and stimulating concerted development. In the new situation when the unconditional compliance with the UN Charter is of exceptional importance, the parties are resolved to make further efforts aimed at strengthening the UN system.

The parties believe that, in the area of safeguarding international peace and security, the coordinating role must be played by the UN with its authority, universality and unique experience. It is necessary to make concerted efforts to build, with the UN playing the central role, a comprehensive system for opposing new challenges and threats for the purpose of ensuring international stability, security and predictable development. Such a system must meet the vital interests of each state, ensure a long-term socio-economic development and stability, correspond to the principle of indivisibility of international security, be based on norms and principles of international law, above all the UN Charter. It must have a global character, be the widest in scope, and ensure the adoption of comprehensive solutions with account for interrelation between the new threats and challenges.

VIII. Russia and China maintain a permanent dialogue on the subject area of strategic stability. The sides are unanimous that in conditions of a new situation in the area of international security, the comprehensive maintenance of global strategic stability, active stimulation of the process of disarmament and the strengthening of multilateral control over arms, effective prevention of the proliferation of weapons of mass destruction and the means of their delivery meet the interests of all states. The parties will continue to further strengthen the coordination and cooperation at all levels, contribute to building up international efforts in the above-listed areas. At the Conference on Disarmament, Russia and China have come out with a joint draft of the basis elements of a future international-legal agreement on preventing the deployment of weapons in outer space, the use or threat of force in regard to space objects. The parties will continue the appropriate work on these questions in cooperation with other states.

IX. Russia and China believe it is necessary in the near future to take measures to restore internal stability in Iraq. The priority task is to settle the humanitarian situation in that country. The sides agreed to continue efforts in this direction and to provide further help to the Iraqi people. The parties state that the Iraqi crisis must be returned into the mainstream of political settlement within the UN framework. The central role in the post-war reconstruction of Iraq must be assigned to the United Nations. Russia and China are convinced that the appropriate settlement of the Iraqi problem—one of the most complex in the modern world — is possible only within the UN framework, based on the appropriate resolutions of the UN Security Council.

The parties believe that it is necessary to guarantee Iraq's sovereignty, political independence and territorial integrity, to respect the will and the independent choice of the Iraqi people as well as its right to dispose of the natural resources of the country. The legitimate rights, interests and concerns of neighboring states and other interested parties must be accommodated in the process of post-war settlement and rehabilitation in Iraq. From the moment of the emergence of the Iraqi crisis, Russia and China, together with the overwhelming majority of the countries of the world have consistently advocated its political, diplomatic settlement, and made vigorous efforts in this direction. This position has earned the respect and broad support of international public.

The parties believe that the interests of the entire world community require making concerted efforts to minimize the damage done to international relations as a result of the war in Iraq. The optimum road for accomplishing the goal is through strengthening the role of multilateral mechanisms, above all the United Nations, in solving problems common to the entire world community, strengthening the international anti-terrorist cooperation, concerted countering of new threats and challenges on the lasting basis of international law.

X. Russia and China attach much significance to the strengthening of security and cooperation in the Asian-Pacific Region for the purposes of securing a stable development and wellbeing of all the states situated there. The parties reaffirm the readiness to continue efforts to establish in the APR a mechanism — according with the regional specificities — of cooperation aiming at securing regional stability and security as well as the enlargement of interaction with other states and regional organizations.

Russia and China invariably proceed from the assumption that the emergence of different bilateral and multilateral mechanisms ought to contribute to enhancing cooperation and agreement within the APR. Such mechanisms must complement each other in accordance with the purposes and principles of the UN Charter, be based on accommodating the reciprocal interests and the commonality of approaches to solving the regional and global problems. The parties believe that the ASEAN Regional Forum (ARF) on matters of security is a major arena of multilateral political dialogue in the region, and advocate its enhanced role on matters of safeguarding regional.

13

The Conflict Roots of Terrorism

National and international conflicts are at the root of terrorism. According to Joshua S. Goldstein, conflicts can be divided into two classes: conflicts of interest and conflicts of ideas. Conflicts of interest include territorial disputes, control of government and economic conflicts. Conflicts of ideas include ethnic conflict, religious conflict, and ideological conflict. This paper analyzes how these conflicts lead to terrorism. Let us first begin by defining terrorism. Terrorism is an act of violence perpetrated against civilians to discredit their government as incapable of protecting them. The goal is to arouse the anger of the population against their impotent government so as to force it to capitulate to the terrorists - that is to meet the demands of the terrorists. Hence, terrorism is the weapon of the weak against the stronger party.

Terrorism has become a household world since September 11, 2001. On that date Arab and Islamic fundamentalist terrorists demolished the Twin Towers of the World Trade Center and the Pentagon in the United States. The death toll was about 3,000 civilians. What caused this terrorist incident and other similar ones? We know all the terrorists involved in the September 11, 2001 catastrophe were Third World nationals. They came from poor countries. True, Saudi Arabia is oil-rich but its wealth is unevenly distributed. Most of its people are poor. Hence, we can agree that the underlying reason for his terrorist incident is economic exploitation, although its proximate cause may be religious and cultural.

The West swindles the mineral and agricultural resources of Third World countries. When a Third World country is rich in mineral or oil resources, its government is placed under bondage to surrender its resources to the Multinational Corporations (MNCs) of Western countries. Mineral or oil-rich country can also be invaded to put its resources under Western control - by reducing its government into vassalage. Young men from these mineral and oil-rich countries seethe with rage at seeing the exploitation of their countries. Even when their country extracts good price for its wealth from the west, they see that money goes to the coffers of the rulers that are under protection by the West.

More over, there is also a "clash of civilizations" between the West and the rest as Samuel Huntington explained it. Citizens in the West earn $10 an hour while citizens of the rest of the world live on $2 a day. The West has installed immigration barriers so as not to share the resources of the earth with poor peoples of the world. The west lives in luxury under the shelter of global apartheid. Third World nationals seethe with rage at being kept jailed at modern prison holes called states. However, talking about global apartheid and economic exploitation is a taboo in the modern world. But talking about religious freedom is acceptable. Hence, terrorists wreck havoc in the West in the name of religion and culture. Yet the real grievance is wealth disparity and economic exploitation.

Religion is important because it offers extraordinary leaders such as Mohammed, Moses and Jesus in whose name to fight. Also it offers reward in the hereafter. But the real struggle is economic. To understand this matter clearly, let us ask why people want religious freedom or the establishment of an Islamic state? Is it not to realize economic prosperity and equality for the exploited and down trodden masses! Hence at the back of all the talk abut religious freedom and establishment of Islamic state is economic justice! This presents the real solution to terrorism to us: end global apartheid! Make the end of global apartheid a 30-year project.

Then to avoid massive inflow of immigrants 30 years later, the West will wholeheartedly support economic development in the Third World. Terrorism will come to an end immediately because the West will be seen as a big brother rather than as a big bully. Also religious equality should be guaranteed to all faiths - until almighty God himself intervenes in human affairs boldly and marvelously (without ambiguity) to support one faith over all others. We will return to the above solution in the conclusion. Below are presented the conflict roots of terrorism.

Territorial Disputes

Territorial disputes take the form of border conflicts, irredentism, demand for a homeland and secession. Some examples of border disputes - cum irredentism - include the Ethio-Somalia conflict over the Somali inhabited territory of Ethiopia known as the Ogaden region, the Eritrean struggle for secession and the recent Ethio-Eritrean conflict. Two pitched battles were fought over the control of the Ogaden between Ethiopia and Somalia in the early 1960s and late 1970s. Now this border dispute has led to terrorism directed at Ethiopia by Al-Ittihad Islamiya, a Somali terrorist organization.

Territorial conflict in the form of demand for homeland is exemplified by the conflict between Israel and Palestinian people. Palestinians want to establish an independent state in the West Bank and Gaza strip. Israel is not amenable to the demand for security reasons. It fears that once

Palestinians establish an independent state with its own armed forces, they will quickly invade the Israeli state to seize more territory. The result of the stand off has been long standing terrorist activity by Palestinians against Israel.

An example of territorial dispute in the form of secession is the Russian conflict with Chechnya. Chechens want an independent state of their own. But Russia can agree only on an autonomous state within the Russian federation. The result has been terrorist acts by Chechens against Russia. These three examples show how a territorial dispute leads to terrorism. In all respects, the weaker party carries out terrorist acts either to inflict damage or to make its cause visible to the international community. Especially the Israel vs. Palestinian dispute has been the main reason for terrorist acts carried out against U.S. citizens by Arab terrorists in the Middle East. This is because the United States is perceived as an ally of Israel and its main arms supplier.

Control of Government

The best example of conflict related to control of government is the recent war between the United States and Iraq. In 1990, Iraq invaded Kuwait. The United States destroyed its war machine while driving it out of Kuwait. Then for more than ten years using intrusive inspections and sanctions it virtually disarmed Iraq of its WMD and even conventional arms. Then the situation became convenient for an all out invasion of Iraq to topple Saddam Hussein. The war took place between March 20, 2003 and May1, 2003. Iraq was occupied and Saddam was captured on December 14, 2003.

The above is a classic war to control government. What has been the result? As expected the result has been terrorist's attacks on United States military men and civilians all over Iraq. Hundreds have died since the end of the war as a result of terrorist acts. Another conflict related to control of government is the India-Pakistan conflict over

Kashmir. Kashmir has been divided between Pakistan and India. But the Indian part of Kashmir, called Jammu and Kashmir, is unstable. Its Moslem population wants union with Pakistan.

Its Hindu population wants to stay with India. India and Pakistan both want to control the government of Jammu and Kashmir. Although the territory is administered by India, the Muslim guerrillas want to take the government out of India's control to eventually unite it with Pakistan. Hence, control to the government is at issue. Because India is not willing to lose Kashmir, Muslim separatists have been carrying out terrorist acts against India. The above the examples of conflict over control of government show that alien rule has almost always led to terrorism by subjugated nationals.

Economic Conflicts

Economic conflicts include conflicts over foreign investment, debt, terms of trade, activities of Multi-National Corporations (MNCs) and drug trafficking. However, economic conflicts are rarely the immediate causes of terrorism. Yet, they are the main underlying causes of terrorism. Wealth sharing is a taboo subject in international relations. But religious freedom and cultural equality are acceptable subjects for discussion. Hence, terrorists wreck havoc in the name of religious and cultural grievances. But religion and cultural demands are euphemism for economic demands. Why do terrorists care about religion and culture? Is it not to usher in economic prosperity a justice in their countries?

Moreover, conflict in the Persian Gulf is rooted in economic interest, namely free flow of oil. While those who can manage it can send their armies to assure free flow of oil, those who cannot assure themselves equitable distribution of its income engage in terrorist activities. The West has now terrorized all resource rich Third World countries, saying in effect, "What is mine is mine, but what is yours is negotiable!" Resource rich Third World countries are now giving up their nuclear weapons ambitions for fear it can be used as an excuse to rob them of their resources.

While the West carried out its brand of world terrorism to assure itself of continuous economic exploitation of Third World countries, nationals of these poor countries are resorting to the weapon of the weak - terrorism. At one time, there was a call for New International Economic Order (NIEO) to share the world's resources equitably. But nothing came of it. Hence, since the West has made wealth sharing non-negotiable subject, it is now being haunted with terrorism in the name of religion.

Ethnic Conflicts

Ethnic conflicts have become prevalence since the end of the Cold War. Here, we will look at two examples. One example is the conflict between the Ethiopian government and the Oromo Liberation Front (OLF). The OLF was a participant in the All-Nationalities Conference that took place in Ethiopia in 1991. But it left mainstream Ethiopian politics to demand secession of the Oromo inhabited territories of Ethiopia. It claims to be spokesman for the Oromo ethnic group. It wants to establish an independent Oromo state.

However, although secession is constitutionally guaranteed to all nations of Ethiopia, the Ethiopian government refused to let Oromo state go. Why? Because the Oromo people as a whole do not want to secede. Oromo Peoples Democratic Organization (OPDO) is part of the coalition of parties that form the ruling EPRDF party. But OLF is now engaged in frequent terrorist acts against the Ethiopian government. The second example of ethnic conflict is the Chechnya conflict with Russia. Chechnya is inhabited by Chechens, who form the majority ethnic group, and other ethnic groups including Russians.

Ethnic Chechens want their own state. But Russia can only grant them autonomy within the Russian federation. As a result of this conflict, Chechens are now engaged in terrorist attacks against Russia. These two examples show that ethnic conflict has led to terrorist activities. But as the religious question, ethnic conflict is a cloak for economic prosperity. Why do ethnic groups want a state of their own? It is not to enjoy economic prosperity in their state? So economic conflict is the underlying cause of ethnic terrorism.

Religious Conflicts

Many conflicts in the world today are traceable to religious disagreements. Examples of such conflicts include the conflicts in Northern Ireland between Catholics and Protestants, the conflict in Kashmir between Moslems and Hindus, the conflict in Chechnya between Moslems and Christians, and the conflict between al Qaeda and the United States and the West. As has been noted by many authors, religious conflicts are often bitter and turn to be struggles to death. To elaborate on the above examples a bit, we note that religious conflicts are often accompanied with conflicts over territory, government, and economic matters. In Northern Ireland, Catholics want union with Ireland while Protestants want union with Britain.

In Kashmir Moslems want union with Pakistan while Hindus want union with India. In Chechnya, Moslem Chechens want independent state of their own while the minority ethnic Russians who are Christians want federation with Russia. Yet, by far the most talked about religious conflict is the one between al Qaeda and the United States. Al Qaeda which means "the base" or "the camp" is an Islamic terrorist organization which seeks to become the base or the camp from which worldwide Islamic revolution will be fought. Its origins can be traced to the 1979 invasion of Afghanistan by Soviet Union. Osama Bin Laden joined the struggle (Guerrilla Warfare) against the Soviet Union in support of Muslim Afghanistan fighters.

In the late 1980s, Bin Laden's followers become known as Al Qaeda members. The declaration of war against the United States by al Qaeda is due to the fact that the United States refused to get out from the Middle East, especially from Saudi Arabia after the first Gulf War. Bin Laden does not want an infidel force to stay in the Holy Land of Islam. All the above religious conflicts have led to terrorism regionally and internationally - but they are economic in nature as we will see later.

Ideological Conflicts

Ideological conflicts were important during the cold war. At present, they have been replaced by conflicts among civilizations. In the heyday of the cold war the communist and capitalist world engaged in overt and covert conflicts. The covert acts were carried out by KGB for communists and CIA for capitalists. Each of these secret services carried out terrorist operations all over the world. However, they did so through local intermediaries. Hence, the terrorist acts are hard to trace to the KGB and the CIA. Mostly this terrorist acts took the form of assassinations or attempted assassination of public figures in the Third World. One infamous assassination attempt was against the Pope of the Roman Catholic Church!

Be that as it may, nowadays ideological conflicts are replaced by civilization conflicts involving the West against the rest. The current problem is the wealth disparity between OECD nations and Third World nations. Most of the OELD nations are in North America and Europe. The Third World encompasses the rest of the world except Japan and Australia-New Zealand. The conflict between these camps of nations is profound. Although we say civilization conflict, actually the conflict is economic. It is just that the rich nations belong to just one civilization.

Both ideological and civilizational conflicts are facets of economic conflicts. Ideological conflict was a conflict over the division of the Third world as sphere of influence. This was economic conflict - conflict over natural resources and markets. The economic conflict and the west trying to gobble everything in the world, and the rest of the world protecting its own. This problem has led to terrorism by the poor.

Observations

Terrorism is a crime as murder is a crime. Terrorism is even more heinous in that it targets civilians. The fact that terrorism is perpetrated by poor people from the Third World, and the fact that it is rooted in economic exploitation and oppression does not justify its occurrence. Terrorism has to be stamped out wherever it exists. Having said this we must also agree that the West is a creator of its own problem. Terrorism against the west is due to the fact that the West seeks to gobble the cream of the world's wealth leaving only the residue for poor people of the world to live on. Hence, the solution for terrorism is equitable sharing of the worlds wealth hand in hand with religious and cultural equality until God himself shows the world which region he approves.

On need not be a Marxist to believe that economic interest makes the world go round. Even psychologists believe that physical needs have to be satisfied before all other needs are considered. Hence, it cannot be brushed aside the fact that it is the bread and butter issue that leads to most conflicts in the world. Yet to avoid considering solutions for the sword gash economic woes of the Third World, the West engages in interminable litany over its pin pricks of economic problems. Hence, it is apparent that unless the world agrees to dismantle immigration barriers within 30 years, global poverty will not be eliminated. If the West expects it will be flooded with new comers from all over the world after 30 years, it will be in hurry to develop every country in the world to let people say where they are, enjoying riches where they are.

This means that the ultimate answer for terrorism is a global confederacy of nations or states. Every scholar worthy of his salt agrees that a world government is the final solution for all the ills that afflict the world. Moreover, modern technology of transpiration and communication has made it now easy to consider a world state. It is only greed, nationalism and racism that keep the world's people separated. But greed, nationalism, and racism are dysfunctional human behaviour. They have to be overcome. The first line of attack to overcome them is to end the global apartheid. Once every one can live everywhere he likes, he will see people everywhere as sharing a common destiny. It will be easier for such person to overcome greed, nationalism and racism.

Just note what is happening in Europe. There is freedom of movement and establishment of residence. As a result, once bickering European countries have become fraternal nations. Moreover, it is now unthinkable for France to sponsor terrorists to wreck in Germany and vice versa. In short, to end global terrorism the West must agree for eventual dismantling of immigration barriers. It must start serious planning for a world government by the mid of the current century. If it does this thing, the West will be seen as a big brother rather than as a big bully. Nobody will target it for terrorist attack. The sad fact is that the above measures are hard for present-day greedy and racist people to contemplate. Hence, we must wait for almighty God to undertake them.

14

Links of Terrorism and Globalization

Globalization Defined

While a precise definition of the term has yet to be established, many of the currently employed definitions use similar concepts. The University of Colorado at Boulder (2002) describes the global economy as one in which the main international players are corporations and lacking a structure tied to national boundaries. Refusing to assign a specific definition to the term, the World Bank (2000) describes it primarily as "the observation that in recent years a quickly rising share of economic activity in the world seems to be taking place between people who live in different countries," or, more simply, an increase in international economic activities. The Center for Strategic & International Studies (2002) attempts to precisely define globalization, calling it "a process of interaction and integration among the people, companies, and governments of different nations, a process driven by international trade and investment and aided by information technology."

The International Monetary Fund (2000) offers the broadest summary of globalization, referring to it as "the increasing integration of economies around the world, particularly through trade and financial flows," adding,

"The term sometimes also refers to the movement of people (labor) and knowledge (technology) across international borders. There are also broader cultural, political and environmental dimensions of globalization." Globalization is "the increased mobility of goods, services, labour, technology and capital throughout the world," according to the Government of Canada (2005). Rainer Tetzlaff (1998) writes that globalization encompasses many aspects, including increasing international transactions, new communications technologies, an increasing complex division of labor and goods distribution, quick turnover of concepts and consumer patterns, and a significant increase in transnational institutions and political movements.

Globalization is "a process of growing interdependence between all people of this planet," according to the International Labour Organization (1996) and mentions economical interdependence. Even the cynical Progressive Living organization (2001) talks about globalization from an economic standpoint, calling it "a process, well underway, which trends toward the undermining of national sovereignty, and therefore citizen's [sic] rights, in favor of the economic interests of gigantic transnational corporations."

All of these definitions of the term agree on the economic aspect of globalization. The process began as one of increasingly international business dealings. However, it is ignorant to not consider other aspects of globalization. A good definition for it is an economically-driven process of business which also makes ideas, cultural behaviours, technologies, and politics global concepts and lead to greater interaction among previously separated groups and/or nations. It seems that this is the most succinct and precise the definition of globalization can be without ignoring many important aspects of it as some of the previously mentioned definitions do.

Globalization and Terrorism

In recent years, the world has seen many terrorist attacks or attempted attacks in locations other than where the terrorist(s) originated from. Notably, the majority of these attacks involved Muslim extremist groups. A Madrid train was bombed, as was a London subway. United States embassies in African nations were attacked. Airplanes were hijacked and flown into the World Trade Center in New York. Australia narrowly avoided a terrorist attack. In each of these cases, the terrorists did not come from the country that was targeted.

When the media covers the fight against terrorists, people often hear that a government is doing something to stop them without sending any military personnel somewhere in response. Instead, financial assets are frozen to slow terrorists. Terrorist websites may be taken offline. Group cells may be discovered within a targeted country and be shut down by local, state, and/or federal law enforcement officers. Considering what is known about globalization and the current situation of international terrorist activity, one could draw a correlation between globalization and terrorism. It certainly seems that the two are connected.

In a speech at the World Media Conference, John O'Sullivan (2004) identified four components of what he called the "world crisis:" globalization itself, the mass migration of people over frontiers and the consequent spread of ethnic diasporas, the increased power of religion over secular philosophies, and the extension of the powers and influence of transnational organizations. Are globalization and terrorism linked in any way(s)? If so, how are they linked? By answering these questions, it may be possible to see if globalization causes international terrorism, if international terrorism is simply an unfortunate side effect of globalization or some of its aspects, or if no link exists between the two.

Globalization Facilitating Terrorism

Some aspects of globalization facilitate terrorism. At its basest meaning, globalization means internationalization. Something is taken from a national setting and projected across the world. Certain nations adopt this, others reject it. When most nations do accept it and adopt it, globalization is taking place. Cronin (2002) suggests that terrorism cemented itself as an international phenomenon in the 1970s and 1980s, "evolving in part... in reaction to the dramatic explosion of international media influence." At this point in time, news media was truly becoming international in scope. Many broadcasting companies maintained correspondents or sister stations in other nations, sharing information back and forth.

This would lead to the first visions of terrorism for many peoples who had never seen it. Presently, the media can be responsible for perpetuating the climate of international terror. "For example, there may no longer be... a globally organised terror network, but... the media have globalised our perception of terror". Another aspect to this concept is that the media can be used by terrorists for their purposes. Campbell (2001) reminds his readers Osama bin Laden released his now-infamous recorded statements using instruments of globalization. Many have seen video of bin Laden on American media outlets even though it was originally released to regional network Al-Jazeera.

International media certainly is not the main byproduct that facilitates terror. Perhaps the main facilitator stemming from globalization is communications technologies. There are many devices taken for granted in Western society that changed the way terrorists operate, especially digital communications device. Clansmen fighting Americans in Somalia in the early 1990s used digital phones that could not be tapped. The internet, mobile phones, and instant messaging have given many terrorist groups a truly global reach. Leading up to the September 11 attacks, al-Qaeda operatives used Yahoo e-mail, while the presumed leader made reservations online and other members researched topics such as using crop dusters to release chemical agents. Perhaps even more troubling is that these technologies can be used to disperse terrorists to different locations yet stay connected.

Cells can stay in touch through internet communications while websites spread ideologies. It is estimated that al-Qaeda operates in over sixty countries now as a result of using technologies inspired by globalization. According to Campbell (2001), many things sophisticated Western societies have adopted to become more efficient are leaving them more vulnerable to attacks. This includes policies of free trade, relaxed immigration policies, and streamlined border crossing policies. Rojecki (2005) claims the "transportation infrastructures that had been credited by some... had been used by terrorists." This includes both national and international travel systems.

Even financial systems created to make international business simpler can be used for terror instead. Cronin (2002) points out that the fluid movement of financial resources can help terrorists, citing the United States' invasion as an example. While the allied forces closed in on the Taliban, money collected by small businessmen was moved across the border by operatives and transferred through an informal banking system to the United Arab Emirates. From there, it became gold bullion and was sent around the world before it could be seized. More concerning is the way organizations are beginning to gather funds to operate. There are many groups with global financing networks, most of them recognized as foreign terrorist organizations. Their sources include nonprofit organizations and charities (whose donors may or may not be aware of their monies' use), companies which send revenue to illegal activities, illegal enterprises, and websites set up for donations.

"The terrorist attacks showed that political globalization is as powerful a phenomenon as the globalization of the economy". To deal with ever-increasing international relations, many organizations were set up, including the United Nations, the North American Treaty Organizations, the Organization of American States, and so on. In these forums, many people can come together to share ideas. At the same time, similar forums provide a hub for ideas and processes of coordination and cooperation used by terrorists. It is apparent that many things inspired to grow or be created by globalization have unexpectedly been used to facilitate terrorist operations.

The international media has made the world much more aware of their aims and activities. Communications technologies have been used to frustrate opposition forces ore ease operations within terrorist groups. Modern conveniences and economic policies have even been known to facilitate terror in some way. International financial systems can help terrorists hide their assets or gather funds. Political globalization can help terrorists meet and share ideas and procedures. It is not a stretch to claim that there are many aspects of globalization that have unfortunately been used to help terrorists.

Globalization Cause Terrorism

Although a peripheral link between globalization and terrorism has been established, it does not answer a simpler question. Does globalization cause international terrorism? Haydar Bao is quoted by Kuru (2005) as saying, "'Globalization is a concept originating from the West which has became [sic] a façade to adamantly impose particular ideas on underdeveloped countries, such as the claim that the borders are removed and nations are cooperating by ignoring their economic, cultural, and civilizational differences.'" There are a few hypotheses in support of the idea. These hypotheses fall into four main categories:

cultural differences, economic disparity, political frustration, and clashing market systems.

There are also claims that globalization and international terrorism are not linked at all. Foreign Policy (2005) found "little correlation between a country's level of global integration and the number of significant international terrorist attacks on its soil." It even claims globalization may help countries combat terrorism. However, this study solely looks at numbers; the question to be answered here cannot rely solely on quantitative data.

Cultural differences introduced by globalization are thought of as the main cause of international terrorism. If the hypothesis is true that cultural differences cause international terrorism, then it can certainly be said that globalization indirectly causes terrorism. Cronin (2002) states, "Foreign intrusions and growing awareness of shrinking global space have created incentives to use the ideal asymmetrical weapon, terrorism, for more ambitious purposes." She also says indigenous peoples blame the perceived corruption of their customs, religions, and languages on an international system American behaviour unconsciously molds. The CQ Researcher (2001) mentions cultural differences as a source of conflict many times. Conservative societies are offended by the media image of the United States.

There may not be enough solid evidence of cultural differences inciting **terrorism** though. Campbell (2001) writes, "Debates within [the Middle East] center only in the most trivial way on Western 'contamination,' such as by pop music and video games, of their cultures." Rojecki (2005) even says the Huntington hypothesis (culture as the major source of anti-globalization) "receives comparatively little support in [the media], perhaps because of the Bush administration's strenuous efforts to divide… al-Qaeda from Islam in general." It seems that cultural hypotheses for international terrorism lack solid support and are only popular because they take into account the most obvious differences between the West and Middle East.

Economic disparity is another source of hypotheses concerning globalization and international terrorism. The recent invasion of Iraq portrays an "image of the West as an enlightened but militarized and muscular liberator," and "recoups the reality of the global North as... a site of mass consumption in a world of horrifying need". The CQ Researcher (2001) also explores economic disparity as a source of terrorism. "'With globalization, people tend to compare themselves with bigger and bigger groups, and if you're in a poor village in Egypt what you see in U.S. television sitcoms are people with a lot of money,'" David Byman is quoted.

However, economic disparity alone does not seem like it would inspire international terrorism, no matter how well-off Western nations are compared to the rest of the world. There are plenty of nations that are as bad as or worse-off than the Middle East that do not engage in international terrorist activity. That point alone discredits the economic disparity hypothesis. The category of political frustration has two different theories concerning globalization and terrorism. The first theory, presented by Kuru, claims, "Globalization challenges a specific type of state, one that aims to homogenize its citizens through sociocultural policies."

This is true of the Middle East and untrue of Western nations. Western nations, being mainly democratic, do not attempt to lump their citizens together as one; rather, a great deal of diversity is present in them. In the Middle East, internal strife is intense, as one group of leaders tries to claim power and keep all people under its law. It does not seem that this challenge should concern leaders very much, considering they constantly struggle against internal opponents. It seems the leader could simply ban access to any international influence.

The other type of theory in this category is blaming the West for internal strife. Most of the time, this involves Western nations interfering and installing unfit leaders. As far as politics are concerned, Rojecki (2005), states, "Globalization is a cover for reinforcing American dominance with the UN as a fig leaf... the United States is said to support corrupt regimes that routinely violate human rights." Carmody (2005) agrees with this idea, saying, "Support for repressive governments... are likely to prove unstable as [it generates] 'blowback,' unintended negative consequences." History has seen Western installation of repressive regimes throughout the world, so this point has more bearing than the former.

Despite any Western nations' actions to install ineffective governments, it seems the affected nations are no better at helping themselves. The CQ Researcher (2001) points out, "The Muslim world never underwent a movement like the 18th-century Enlightenment in the West, which hastened the demise of religious influence in government." Considering the tendency of the region to reject secular government, it seems the best government to be installed, if secular, would be rejected. Western nations, wary of Islamic terror, cannot be blamed for avoiding the installation of Islamic governments.

The final type of hypothesis considers clashing markets, a concept that has not been considered enough. Mousseau pins the problem of international terrorism solely on this aspect of globalization, stating, "In this mixed economy, the clash of clientalist and market cultures can lead to illiberal and unstable democracy, military dictatorship, state failure, sectarian violence, or some combination thereof." It seems that this scenario could lead to the conditions Carmody (2005) claims are responsible for providing opportunity for transnational terrorism, "Islamic fundamentalism... 'failed states,' and the lack of effective territorial control."

Clientalist societies and market societies are naturally clashing entities. To summarize, clientalist societies see cooperation as the exchange of gifts, base trust on life-long friendships within small, approved groups, and are very hierarchical. Middle Eastern nations are clientalist societies. Market societies place less emphasis on small, approved group loyalty and encourage cooperation with new groups and base loyalty on an agreed-upon sanctity of contracts. Western nations are market societies. "From the clientalist perspective, however, those with market values are from out-groups and thus are untrustworthy.

Moreover, by expressing self-interest, individuals with market values... appear to have no culture and are seemingly interested in little beyond the crude pursuit of material gain". When this concept is paired with the fact that when people in developing countries see the breakdown of traditional relationships and the surfacing of zero-sum anarchy, they relate them to growing Westernization of their societies, it is not difficult to see that there is potential in this hypothesis. There are two more factors within clientalist societies that contribute to international terrorism. First, privileged persons often emerge as terrorist leaders because they have the most to lose from globalization. They exploit the hierarchical structure and gather many patrons from the economically lowest parts of society.

To keep their patrons' loyalty, leaders must demonstrate strength. Second, in this society's perspective, individuals are responsible for the actions of the entire group. Therefore, terrorist attacks that kill innocent people are justified because leaders are showing strength by killing guilty people. The hypothesis of clashing market systems is the best explanation for international terrorism. It does need to be further researched and tested to confirm its plausibility, but it definitely seems to be the most rational explanation for international terrorism. Mousseau (2002) sums up his hypothesis by saying, "The underlying cause of terror: the deeply embedded anti-market rage brought on by the forces of globalization."

Globalization is an economically-driven process of business which also makes ideas, cultural behaviours, technologies, and politics global concepts and lead to greater interaction among previously separated groups and/or nations. Recent terrorist attacks and attempted attacks have raised the question: Are globalization and international terrorism connected? There are aspects to globalization that have inadvertently facilitated the rise of international terrorism. International media, communications technologies, conveniences, and international finances have facilitated terrorism on a global scale. The more important question is: Does globalization cause terrorism? The answer to that is unclear. There are many hypotheses, considering cultural differences, economic disparity, political frustration, and clashing market systems. The concept of clashing market systems seems to best answer the question. The theory definitely finds globalization greatly contributes to international terrorism but is not itself the only cause. However, the theory should be further tested and researched to verify its worth.

Terrorism and the All-Hazards Model

Terrorism is not like natural or even other man-made hazards. But, then again, a tornado is not like a hurricane and certainly not like an earthquake. The argument that the all-hazards model cannot accommodate hazards like terrorism – especially bioterrorism – is most often based upon a fundamental misunderstanding of the model. "All-hazards" does not literally mean being prepared for any and all hazards that might manifest themselves in a particular community, state, or nation. What it does mean is that there are things that commonly occur in many kinds of disasters, such as the need for emergency warning or mass evacuation, that can be addressed in a general plan and that that plan can provide the basis for responding to unexpected events. Emergency plans never, or virtually never, cover everything that might be required in a disaster. Indeed, the requirements for evacuation for flood may differ significantly from those required for evacuation during a hazardous materials spill.

Plans need to be adaptable to circumstances and emergency managers and other officials, whether they be elected public officials or corporate officers, also need to be adaptable, innovative, and, when necessary, improvisational. The theory is that "all-hazards" plans can provide a basic framework for responding to a wide variety disasters, but planners typically address the kinds of disasters that might be expected to occur. Emergency planning normally begins with the identification of the disasters that have occurred in a community in the recent past. These are the known and, generally, the most probable hazards. Planners may then focus on the disasters that have occurred in the distant past by going through newspaper archives, history books, and other documents and by interviewing long-time residents. Other hazards may be added to the list if it is determined that there may be some probability of them causing risk to life and/or property or to the environment. New highways and rail lines mean more potential for hazardous materials accidents, for example. These are the probable threats.

There may be some talk of possible threats and some of them may be addressed in the plan, as well. The media, political leaders, influential residents, or influential participants in the planning process or the larger community may encourage attention to hazards of very low probability or even of no discernible possibility. Media attention can make hazards and disasters seem much worse or more frequent than they really are. That is the so-called "CNN effect." Personal and family traumas may create champions for lesser risks. The point is that these less probable or even improbable hazards may be included in the planning. That's politics and the planning process is, after all, political as well as technical. It is also human nature. If the community is lucky, the planners give greatest attention to the biggest risks. All-hazards planning, then, are based upon the most likely disasters and the most "popular." Terrorism is a hazard of uncertain probability for most communities and organizations.

The question is whether terrorism is so different from other threats that the "all-hazards" approach is inappropriate or ineffective. Might officials need to issue public warnings, order evacuations or sheltering-in-place, call out law enforcement and fire service and EMS personnel, involve hospitals and other medical resources, or mobilize volunteers? To the extent that terrorist incidents might even resemble natural or technological disasters, the response may be very similar. A bridge or building collapse, a fire, an explosion, a power outage, and even a flood might result from terrorist actions. Certainly the responses to the World Trade Center towers and Pentagon attacks were much like responses to fires and structural failures. While law enforcement officials were concerned with the preservation of evidence, the emergency responses were much as they would have been to a "regular" disaster – an act of God rather than an act of man. Emergency planning now may include fire and EMS protocols to minimize disturbance of evidence, but the basic response requirements remain.

Bioterrorist attack may require quarantine, special medical response, and other extraordinary measures, including dealing with mass casualties on a scale unlike even the largest natural disasters, but the basic plan is a beginning place for dealing with such incidents. More importantly, community response will be guided by the plans in place, likely an all-hazards plan. That plan should address not only bioterrorism but flu and other naturally occurring pandemics. All-hazards planning have the virtue of being cost effective in terms of time and money. It is cheaper to develop and easier to remember a single plan even if one has to wade through annexes to provide guidance for dealing with specific issues. Hazardous materials accidents do require understanding of the chemicals involved and technical expertise to minimize damage and protect lives. Structural failures raise other issues concerning the conduct of emergency response in unstable and unsafe environs. Floods raise public health issues, as well as hazardous materials issues.

What the all-hazards approach can contribute to the effort to deal with terrorism in its many forms is a basic framework for structuring the emergency response, preparing for the response, and recovering from attacks, as well as developing appropriate measures to prevent or reduce the impact of the attacks – whatever form the attacks may take. It is also important to remember that the threat of terrorism is less certain than other threats. Indeed, the threat of earthquakes in California and the Pacific Northwest is much more certain than the threat of terrorism, consequently investments in capacity to deal with risks to life and property should be based upon that priority. Similarly, the threat of hurricanes is more certain along the Gulf and East coast than the threat of terrorism. As Hurricane Charley recently demonstrated, the level of destruction may be even greater than that we have experienced in terrorist attacks. Building capacity to deal with the most probable events will increase capacity to deal with less probable events. For private firms, unless they are a likely target of terrorists or are located adjacent to such a target, the biggest threat may well be workplace violence of other sorts.

Physical security, from locked doors and closed circuit television systems to armed guards and employee identification cards, can address a variety of threats. In short, precautions to deal with criminal intruders, disgruntled employees, angry spouses, and enraged clients can also serve as foundation for an anti-terrorism programme and an all-hazards plan can provide the framework for a response. Finally, the all-hazards approach encourages a broader perspective. Attention to the potential to prevent or reduce the impact of hazards is important. The Department of Homeland Security has been focused on the prevention of terrorist incidents, even though the department's mission statement also mentions reducing the impact of incidences that do occur. Mitigation efforts can reduce the political benefits of terrorist violence and the psychological impact. Recovery planning can reduce the social and economic impact, as well. All-hazards planning do encourage a broader perspective on risks and how to deal with them and a broader foundation on which to build effective programs to manage hazards and disasters.

15

Political Necessity of Terrorism

It has become something of a cliché to note that there are over 200 definitions of terrorism in existence within the broader terrorism studies literature; that many terrorism scholars have given up on the definitional debate and use the term unreflectively; and that such a state of affairs hampers theoretical progress and skews terrorism research in unhelpful ways. However, the significance and consequences of the definitional debate go far beyond such narrow academic confines, important as they are to the field. Rather, it is central to the ideology and practices of the global war on terror, the constitution of terrorism as a legal subject in domestic counter- terrorism and the construction of knowledge and commonsense about what has been designated one of the defining security issues of our time.

Furthermore, it has substantial indirect consequences for individuals and groups labelled as terrorists, who may then be legally subject to torture, rendition and internment without trial, and for the 'suspect communities' they belong to. In this, I attempt to argue that despite a number of serious political and ontological obstacles to the definition of terrorism, it should be possible to agree on a clear set of criteria that can be employed to distinguish and conceptualise terrorism as a unique form of political violence.

There are a great many advantages to adopting these definitional criteria. More importantly, I want to argue that, in addition to the conceptual benefits, there are important political-normative imperatives for retaining terrorism as a central organising concept for the field. I begin the paper by discussing some of the main challenges in defining terrorism and the kinds of knowledge practices this has resulted in to date. In the second section, I outline a set of criteria that analysts can employ to distinguish terrorism from other forms of political violence. The final section of the paper attempts to demonstrate how this approach to terrorism can play a role in progressive politics and an emancipatory project.

The Constitution of Terrorism

The definitional debate in terrorism studies has reached something of a stalemate. Not only is there no agreed definition among scholars, but an analysis of 490 articles published in the leading terrorism studies journals between 1990 and 1999 revealed that only eight or 1.6 percent of them could be regarded as conceptually-oriented papers. This suggests that many scholars have largely given up on the challenging theoretical debates surrounding the central concept of the field. An examination of the broader terrorism studies literature suggests four main approaches and practices towards the definition and conceptualisation of terrorism. Arguably, the most frequent practice, particularly amongst scholars who are newly arrived to the subject, is to simply use the term without defining it, on the misguided assumption that it is widely understood and accepted. Such an approach is problematic for a number of very obvious reasons, not least because terrorism is a highly emotive and divisive concept which different scholars and societies have often understood in very different ways.

A second approach, confined mainly to political leaders and security officials, but also to a surprising number of researchers and media pundits, is to define terrorism as an ideology or movement. Although groups specializing solely in terror do sometimes form, they are extremely rare and typically they remain highly unstable and ephemeral. There are very few such groups operating today. In reality, most terrorism occurs in the context of wider political struggles in which the use of terror is one strategy among other more routine forms of contentious action. As Charles Tilly puts it, 'Properly understood, terror is a strategy, not a creed. Terrorists range across a wide spectrum of organizations, circumstances, and beliefs.' Third, it is not uncommon to see researchers adopt an actor-based definition in the literature, whereby terrorism is defined as a particular form of political violence committed by non-state actors who attack civilians. Bruce Hoffman, for example, argues that terrorism involves violence 'perpetrated by a subnational group or non- state entity.'

This is in keeping with the U.S. State Department's highly influential definition of terrorism, which conceives of terrorism as 'premeditated, politically motivated violence perpetuated against noncombatant targets by subnational groups or clandestine agents, usually intended to influence an audience.' For scholars who adopt this definition, terrorism is largely indistinguishable from insurgency, militancy, guerrilla warfare and the like. More importantly, inherent to this approach is an assumption that while states may commit atrocities, engage in political repression or torture opponents, this nonetheless does not constitute terrorism, in large part because states have the sovereign right to use force. From this perspective, definitions of terrorism hinge on questions of legitimacy and sovereignty and the nature of the actor who employs the violence. As I will argue below, actor-based approaches to the definition of terrorism are both analytically untenable and politically suspect. Lastly, and most commonly among the leading scholars in the field, terrorism is defined as a violent strategy or tactic that actors employ in pursuit of particular political goals.

That is, terrorism is defined and understood by the nature and characteristics of the act itself, rather than the nature of actor, and is conceived as a particular kind of political action directed towards certain strategic goals rather than as a broad ideology or movement. Louise Richardson for example, defines terrorism as 'politically motivated violence directed against non combatants or symbolic targets which is designed to communicate a message to a broader audience.' Crucially, such a definitional approach accepts that states are also actors who can and frequently do adopt strategies of terrorism and commit terrorist acts. This is a useful formulation that provides the basis for the identifying criteria I present below.

In part due to these definitional approaches, research on terrorism in the broader field has been characterised by a number of unfortunate tendencies. An initial tendency widely noted by some critics of the field is the selection bias of much terrorism research whereby the terrorism label is applied almost solely to non-state groups opposed to Western interests and not to those groups supported by Western states – even when they commit identical acts of civilian-directed violence such as hijackings, bombings, kidnappings and assassinations. Thus, while left-wing groups have always received an inordinate amount of attention in the terrorism studies literature, right-wing groups like the Contras, anti-Castro groups, UNITA, RENAMO, various Afghan factions, numerous Latin American death squads, and today a number of Iraqi death squads today have remained scandalously understudied.

Although this is in part the result of the definitional practices noted above, it is also the result of an understandable but avoidable ideological bias amongst many Western scholars who adopt the interests of their own governments. Another more serious feature is that the field has been widely criticised for its failure to provide sustained analysis (and moral condemnation) of state terrorism specifically.

Indicative of the almost exclusive focus on 'terrorism from below' as opposed to 'terrorism from above' is the finding that only 12 or less than two percent of articles from 1990 to 1999 in the core terrorism studies journals focused on state terrorism, and that only 12 of the 768 pages in the *Encyclopaedia of World Terrorism* (1997) examined state terrorism in any form. In part, this is due to the not infrequent practice noted above of defining terrorism exclusively as a form of non- state violence. However, there are also a great many prominent scholars who accept that objectively terrorism is a strategy of political violence which any actor can employ, including states, but then simply refuse to examine cases of state terrorism in their research.

Walter Laqueur, arguably one of the founders of terrorism studies, is emblematic of this practice: he openly accepts that states have killed many more people and caused far more material and social destruction than 'terrorism from below', but then argues that this is simply not the terrorism he wishes to examine. It is perfectly understandable that scholars would wish to focus on particular subjects, but when an entire field neglects what is a very important dimension of the phenomenon, it raises troubling questions about the ideological orientation and political objectivity of the overall field. Clearly, there are reasons for concern over this state of affairs. From a political-normative perspective it makes the field appear biased towards Western state interests and complicit in the terroristic practices Western states have regularly employed over the past two hundred years.

That is, the failure to analyse state terrorism or to condemn it in the same morally assured terms as non-state terrorism – particularly the well-documented use of political terror by Western states during the colonial period, the 'terror bombing' during World War II and other conflicts, cold war counter-insurgency and pro-insurgency campaigns, the active sponsorship of right-wing non-state terrorist groups and the widespread use of torture during certain counter-terrorism campaigns, among others – appears to many observers as pro- Western bias and a toleration of certain forms of state-practiced terrorism. In addition, it represents a breakdown of scholarly procedure and a self- imposed intellectual blindness. It is intellectual unsustainable to argue that states cannot practice terrorism against their own people and against other states – that a car bomb detonated on a city street by clandestine state agents is not an act of terrorism, but an identical attack by non-state actors is, for example.

Or that the kidnap, torture and murder of a civilian by agents of the state is not terrorism, but the same act by a non-state group is terrorism. Moreover, accepting that terrorism can only really be described according to the nature and quality of the particular act of violence – rather than the purported legitimacy of the actor who commits it (states who employ terror as a mode of governance arguably lack legitimacy, in any case) – has a number of serious consequences and implications. In the first place, it raises serious questions about the broader focus of the field and the empirical foundations it is based on. That is, while non-state terrorists have killed tens of thousands and caused significant damage during the past century and a half, the acceptance that 'states can be terrorists, too' reveals that some individual states have been responsible for more terrorism than all non-state terrorist groups put together.

A conservative estimate of state-instigated mass murder, forcible starvations and genocide against civilians for example, suggests that governments have been responsible for 170-200 millions deaths in the twentieth century alone. Even if only a small proportion of these deaths can be strictly defined as state terrorism, the few hundred deaths caused every year by non-state terrorists pales beside the massive death, destruction and de-stabilisation caused by states. Moreover, a great many states continue to employ terrorism on a massive scale against their people today in places like Colombia, Haiti, Algeria, Zimbabwe, Myanmar, Uzbekistan, Kashmir, Palestine, Chechnya, Tibet, North Korea, Indonesia, the Philippines and elsewhere. And yet, the broader terrorism studies field does not include statistics on state terrorism in any of its recognised data bases, nor does it expend any real effort trying to understand the nature, causes, strategies and outcomes of state terrorism.

It is a serious analytical failure when an entire field largely fails to examine what is arguably the most serious aspect of the subject. It would be comparable to an imaginary situation in which criminologists focused most of their research on anti-social behaviour and burglaries, and failed to study in any systematic way the extent and causes of domestic violence, rape, murder, sexual abuse or other serious crimes. Another important consequence of the acceptance of the reality of state terrorism is the need to re-conceptualise some of the accepted truisms regarding the nature of terrorism. It is not the case for example, that terrorism is solely the 'weapon of the weak'; it can also be true that 'the stronger the state, the stronger the temptation to rule through a regime of terror'. In fact, the history of terrorism would suggest that strong actors use terror far more frequently than weak ones. Moreover, it is clear that in contradistinction to popular beliefs, terrorism can be employed during war as well as during peace, when for example, states bomb civilian targets of no military value for the sole purpose of terrorising a population into surrender – a case of frightening one group of people in order to produce a political change in another.

Similarly, counter-terrorism itself can become terrorism when it fails to distinguish between the innocent and the guilty, it is highly disproportionate, it aims to terrify or intimidate the wider population or a particular community into submission and when it is co-opted to serve a political agenda. In the end, there are important ethical-normative implications for the notion that states can be terrorists too, particularly in the current climate where virtually every state and international organisation has adopted new anti-terrorist legislation and where military force – including 'strategic bombing' – is being used as counter- terrorism tool in the so-called war on terror. At the very least, scholars should be highly suspicious of any and all attempts by states to define terrorism in ways that conveniently mean that no matter what they or their agents do, it cannot be considered terrorism.

They should refuse to accede to the common practice of exempting state officials from charges of terrorism, if no other reason than that: There is something morally suspicious; however, about people making laws that apply to everyone else accept themselves. The sheer fact that politicians have entered into a mutual-protection pact not to prosecute one another as 'terrorists' cannot change any logical or deontological facts of the matter. If what they do is otherwise indistinguishable from what is done by non-state actors that we would deem to be terroristic, then the acts of the state officials doing the same thing would be morally wrong for just the same reasons. It is not as if there are no understandable reasons for the continuing failure to agree a definition of the field's central concept. In the first place, some of the key concepts at the heart of the definition of terrorism are extremely subjective and difficult to determine objectively. Most definitions of terrorism by leading scholars for example, describe it as a form of 'illegitimate' violence directed towards 'innocent' civilians that is 'intended' to intimidate or terrify an audience for 'political' purposes.

The question of what makes an act of violence legitimate or not, who counts as a civilian, how innocence can be measured, what the real intentions of often clandestine actors might be and what counts as a political aim, are all highly contested and subject to competing claims. As a consequence, in practice it is often the politically and culturally determined legitimacy of the particular group under scrutiny that determines whether its actions are labelled as 'terrorism' and not necessarily the characteristics inherent to the violence itself. Much more significantly however, terrorism is not a causally coherent, free- standing phenomenon which can be defined in terms of characteristics inherent to the violence itself. It lacks a clear ontological status – which actually makes an objective definition impossible. As two leading figures in the field put it, 'The nature of terrorism is not inherent in the violent act itself. One and the same act... can be terrorist or not, depending on intention and circumstance'. The bombing of civilians for example, is not always or inherently a terrorist act; it may be the unintentional consequence of a military operation during war, for example.

The reality is that terrorism is a social fact rather than a brute fact. Although acts of violence are experienced as brute facts, the wider cultural-political meaning of those acts as 'terrorism' for example is decided through symbolic labelling, social agreement and a range of inter-subjective practices. That is, as a phenomenon, terrorism is constituted by the discursive practices which make it 'real', including among others: the labelling of certain acts and groups by authoritative actors, such as the annual State Department reports; the legal definitions contained within criminal and international law; the compiling of statistics on terrorism by the CIA, RAND, and various academics and think-tanks; the ascriptions of different groups and acts as 'terrorist' in the media; and the like. Actions and actors are constituted and reconstituted as terrorism in a continuous flow of social and political discourse.

Moreover, analyses of these discourses reveal significant variation and instabilities between and within institutions, as well as shifts over time in the way terrorism is discursively constructed and delineated. For example, before the late

1960s, there was virtually no 'terrorism' spoken of by politicians, the media or academics; there were instead numerous references to 'bombings', 'kidnappings', 'assassinations', 'hijackings' and the like. The current discourse of terrorism used by scholars, politicians and the media is in fact, a very recent invention. Similarly, in the 1980s, the Afghan Mujahidin were described as 'freedom fighters' before they were later reconstructed as 'Islamic terrorists'. Numerous other groups and states have experienced the same kind of discursive transformation from 'terrorist' or 'state- sponsor of terrorism' to 'freedom fighter', 'political leader' or 'ally in the war on terror'.

In an important sense then, terrorism does not exist outside of the definitions and practices which seek to enclose it. Just as 'races' do not exist objectively 'out there', but classifications of humankind does, so too 'terrorism' does not exist but classifications of different forms of political violence does. A pertinent illustration of the ontological instability of the terrorism label is the observation that there are no less than four recognised 'terrorists' who have gone on to win the Nobel Peace Prize: Menachim Begin, Sean McBride, Nelson Mandela and Yassir Arafat. Clearly, even within the confines of contemporary terrorism discourse 'once a terrorist is not always a terrorist'. It depends upon the current political context and the dominant discourses which determine and constitute it. It is for this reason, among others, that some scholars argue that the term should be avoided or eschewed altogether in academic research. These scholars suggest that the appropriate focus of study is not the terrorism that exists out there 'in reality', but the discourses of terrorism and the discursive practices that construct terrorism as a political and cultural subject.

Another set of scholars argue more prosaically that terrorism is a political-cultural label, an act of de-legitimisation and no group ever accepts its designation as 'terrorist'; that it has been abused by political interests and that it has too many negative cultural and political connotations to retain any real analytical value. While these are cogent and challenging arguments, as I will argue below, I don't believe that this means we should abandon the attempt to carefully and consistently determine which acts should be considered terrorist, or that we cannot agree on a set of fairly clear identifying criteria which can be employed for research purposes.

Argument for Terrorism

It is my argument here that in spite of its insecure ontological status, its negative cultural-political baggage and its frequent misuse by political and academic actors, there are a number of important political and normative reasons for retaining the term 'terrorism' as an organising concept for the field. I want to further suggest that the term can serve a useful function within a broader emancipatory project – that it can inform and strengthen a progressive politics. However, in order to achieve these lofty goals, scholars need to adopt the aims and commitments of a more 'critical' approach to terrorism. Politically, there are a number of reasons why we should retain the term terrorism and engage in sustained and rigorous discursive struggle over its constitution and knowledge production. Most obviously, the term now has widespread political and cultural currency. It is the organising concept for a vast array of powerful political institutions, processes and practices in contemporary society, and scholars who refuse to employ or engage with it risk marginalising their views and their access to power.

The term also clearly retains a great deal of academic currency. There is now a whole field of research, teaching and advocacy surrounding the concept of terrorism, with numerous journals, conferences, teaching programmes, think-tanks, research centres, funding opportunities and advisory posts in existence. To refuse to employ the term or engage in debates about its definition and application in research is again, to risk marginalisation and irrelevance within this broader scholarly context. Most importantly however, there is a compelling normative imperative to retain a term that de-legitimises particular kinds of violence directed against civilians and which instrumentalises human suffering for the purposes of influencing an audience.

Of course, the normative power of the terrorism label is highly dependent upon its consistent application to all qualifying cases, even when committed by Western states or their allies; the selectivity and bias of terrorism scholars and political leaders in the past has seriously undermined this project by making it appear that the term is reserved for the enemies of the West. However, I would argue that this provides a reason for critical engagement rather than withdrawal and capitulation in the discursive struggle. Although terrorism can never be adequately defined due to its unstable ontological status, I want to argue that it can, and should, be described according to a set of identifiable and unique characteristics which delineate it from other forms of political violence. Furthermore, a review of the broader terrorism studies literature would suggest that the following conception of terrorism has broad support from many leading scholars in the field and could form the basis of a consensus over how to conceptualise it. Such an approach moreover, has several advantages over most of the existing approaches I outlined above. I suggest that as a form of political violence, terrorism can be described according to four main characteristics.

First, terrorism is an intentional and pre-determined strategy of political violence. This suggests its rational and instrumental basis. It also implies that any actor (states, groups or individuals) can employ it in pursuit of strategic goals and that once a terrorist is not always a terrorist – it does not imply a kind of essential identity. Importantly, it also implies political motivations, as a way of distinguishing terrorism from other forms of violence designed to terrify, such as the intimidation of communities by organised criminals seeking to obtain financial reward, the terror caused by a serial killer, or the fear caused by a one-off mass killing. Lastly, it implies forethought and intentionality, as opposed to the terror induced by rioting or communal disturbances, for example. Second, the targets of terrorist violence are not necessarily the victims of the violence, but rather the audiences to the violence. From this perspective, terrorism is a form of political communication rather than direct military action.

An important distinction here is that terrorism instrumentalises its victims; unlike the actions of soldiers in war who seek to directly degrade the material ability of the enemy to continue fighting, the victims of terrorism are chosen instead for symbolic reasons. An important point here is that states which try to hide their involvement in civilian- directed violence may still be sending a powerful message to the society or social groups they wish to intimidate. The use of disappearances as a strategy of terrorism for example, sends a message that the state is omnipotent, omnipresent and ruthless in rooting out opponents, as does kidnap and torture. In other cases, state terrorism may be both instrumental and direct: killing a union organiser for example, both weakens the union and sends a message to potential union leaders and the society they come from. Third, and related to the previous point, terrorism is intended to cause fear and intimidate.

This is the central purpose of the violence and not just the unintended consequence, although it can be argued that there is a certain kind of intentionality when actors engage in actions they can be sure which will causes terror and intimidate, such as using airpower to bomb civilian areas. Moreover, the intention to cause fear can be usually be deduced from the targets, context and foreseen consequences of the violence. Bombs in public places or the widespread use of torture against regime opponents for example, are clearly intended to terrify the wider society. Lastly, terrorism is aimed primarily but not solely at civilians. Here I differ with some scholars in that I argue that it is often unhelpful to try and maintain civilian - military or combatant-non-combatant distinctions in conceptualising terrorism. I agree with Goodin in this regard that such distinctions can in fact, be counter-productive, as they provide actors with legitimation for other forms of equally abhorrent forms of violence.

A violent campaign aimed at police officers or off-duty military personnel was intended to cause fear and intimidate the wider society or a certain section of society for example, would still constitute terrorism even though it avoided targeting civilians. Similarly, certain actions during war which were aimed solely at terrorising enemy soldiers and their civilian audience, rather than for military-strategic reasons – such as the use of certain militarily ineffective but demoralising chemical weapons or the bombing of civilian areas which possessed no strategic targets, for example – could also be considered terrorism. There are a number of clear advantages to employing such a conception of terrorism. In the first instance, it does not artificially and illogically limit the phenomenon by the nature of the actor (as some definitions do), but includes state terrorism, gender-based terrorism, and non-state terrorism. Second, it does not limit the analysis to peace but also includes the behaviour of actors in war, the site of a great deal of concentrated political violence.

Lastly, as mentioned, it can be argued that there is already a consensus on these criteria among the leading terrorism scholars, as their definitions tend to incorporate all these elements. From this perspective, the main issue is not that we do not know what terrorism is or that we cannot clearly identify it; it is rather that the application of the definition is too often restricted – for whatever reason – to a narrow set of actors that happens to coincide with the current strategic interests of Western powers. During the cold war, most terrorism research focused on left-wing non-state groups; today, most terrorism research focuses on so-called 'Islamic terrorism'. This inconsistent application both distorts the focus of the field and undermines the emancipatory project.

Terrorism and Emancipation

As I have conceived it above, in addition to its analytical advantages, the terrorism label could be employed as means to advancing an emancipatory project and progressive politics in a number of respects. At the most basic level, employing the above criteria effects to de-legitimise forms of violence that instrumentalise human beings for the purposes of political communication, whether they are civilians or combatants. Related to this, it further de-legitimises all forms of civilian-directed violence, including the direct targeting of civilians during war. Most importantly, however, this approach to terrorism brings back states as a subject for analysis and holds them accountable for actions that many recognise as terrorism but which is rarely acknowledged as terrorism, even by terrorism scholars. This is a critical task, given that state terrorism is objectively far more serious and far more entrenched in political institutions and forms of governance than non-state terrorism. In this sense, the identifying criteria set out above functions to set the limits of legitimate state violence, despite the frequent attempt to justify terroristic forms of violence by reference to doctrines of state sovereignty and the legitimate use of political violence.

The criteria can also be used to scrutinise state practices during counter-terrorism and counter-insurgency which more often than not morphs into terrorism when it fails to distinguish between the innocent and the guilty, is highly disproportionate, or aims to terrify and intimidate the wider population or a particular community into submission. Similarly, it can be used to evaluate state practices during times of war, identifying those occasions when military actions go beyond strategic necessity to the use of force for the purpose of intimidating and demoralising civilians. In short, these criteria provide a strict set of criteria for the evaluation of actions by any and all actors who are in conflict. As such, they have the potential to strengthen the norms relating to the limits of political violence, thereby improving human security and progressive politics. Importantly, the broad social and academic consensus, as well as the relevant legal precepts, is already in place for proscribing and de-legitimising actions that fall within the categories of illegitimate, terrorist violence outlined above.

However, in order to make this work in everyday scholarly practice, I would argue that terrorism scholars in particular would need to adhere to a set of core ontological, methodological and normative commitments. These have been outlined in detail elsewhere, but would include, among others: an acute sensitivity to the politics of labelling in the terrorism field and an acceptance of the insecure ontological status of the term; transparency about their own values and political standpoints, particularly as they relate to the geo-political interests of Western states; a willingness to expand their focus of research to include the use of terrorism by states; adherence to a set of responsible research ethics; and a commitment to normative values and a broadly defined notion of emancipation.

In particular, terrorism scholars must recognise the cultural-political biases they hold and aim for consistency of application of the criteria set out. Specifically, they must demonstrate a willingness to scrutinise and condemn the actions and intentions of their own states when they cross the line into terrorism. This is in fact, the biggest problem facing the field in this area. It is not that terrorism scholars do not recognise the use of terrorism by states; it is rather that they limit the focus of their research largely to non-state groups that are opposed to Western interests and fail to acknowledge the long history of involvement of their own states or allied states in terrorism.

In this, I have attempted to demonstrate that even though terrorism is impossible to define and the study of terrorism is beset by some unhelpful biases and knowledge practices, it is both possible and necessary to retain the terrorism term as a focus for research. I have further suggested that as an analytical term, terrorism can potentially play an important normative function. However, in order to realise this potential, terrorism scholars need to acknowledge and accept the ethico-political content of their subject and commit themselves to a number of transparent principles. The consequences of failing to do so are that the field remains unbalanced, politically biased and highly limited in its focus.

More importantly, unless these imbalances are addressed the field is in danger of providing academic legitimacy to the current efforts of certain Western governments in the ongoing war on terror. That is, scholars risk reinforcing the view that terrorism is solely a problem of non-state groups and individuals, and that states are immune from condemnation or sustained scholarly analysis. Considering some of the morally questionable and counter-productive policies at the heart of this global campaign – such as extraordinary rendition, the widespread use of torture, internment at Guantanamo Bay, pre-emptive war, extra- judicial killing of terrorist suspects, shoot-to-kill policies, intrusive surveillance, aid and support for authoritarian regimes and the like – this should sound a clarion call for concerted action to scholars in the field.

16

Patterns of Global Terrorism

Incidents of terrorism in East Asia increased in 1997. Continuing defections from the Khmer Rouge to Cambodian forces reduced the threat from the terrorist group, but guerrillas in the Cambodian provinces have been responsible for deadly attacks on foreigners. The unstable political situation in Cambodia has led to marked political violence, and the most significant act of terrorism there was a grenade attack on an opposition political rally in March, which left 19 persons dead and injured more than 100, including a US citizen. In October, the Secretary of State designated the Khmer Rouge as a foreign terrorist organization pursuant to the Antiterrorism and Effective Death Penalty Act of 1996.

In the Philippines, implementation of a peace agreement with insurgent groups has reduced fighting with government forces, but former members of these insurgent groups and members of Philippine terrorist organizations continued attacks. Foreigners number among their victims. In October, the Secretary of State designated one of these terrorist organizations, the Abu Sayyaf Group, as a foreign terrorist organization pursuant to the Antiterrorism and Effective Death Penalty Act of 1996. In China and Indonesia, separatist violence not targeted against foreigners but having the potential to claim foreigners as collateral victims continued.

In Japan, the trial of the leader of Aum Shinrikyo, the group responsible for the sarin gas attack on the Tokyo subway system in 1995 continued. A government panel decided not to invoke an Anti-Subversive Law to ban Aum Shinrikyo, concluding that the group poses no future threat, although the group continued to operate and to recruit new members. In October, the Secretary of State designated Aum Shinrikyo as a foreign terrorist organization pursuant to the Antiterrorism and Effective Death Penalty Act of 1996. In South Asia, many of the factions involved in the Afghanistan civil war—including large numbers of Egyptians, Algerians, Palestinians, and Saudis—continued to provide haven to terrorists by facilitating the operation of training camps in areas under their control. The factions remain engaged in a struggle for political and military supremacy over the country.

Efforts to ascertain the fate of the four Western hostages kidnapped in July 1995 in Kashmir by affiliates of the Harakat ul-Ansar (HUA) continued through 1997. There is no evidence to corroborate claims by multiple Kashmiri militant sources that the hostages were killed in December 1995. In October, the HUA was designated a foreign terrorist organization pursuant to the Antiterrorism and Effective Death Penalty Act of 1996. In Pakistan, deadly incidents of sectarian violence, particularly in Sindh and Punjab Provinces, continued throughout 1997. In November, four US employees of Union Texas Petroleum and their Pakistani driver were murdered in Karachi when the vehicle in which they were riding was attacked 1 mile from the US Consulate in Karachi. In addition, five Iranian Air Force technicians were killed in September in Rawalpindi.

There continue to be credible reports of official Pakistani support for Kashmiri militant groups that engage in terrorism, such as the HUA. In Sri Lanka, the Liberation Tigers of Tamil Eelam (LTTE) showed no signs of abandoning their campaign to cripple the Sri Lankan economy and target government officials. The group retains its ability to strike in the heart of Colombo, as demonstrated by an October bomb attack on the World Trade Center in the financial district that was reminiscent of the January 1996 truck bomb attack that destroyed the Central Bank. The LTTE was designated a foreign terrorist organization in October pursuant to the Antiterrorism and Effective Death Penalty Act of 1996.

Afghanistan

Islamic extremists from around the world—including large numbers of Egyptians, Algerians, Palestinians, and Saudis—continued to use Afghanistan as a training ground and home base from which to operate in 1997. The Taliban, as well as many of the other combatants in the Afghan civil war, facilitated the operation of training and indoctrination facilities for non-Afghans in the territories they controlled. Several Afghani factions also provided logistic support, free passage, and sometimes passports to the members of various terrorist organizations. These individuals, in turn, were involved in fighting in Bosnia and Herzegovina, Chechnya, Tajikistan, Kashmir, the Philippines, and parts of the Middle East.

Saudi-born terrorist financier Usama Bin Laden relocated from Jalalabad to the Taliban's capital of Qandahar in early 1997 and established a new base of operations. He continued to incite violence against the United States, particularly against US forces in Saudi Arabia. Bin Ladin called on Muslims to retaliate against the US prosecutor in the Mir Aimal Kansi trial for disparaging comments he made about Pakistanis and praised the Pakistan-based Kashmiri group HUA in the wake of its formal designation as a foreign terrorist organization by the United States. According to the Pakistani press, following Kansi's rendition to the United States, Bin Ladin warned the United States that, if it attempted his capture, he would "teach them a lesson similar to the lesson they were taught in Somalia."

Burma

The explosion in April of a parcel bomb at the house of a senior official in Burma's military-led government was the most significant terrorist event in Burma in 1997. The blast killed the adult daughter of Lieutenant-General Tin Oo, Secretary Number Two of the ruling State Law and Order Restoration Council. No group or individual claimed responsibility for the attack, but the Government of Burma attributes the act to Burmese antigovernment activists in Japan; the package bore Japanese stamps and postmarks. The Burmese expatriate and student community in Japan denies any involvement in the incident.

Cambodia

Continued defections from the Khmer Rouge to the government and the split of the group into pro- and anti-Pol Pot factions have greatly reduced the threat it poses. Nevertheless, the hardliners based in the Khmer Rouge stronghold at Anlong Veng regularly launched guerrilla-style attacks on government troops in several provinces from July onward. Guerrillas are also suspected in two deadly attacks against ethnic Vietnamese civilians in Cambodia, but they have denied playing a role in the disappearance of two Filipino and two Malaysian employees of a logging company in December 1997.

The most significant terrorist incident in Cambodia in 1997 was the grenade attack on an opposition political rally on 30 March. Nineteen persons were killed in the attack, and more than 100 were injured, including one US citizen. Those responsible for the attack have not yet been apprehended. Reacting to political violence throughout July, Second Prime Minister Hun Sen announced an eight-point program in August designed to improve the security situation in Cambodia. The new measures include government crackdowns on illegal roadblocks and weapons and a ban on tinted windows intended to discourage kidnapping and arms smuggling.

The fate of British mine clearing expert Christopher Howes, allegedly kidnapped by the Khmer Rouge in March 1996, remained unresolved in 1997. Unconfirmed reporting suggested Howes was with forces loyal to Pol Pot, and some Cambodian officials expressed fears publicly that he had been killed. In May, Khmer Rouge leader Khieu Samphan denied any knowledge of Howes' whereabouts.

China

There were no incidents of international terrorism in China in 1997, but Uygur separatists continued a campaign of violence. The Uygurs are a Chinese Muslim ethnic minority group concentrated in the Xinjiang Autonomous Region in far western China. In February, Uygur separatists conducted a series of bus bombings in Urumqi that killed nine persons and wounded 74. Uygur rioting earlier in the month in the city of Yining caused as many as 200 deaths. Uygur exiles in Turkey claimed responsibility for a small pipe bomb that exploded on a bus in Beijing in March and which killed three persons and injured eight. In August, Uygur separatists were blamed for killing five persons, including two policemen. The Chinese Government executed several individuals involved in both the rioting and bombings. Beijing claims that support for the Uygurs is coming from neighboring countries, an accusation these countries deny.

India

Security problems persist in India as a result of insurgencies in Kashmir and in the northeast. The violence also has spread to New Delhi; there were more than 25 bombings in the city in 1997—mainly in the marketplaces and buses of old Delhi—that left 10 persons dead and more than 200 injured. These attacks appeared to be aimed at spreading terror among the public rather than causing casualties. Nearly 100 bombings with similar characteristics took place elsewhere in the country in 1997, most with no claims of responsibility. Although foreigners were not the likely targets of these attacks, foreign tourists were injured in a train bombing outside Delhi in October.

The Indian and Pakistani Governments each claim that the intelligence service of the other country sponsors bombings on its territory. The Government of Pakistan acknowledges that it continues to provide moral, political, and diplomatic support to Kashmiri militants but denies allegations of other assistance. Reports continued in 1997, however, of official Pakistani support to militants fighting in Kashmir.

Indonesia

Separatist groups in East Timor apparently continued to target non-combatants and were involved in several bomb making activities in 1997. In Irian Jaya, an attack allegedly by the separatist Free Papua Organization against a road surveying crew in April left two civilians dead.

Japan

The trials of Aum Shinrikyo leader Shoko Asahara and other members of the sect continued in 1997. Prosecutors reduced the number of victims listed in the indictments against Asahara to speed up the proceedings, which entered their second year. In addition to the murder charges stemming from the March 1995 sarin nerve gas attack on the Tokyo subway system, Asahara faces 16 other charges ranging from kidnapping and murder to illegal production of drugs and weapons. Nine former Aum members pleaded guilty or received sentences from 22 months to 17 years for crimes they committed on behalf of Asahara; one Aum member was acquitted of forcibly confining other cult members.

Despite the legal proceedings against Asahara and other members, what remained of Aum following the arrests of 1996 continued to exist, operate, and even recruit new members in Japan in 1997? In January a government panel decided not to invoke the Anti-Subversive Law against Aum Shinrikyo, which would have outlawed the sect. The panel ruled that Aum posed no future threat to Japanese society because it was financially bankrupt and most of its followers wanted by the police had been arrested.

Several members of the Japanese Red Army (JRA) were arrested in 1997. Five members were convicted in Lebanon on various charges related to forgery and illegal residency and sentenced to three years in prison. Another member, Jun Nishikawa, was captured in Bolivia and deported to Japan where he was indicted for his role in the 1977 hijacking of a Japanese Airlines flight.

Tsutomu Shirosaki was captured in 1996 and brought to the United States to stand trial for offenses arising from a rocket attack against the US Embassy in Jakarta, Indonesia, in 1986. He was convicted in Washington, DC, of assault with the intent to kill, attempted first degree murder of internationally protected persons, attempted destruction of buildings and property in the special maritime and territorial jurisdiction of the United States, and the committing of a violent attack on the official premises of internationally protected persons. (In February 1998, he was sentenced to 30 years in prison.) Seven hardcore JRA members remain at large.

Pakistan

In November four US employees of Union Texas Petroleum and their Pakistani driver were murdered in Karachi when the vehicle in which they were traveling was attacked 1 mile from the US Consulate in Karachi. Shortly after the incident, two separate claims of responsibility for the killings were made: the Aimal Khufia Action Committee—a previously unknown group—and the Islami Inqilabi Mahaz, a Lahore-based group of Afghan veterans. Both groups cited as the motive for the attack the conviction of Mir Aimal Kansi, a Pakistani national who was tried in the United States in November for the murder of two CIA employees and the wounding of three others outside CIA Headquarters in 1993. Kansi was found guilty and sentenced to death.

Deadly incidents of sectarian violence, particularly in Punjab Province, surged in 1997. According to press reports, 200 people died during the year. In addition, five Iranian Air Force technicians were killed in September in Rawalpindi. Lashkar-i-Jhangvi, a violent offshoot of the anti-Shiite Sunni group Sipah-i-Sahaba Pakistan, claimed responsibility. The Iranian Government-controlled press holds Pakistan responsible for failing to stop the attack and accused the United States of conspiring in the murders.

The United States designated the HUA a foreign terrorist organization in October. This group is responsible for the still unresolved July 1995 kidnapping of six Westerners in Kashmir; one of the six, a US citizen, managed to escape, but a Norwegian hostage was killed in August 1995. Ramzi Ahmed Yousef, who was extradited from Pakistan to the United States in 1995, was convicted in New York in November for his role in the 1993 World Trade Center bombing in New York City.

Philippines

The Philippine Government began implementing terms of a peace agreement signed with the Moro National Liberation Front (MNLF) in 1996 and continued efforts to negotiate a peace agreement with the Moro Islamic Liberation Front (MILF). The government began the process of integrating former MNLF rebels into the Philippine military. A cease-fire with the MILF reduced the fighting that peaked in the first half of 1997, but the two sides failed to agree on a more comprehensive arrangement. The MILF and the smaller Abu Sayyaf Group continue to fight for a separate Islamic state in the southern Philippines.

Muslim rebels in the southern Philippines conducted

several attacks against foreigners in 1997. A Japanese businessman and three Filipino boys were kidnapped in June by members of the Abu Sayyaf Group. A rescue operation by the Philippine military freed the Japanese hostage. A German businessman was abducted in September by former members of the MNLF and was released in December only after his family agreed to pay the kidnappers some $100,000 in ransom. In separate incidents in October and November, former MNLF members abducted priests—one Irish and one Belgian—and demanded payment of funds owed them under a government rehabilitation program. The captives were released after the government agreed to expedite disbursal of the funds.

The government had mixed results in its efforts against communist rebels in 1997. Philippine police captured some key communist personnel. The government again suspended negotiations with the political arm of the communist New People's Army (NPA) in late 1997 following an upsurge in small-scale attacks by the NPA on police and government units. In May communist guerrillas ambushed a vehicle owned by a subcontractor of a major US firm, killing two Filipino employees. In December, New People's Army rebels ambushed two army detachments and abducted 21 paramilitary troops in Davao City in Mindanao. The government pledged to revisit the issue of a dialogue with the communists if acceptable circumstances could be met. Another communist rebel group, the Alex Boncayao Brigade, is not participating in peace talks with the government.

In September a previously unknown group calling itself the Filipino Soldiers for the Nation claimed responsibility for grenade attacks at bus terminals in Manila and Bulcalan City that killed six persons and wounded 65. Press reports indicated the group claimed to favor a constitutionally prohibited second term for President Ramos. The Ramos government strongly condemned the attacks and blamed them on unknown provocateurs.

The Philippine Government continued its strong support for international cooperation against terrorism and actively sought to build a multilateral approach to counterterrorism in regional and other forums. The government cooperated in providing additional personnel to protect likely targets and to identify, investigate, and act against likely terrorists. The government quickly responded when a US company experienced what appeared to be an NPA attack on one of its subcontractors in Quezon, and officials at the Cabinet level met with company executives to discuss what could be done to improve security.

Sri Lanka

The Liberation Tigers of Tamil Eelam continued its terrorist activities in 1997, attacking government troops, economic infrastructure targets, and assassinating political opponents. The LTTE's most spectacular terrorist attack in 1997 was a truck bombing directed at the newly opened Colombo World Trade Center on 15 October. The explosion injured more than 100 persons, including many foreigners, and caused significant collateral damage to nearby buildings. Eighteen persons—including LTTE suicide bombers, hotel security guards, and Sri Lankan security forces—died in the explosion and aftermath. Two of the terrorists were shot by Sri Lankan authorities as they tried to escape, and another three killed them to avoid capture. One of the bombers lobbed a grenade into a monastery yard as he fled the scene, killing one monk.

In two separate incidents in June in the Tricomalee area, the LTTE assassinated two legislators and nine other civilians. Also, during the summer months, naval elements of the LTTE conducted several attacks on commercial shipping, including numerous foreign vessels. In July LTTE rebels abducted the crew of an empty passenger ferry and set fire to the vessel. The captain and a crewmember—both Indonesian—were released after three days. Also in July, the LTTE stormed a North Korean cargo ship after it delivered a shipment of food and other goods for civilians on the Jaffna Peninsula, killing one of the vessel's 38 North Korean crewmembers in the process. The Tigers freed its North Korean captives five days later and eventually returned the vessel. Sri Lankan authorities charged the LTTE with the July hijacking of a shipment of more than 32,000 mortar rounds bound for the Sri Lankan military. In September the LTTE used rocket-propelled grenades to attack a Panamanian-flagged Chinese-owned merchant ship chartered by a US chemical company to load minerals for export. As many as 20 persons, including five Chinese crewmembers, were reported killed, wounded, or missing from the attack.

In August a group calling itself the Internet Black Tigers (IBT) claimed responsibility for e-mail harassment of several Sri Lankan missions around the world. The group claimed in Internet postings to be an elite department of the LTTE specializing in "suicide e-mail bombings" with the goal of countering Sri Lankan Government propaganda disseminated electronically. The IBT stated that the attacks were only warnings.

The Sri Lankan Government strongly supports international efforts to address the problem of terrorism. (It was the first to sign the International Convention for the Suppression of Terrorist Bombings in January 1998.) Colombo was quick to condemn terrorist attacks in other countries and raised terrorism issues in several international venues, including the UN General Assembly and the Commonwealth heads of government meeting in Edinburgh. No confirmed cases of LTTE or other terrorist groups targeting US citizens in Sri Lanka occurred in 1997. The LTTE was among the 30 groups designated as foreign terrorist organizations by the United States on 8 October.

Thailand

An appeals court in Thailand upheld the conviction and death sentence passed on an Iranian convicted of a 1994 plot to bomb the Israeli Embassy in Bangkok. The defendant, Hossein Dastgiri, has appealed to the Supreme Court. Muslim separatist groups in southern Thailand carried out a series of bombings and other violent attacks in 1997. Bomb attacks in October killed seven persons, and a bombing of a Chinese religious festival in December killed three and wounded 15. Government authorities credited separatist groups with assassinating 11 policemen in a two-month period and blowing up a railroad in May.

Vietnam

A Vietnamese court sentenced two persons to death and three others to life in prison for carrying out a grenade attack on the waterfront in Ho Chi Minh City in 1994, in which 20 persons, including 10 foreigners, were injured. The five were part of the "Vietnam Front for Regime Restoration," an antigovernment exile group based in the United States.

Europe and Eurasia Overview

The number of terrorist incidents in Western Europe remained low during 1997. Terrorist acts by the Kurdistan Workers' Party (PKK) declined in Germany as PKK leader Ocalan attempted to get out from under Germany's tough sanctions on terrorist organizations. Spain and France continued to cooperate in bringing to justice members of the Basque Fatherland and Liberty (ETA) terrorist organization, while Spanish authorities have offered to negotiate with Basque groups that foreswear violence. Spanish authorities arrested, tried, and jailed the leadership of the ETA's political wing, the Herri Batasuna.

Although no major terrorist acts took place in France, security forces maintained a high public visibility as a precaution against repeats of the deadly 1996 bombing of a commuter train in Paris. In Germany, acts of terrorist violence attributable to the PKK declined, although the PKK remains actively engaged in criminal activities, principally extortion and aggravated assault. A judgment by a court in Berlin in April in the so-called Mykonos trial found that the highest levels of Iran's political leadership followed a deliberate policy of murdering political opponents who lived outside the country. In March 1996 a German court had issued an arrest warrant for former Iranian Minister of Intelligence and Security Ali Fallahian in this case.

In the United Kingdom, the Irish Republican Army (IRA) announced another cease-fire, thereby making it possible for Sinn Fein to join the multiparty talks on Northern Ireland's future. Recalcitrant elements on both the Republican and Loyalist sides, however, showed their determination to continue the armed struggle over whether Northern Ireland should remain part of the United Kingdom or be united with the Republic of Ireland. At the end of the year, Republican prisoners in Belfast's Maze prison shot a rival prisoner, Loyalist terrorist leader Billy "King Rat" Wright. Within a day Wright's followers shot and killed a former IRA member in County Tyrone, and several other killings of Catholics followed.

Greek Government efforts during 1997 to crack down on indigenous terrorism continue to yield few successes. There has been no known progress in bringing members of the 17 November terrorist organization to justice. A major suspect in the 1986 bombing of the La Belle discotheque was extradited to Germany, however. An Italian Red Brigades terrorist who had been living freely in Greece for 12 years was arrested and entered into extradition proceedings.

In eastern Turkey, authorities and security forces remain locked in a war of attrition with the terrorist group PKK. There are also signs that the DHKP/C (formerly the

Dev Sol terrorist organization) may be resurfacing and targeting Turkish Government figures and US military and commercial interests. There were numerous attacks targeted against the international presence in Bosnia and Herzegovina, most consisting of small-scale bombings.

Terrorist acts and threats have been triggered by dissatisfaction over the international community's handling of voter registration procedures, the return of refugees, and the apprehension of suspected war criminals. In Russia, although the armed conflict between Federal forces and Chechen separatists has been resolved, there were numerous incidents of kidnapping and other acts. In Tajikistan, violence claimed the lives of Russian servicemen and a French humanitarian aid worker. Azerbaijan and Georgia also saw continued ethnic-related terrorist violence.

Austria

In October, Austrian police arrested a man suspected of a xenophobic letter bomb campaign since 1993 that has claimed the lives of four members of the Roma (gypsy) minority in Burgenland Province and injured 15 persons in Austria and Germany. The ongoing investigation convinced Austrian authorities that the suspect acted his own and invented the name Bavarian Liberation Army, which was used in claims of responsibility for most of the bombings.

In June an Austrian investigative judge interrogated international terrorist Illich Ramirez Sanchez, alias "Carlos the Jackal," who is incarcerated in Paris. The terrorist is believed to have masterminded the terrorist attack on the OPEC Headquarters in Vienna in 1975.

Belgium

On 20 June unidentified individuals detonated a bomb at the Turkish Embassy in Brussels. An anonymous caller claimed the attack in the name of the "Gourken Yanikian

Military Unite," a covername used by the Armenian Secret Army for the Liberation of Armenia (ASALA) terrorist organization during the 1980s. ASALA had not conducted terrorist attacks in several years, however, and it is unclear whether the attack was carried out by ASALA, individual Armenians with no terrorist affiliation, or another terrorist group—such as the Kurdistan Workers' Party—using Yanikian as a cover name.

Bosnia and Herzegovina

Numerous attacks occurred against the international presence in Bosnia and Herzegovina during 1997. Most of these attacks consisted of small-scale bombings that resulted in material damage and few casualties. However, during the visit of Pope John Paul II to Bosnia and Herzegovina in April, an unidentified assailant planted over 23 remote-controlled landmines underneath a bridge that was part of the Pope's motorcade route. Acting on a report from a witness claiming to have seen a suspicious person near the bridge, police discovered and defused the mines a few hours before the Pope's arrival. No group claimed responsibility for the attempted attack.

Following the apprehension of two indicted Bosnian Serb war criminals in Prijedor by the Stabilization Force (SFOR) troops on 10 July, unidentified assailants mounted over 20 improvised bombings against facilities and individuals belonging to the Organization for Security and Cooperation in Europe, the International Police Task Force, and SFOR. In December unknown attackers threw a hand grenade at a Dutch SFOR compound the day after a Dutch SFOR unit apprehended two indicted Bosnian Croat war criminals near Vitez.

Other small-scale bombings against the international community presence in Bosnia and Herzegovina occurred to protest the handling of local elections and voter registration procedures and the return of refugees and displaced persons to their prewar homes. In November, Bosnian security services began an operation to apprehend former mujahedin—foreign Islamic fighters who served in the Bosnian Army during the war—suspected of involvement in a variety of criminal activities, including the murders of several Bosnian Croats and bombings of Croat houses and churches. By yearend, roughly 20 Arab and Bosnian Muslims had been arrested by Bosnian authorities.

Denmark

On 18 January, Danish police arrested several neo-Nazis in connection with the mailing of several letter bombs to targets in the United Kingdom. The bombs, which were mailed from Sweden, were intercepted by Swedish police and safely detonated. The remains of the bombs were provided to Danish police as evidence on 20 January. In September a Danish court sentenced three of the neo-Nazis in connection with this case.

France

French authorities continue to maintain a state of high alert in the aftermath of a wave of terrorist bombings by Algerian Islamic extremists during 1995 and 1996. The French mounted extensive security operations to protect Algeria's 17 consulates in France during the Algerian legislative elections in June, in which an estimated 2 million Algerians resident in France were eligible to vote. On 28 February a bomb exploded outside the American dormitory at Cite Universitaire near Paris. No one was injured in the incident, and no group has claimed responsibility for the attack.

On 29 January 1998 antiterrorism magistrate Jean-Louis Brugiere officially completed his investigation into the 1989 downing of UTA flight 772. French prosecutors are examining his report in advance of a future trial, in absentia, of the Libyan intelligence agents believed to be responsible for the attack.

The trial of notorious international terrorist Illich Ramirez Sanchez, alias "Carlos the Jackal," began in mid-December. Later that month, Ramirez was convicted by a French court for the 1975 murders of two French investigators and a Lebanese national.

Factions of the National Front for the Liberation of Corsica (FLNC) continued to carry out a campaign of low-level bombings, primarily directed against symbolic targets, such as banks and police stations. The vast majority of these bombings took place on Corsica, but several attacks were mounted on the French mainland.

French authorities continued to cooperate closely with their Spanish counterparts during 1997 to track down Basque Fatherland and Liberty (ETA) terrorists operating or seeking refuge in France. French authorities arrested more than 140 suspected ETA members and supporters, tried over 60 of these individuals, and extradited 23 ETA terrorists to Spain, including two of the group's key leaders. In May the French Basque group Ipparratarek claimed responsibility for bombing a fast-food restaurant in Saint Jean de Luz, causing extensive material damage but no injuries.

Georgia

The trial of Jaba Ioselliani, former head of the Georgian Mkhedrioni paramilitary organization, began on 1 December. He and 14 others are accused of conspiring against Georgian President Eduard Shevardnadze, culminating in an assassination attempt against the President in August 1995. The Georgian Government continues to seek the extradition of Igor Giorgadze, former head of the Georgian Security Ministry, from Russia for his alleged involvement in the plot against Shevardnadze.

Germany

PKK leader Abdullah Ocalan, in an ongoing effort to encourage the German Government to lift its four-year-old ban on his organization, reiterated his 1996 public promise to forbid PKK-instigated acts of violence on German soil. Indeed, acts of terrorist violence attributable to the PKK in Germany for the year declined significantly and PKK demonstrations were peaceful. The PKK actively engaged, however, in criminal activities, principally extortion, recruitment, and aggravated assault. (In January 1998 the German Federal prosecutor announced that the PKK would no longer be considered a terrorist organization. However, the German Interior Minister stated that the PKK remains a banned criminal organization in Germany and that German authorities will continue to work on PKK prosecutions.)

German prosecutors indicted the former PKK European spokesman, Kani Yilmaz (a.k.a. Faisal Dunlayiei), charging him with being one of the leaders of a terrorist organization and indirectly participating in two series of arson attacks on Turkish establishments in Germany in June and November 1993. (In February 1998 he was convicted and sentenced to seven and a half years. He was released on parole, however, because he had already served more than half of his sentence in pretrial detention in the United Kingdom and Germany.)

An important terrorism trial in Berlin concluded in April 1997. The Mykonos trial involved five defendants—an Iranian and four Lebanese—suspected in the 1992 killing of Iranian Kurdish dissidents, one of whom was then Secretary General of the Kurdish Democratic Party of Iran (KDPI), in Berlin's Mykonos restaurant. A German judge found the Iranian and three of the Lebanese guilty of the murders. Two defendants, Kazem Darabi and Abbas Rhayel, were sentenced to life in prison. Two others, Youssef Amin and Muhammad Atris, received sentences of 11 years and five years and three months, respectively. The fifth defendant, Ataollah Ayad, was acquitted. The court stated that the Government of Iran had followed a deliberate policy of liquidating the regime's opponents who lived outside Iran, including the opposition KDPI.

The judge further stated that the Mykonos murders had been approved at the most senior levels of the Iranian Government by an extra-legal committee whose members included the Minister of Intelligence and Security, the Foreign Minister, the President, and the Supreme Leader. In March 1996 a German court had issued an arrest warrant in this case for Ali Fallahian, the former Iranian Minister of Intelligence and Security.

Germany in November 1997 began the trial of five defendants in the 1986 La Belle discotheque bombing in Berlin, which killed three persons, including two US servicemen, and wounded more than 200, many of them seriously. Both Italy and Greece arrested suspects in the case during 1997 and extradited them to Germany for trial. In his opening remarks, the German prosecutor said the bombing was "definitely an act of assassination commissioned by the Libyan state." German authorities have issued warrants for four Libyan officials for their role in the case. The four are believed to be in Libya.

Greece

Greek Government efforts during 1997 to crack down on indigenous terrorism yielded few successes. Revolutionary Organization 17 November claimed responsibility for its 22nd assassination; previous victims include five US Government employees. On 28 May, Greek shipping tycoon Constantine Peratikos was shot to death in broad daylight on an Athens street. The group issued a manifesto claiming that Peratikos was targeted because he allegedly misused a large government bailout and threatened to close down his shipyard, which would have forced the layoff of 2,000 employees. No member of 17 November has ever been arrested.

Greece's numerous leftist and anarchist groups stepped up the tempo of attacks in 1997, predominantly with Molotov cocktail attacks and low-level bombings against property. Some of the leftist groups—in particular, the Fighting (or Militant) Guerrilla Formation (FGF)—recently have attempted to assassinate Greek officials with improvised explosive devices. For example, the FGF attempted to bomb the home of a former Greek Government counterterrorism adviser in February—the bomb was discovered and dismantled—and also claimed responsibility for a bomb that exploded at the Minister of Development's parliamentary constituency office. No arrests have been made in these cases.

On 1 December, the Athens Court of Appeals overturned a 10-year prison sentence and acquitted suspected terrorist George Balafas of aggravated weapons possession and related indictments, including accessory to murder. Balafas is suspected of having links—if not direct involvement—with the Revolutionary People's Struggle (ELA), one of the country's more deadly terrorist groups. Kurdish nationalist groups—including the terrorist PKK—enjoy widespread sympathy and some support among the Greek public. In April, 157 members of the Greek Parliament signed a petition calling for PKK leader Abdullah Ocalan to be officially invited to Greece.

The Greek Government extradited German citizen Andrea Haeusler to Germany in January for her alleged participation in the 1986 bombing of the La Belle discotheque in Berlin. In November, Greek police arrested former Italian Red Brigade member Enrico Bianco in western Greece and initiated procedures for his extradition to Italy, where he had been convicted in absentia. (A Greek court denied his extradition request in 1998 and Bianco was released.)

Italy

Several incidents in Italy during 1997 involved domestic anarchists, although none of these resulted in casualties. A leftist group called Revolutionary Action claimed responsibility for a bombing on 25 April outside Milan's city hall. In May a hand-grenade was found in a store located near the Uffizi Gallery in Florence. The gallery had been the target of an anarchist bombing in 1993. In November, five days before local elections, a bomb was discovered before it detonated outside the Palace of Justice in Rome, site of Italy's highest court. The investigation is ongoing, but authorities suspect local anarchists were responsible.

In January several unarmed persons broke into the Peruvian Consulate in Padua and defaced the building with graffiti. Although the Peruvian MRTA claimed responsibility for the incident, Italian police believe Italian supporters of MRTA probably were responsible. Eight members of a domestic separatist group took over the bell tower in Venice's main square, Piazza San Marco, on 9 May. The suspects were arrested and tried in July on charges of kidnapping for subversive purposes and unauthorized possession of weapons; all eight were found guilty and received sentences ranging from four years and nine months house arrest to six years in prison.

Italian authorities scored notable successes against foreign terrorists during 1997. In June a court in Turin sentenced five members of the Algerian Armed Islamic Group (GIA) to prison terms of one to three years on charges of forgery and membership in a criminal organization. In August, Italian police arrested Libyan citizen Eter Abulgassem Musbah, a suspect in the 1986 bombing of the La Belle discotheque in Berlin. Abulgassem was promptly extradited to Germany to stand trial for the La Belle bombing. In September, Italian authorities in Bologna arrested 14 foreign nationals suspected of belonging to the

GIA. Nine of the suspects were later released due to lack of evidence.

Russia

In Russia, although the armed conflict between Federal forces and Chechen separatists was resolved, there were numerous incidents of kidnapping. Most of these involved ransom demands, although political motives cannot be excluded. Insurgents have been aided with equipment and training by mujahedin with extensive links to Middle Eastern and Southwest Asian terrorists. According to the Organization for Security and Cooperation in Europe, at yearend 71 hostages remained in captivity, including 15 foreign nationals, five of whom are journalists and 10 are NGO representatives.

Spain

Despite numerous Spanish counterterrorism successes and increased international cooperation with France and Latin American countries, the Basque Fatherland and Liberty (ETA) terrorist group continued its campaign of murder, bombings, kidnappings, and street violence. ETA killed 13 persons last year, as compared to five during 1996. ETA's primary targets remained members of the Spanish security forces and judicial and prison officials, but the group also stepped up attacks against local politicians belonging to the ruling Popular Party. ETA's kidnapping and murder of a Popular Party town councilor in July provoked widespread international condemnation and anti-ETA demonstrations involving millions of people throughout Spain.

The Spanish Government has energetically and successfully sought extradition from countries in which ETA fugitives reside. Spanish-French cooperation during 1997 led to the arrest in France of more than 140 persons directly or indirectly connected with ETA, including several of the group's key leaders. Some 60 ETA activists went to trial in France during the past year, and Spanish authorities negotiated the extradition to Spain of 23 terrorists. Spain also has sought extraditions from Latin American countries, successfully gaining extradition of ETA fugitives from the Dominican Republic and Mexico during 1997.

The Spanish Government moved for the first time in 1997 to prosecute ETA's legal political wing, the Herri Batasuna (HB) political party, on charges of criminal collaboration with a terrorist organization. The charges stemmed from HB's dissemination during the 1996 national election campaign of a video containing footage of ETA terrorists advocating violence. On 1 December sentences of seven years in prison and fines of about $3,500 were announced for all 23 members of HB's executive committee.

The leftwing terrorist group First of October Antifascist Resistance Group (GRAPO) remained inactive during 1997, even though some of the group's leaders were released from prison. Spanish authorities moved forcefully against foreign terrorists in their country, breaking up a ring of the Algerian GIA operating in Valencia in April.

Sweden

In an effort to undermine Sweden's bid to host the summer Olympic Games in the year 2000, "We Who Built Sweden," a previously unknown group, exploded several bombs at Swedish sports stadiums.

Tajikistan

Security for the international community in Tajikistan deteriorated as militant followers of renegade Tajik warlords Rezvon and Bahrom Sodirov resorted again to kidnapping employees of international organizations, a precedent the group established in December 1996. In an incident that began on 4 February, armed militants affiliated with

Bahrom Sodirov took UN and International Committee of the Red Cross (ICRC) personnel, Russian journalists, and the Tajik Security Minister hostage. Russian and Tajik negotiators conceded to Bahrom's demands for safe transport of his brother Rezvon Sodirov and his followers from Afghanistan to a camp outside Dushanbe, as well as for weapons and ammunition, and all the hostages were subsequently released. Authorities captured Bahrom following this incident. On 18 November, Rezvon Sodirov masterminded the kidnapping of two French humanitarian aid workers and demanded Bahrom's release from prison.

The incident ended violently by month's end; one hostage was either released or escaped on 29 November, but the other hostage was fatally wounded on 30 November during a shootout between the kidnappers and government forces in a government rescue attempt. Reports of Rezvon Sodirov's death in the shootout have not been confirmed. Unidentified assailants continued sporadic attacks against Russian servicemen in Tajikistan. On 18 February terrorists, probably followers of Rahmon "Hitler" Sanginov assassinated two ethnic Russian, off-duty US Embassy guards. The assassinations were consistent with a surge in attacks against Russians in Tajikistan; authorities concluded that the victims' affiliation with the US Embassy was not a factor in the attacks.

Turkey

The Turkish Communist Laborers' Party/Leninist (TKEP/L) placed two improvised explosive devices against the wall of the US Consulate in Istanbul on 5 October. The police removed the devices before detonation, but the event marked the first time that the TKEP/L targeted a US Government facility. Ensuing police sweeps reportedly wrapped up the group's leader and most of its senior cadre members.

The virulently anti-US Revolutionary People's Liberation Party/Front (DHKP/C)—formerly known as Dev

Sol—conducted three significant attacks during the year: all were light antiarmor weapon (LAW) rocket attacks against Turkish security facilities in Istanbul. The three attacks were flawed in execution: on 16 June the rocket fired at the Turkish National Police (TNP) headquarters missed and struck a wall; the LAW rocket launched against the Harbiye Officers' Club on 14 July hit the wall of the building but caused only minimal damage; and on 16 September the DHKP/C fired another rocket at the TNP headquarters, which glanced off a wall and broke apart. The TNP's counterterrorism operations against the DHKP/C may be forcing the group to use less experienced cadre members and standoff weapons—such as LAW rockets—rather then the group's preferred close-in handgun assassinations.

The Turkish Islamic fundamentalist group, Vasat, claimed responsibility for throwing a grenade at a book fair in Gaziantep on 14 September, killing one person and injuring 24. The attack was the most egregious by Turkey's increasingly violent Islamic terrorist groups, which include Turkish Hizballah and the Islamic Great Eastern Raiders/Front (IBDA/C). The latter is suspected of masterminding the 2 December bombing of the Ecumenical Patriarchate Cathedral in Istanbul.

PKK activities in Turkey were lower in 1997 than during the previous year, in part due to Turkish military operations into northern Iraq to disrupt the PKK's infrastructure for infiltrating its members into Turkey. PKK leader Abdullah Ocalan, residing in Syria, once again publicly threatened to target Turkey's tourist sites with bombs in an attempt to disrupt the country's vital tourist industry, but these attacks did not materialize.

United Kingdom

In 1997 the IRA continued a campaign of violence begun in February 1996 against Northern Irish police and

UK military and economic targets in Northern Ireland and elsewhere in the United Kingdom. July, however, brought an IRA cessation of hostilities—its second cease-fire in three years—in an effort to secure a place for Sinn Fein, its political wing, in the Ulster peace talks. The IRA cease-fire prompted an increase in activity among Republican and Loyalist splinter terrorist groups opposed to the peace process. The Continuity Army Council (CAC)—also known as the Continuity Irish Republican Army—and the Irish National Liberation Army (INLA) increased their attacks to protest the talks. The Loyalist Volunteer Force (LVF)—a new group in 1997—attacked both Republican activists and Catholic civilians with no paramilitary affiliations.

The IRA increased the frequency of its attacks during the first months of 1997 in anticipation of British elections on 1 May. By 30 April the group had conducted 29 attacks, as compared with 11 in all of 1996. IRA targets included economic and infrastructure targets on the UK mainland, and their attacks caused massive disruption while avoiding civilian casualties:

- Two IRA bombs damaged railway lines in Wilmslow, England, on 26 March.
- IRA bomb warnings closed the M1, M5, and M6 highways, which connect London and points north, on 3 April. Police found and detonated two bombs, one of which contained up to one and a half pounds of Semtex explosive, and several hoax devices.
- IRA bomb threats on 21 April snarled British transportation, with police temporarily closing 17 rail and subway stations: London's Gatwick, Heathrow, Luton, and Stanstead airports; Trafalgar Square; and the eastern dock of the Port of Dover.

The landslide victory of the British Labor Party headed by Tony Blair in the 1 May election led to preliminary talks with Sinn Fein and ultimately to an IRA announcement on 19 July of a cessation of hostilities to take effect the following day. In early September, Sinn Fein leaders agreed to the so-called Mitchell principles of nonviolence—six statements drafted by George Mitchell, currently chairman of the Northern Ireland multiparty talks that commit all parties to renouncing the use of violence, disarming paramilitary groups, and abiding by a peaceful resolution of the Northern Ireland conflict. Sinn Fein thus secured the party's seat in the Ulster peace talks. In response, hardline IRA members called an extraordinary conference to discuss the IRA's future strategy. The conference delegates reaffirmed Sinn Fein's current peace strategy, but some 20 IRA members resigned from the group in protest.

Days later a dozen members of Sinn Fein from Dundalk, Ireland, walked out of a meeting protesting the party's adherence to the Mitchell principles. Since then, most of these dissidents have returned to the fold. However, Bernadette Sands, sister of deceased IRA icon Bobby Sands, reportedly established the "Thirty-Two County Sovereignty Committee" to oppose Sinn Fein's political negotiation and the IRA cease-fire. In October the US Secretary of State did not include the IRA among 30 groups that she officially designated as foreign terrorist organizations under recently passed antiterrorism legislation. The Secretary took note of the 19 July announcement by the IRA of an unequivocal cease-fire. She also noted the subsequent decision by the British Government that the cease-fire was "genuine in word and deed," permitting Sinn Fein to join inclusive, all-party talks in Belfast.

The Department stated that, under these circumstances, the Secretary would continue to review the IRA and that any resumption of violence by the group would have a direct impact on her review. Following the IRA cease-fire, Republican splinter terrorist groups increased their attacks, seeking to replace the IRA as the dominant Republican terrorist group. On 16 September the CAC exploded a car bomb in Markethill, Northern Ireland—a predominantly

Protestant village—causing extensive damage to a police station, a cattle market, and commercial and private premises. The CAC also claimed responsibility for a 30 October bomb attack, which caused minor damage to a British Government office in Londonderry, Northern Ireland.

On 19 November a CAC bomb exploded outside Belfast City Hall, causing minor damage. Gunmen from the INLA murdered a Northern Irish police trainee in Belfast on 9 May. The INLA also carried out several attacks against Northern Irish police and British troops in July during three days of heavy rioting in Belfast over controversial Loyalist parades, injuring five police officers and two Protestant teenagers.

The extremist LVF emerged in February 1997 as a rump of the mainstream Ulster Volunteer Force (UVF), which is maintaining the cease-fire. The LVF is comprised of UVF radicals and other Protestant criminals. It is notorious for its attacks against Republican activists and Northern Irish Catholic civilians with no political or paramilitary affiliations. The LVF claimed responsibility for firebombing Northern Irish tourist information offices on 9 March to protest cross-border arrangements with Ireland. On 12 May LVF terrorists abducted and murdered a veteran member of the Gaelic Athletic Association, a Catholic sports club. The LVF exploded a small bomb in Dundalk, Ireland, on 25 May. Authorities suspect LVF terrorists in the murder of an 18-year-old Catholic girl in Antrim, Northern Ireland.

The girl was shot four times in the head, apparently because she had a Protestant boyfriend. In August unidentified gunmen attacked the homes of two prison guards; although the LVF did not claim responsibility, authorities suspect that the attacks were connected to simultaneous LVF prisoner riots. On 6 August, following a public demand that Catholics stay out of Protestant neighborhoods, LVF members attacked a Catholic taxi driver with Molotov cocktails in Armagh, Northern Ireland. The LVF planted three hoax devices in Dundalk, Ireland, and one small but viable bomb at a Dundalk shopping center on 17 November; bomb experts defused the device. Authorities charged the LVF with the murder of a Catholic man in front of St. Enda's Gaelic Athletic Club in Belfast on 5 December.

On 27 December, INLA members imprisoned in Northern Ireland's Maze Prison assassinated fellow inmate Billy "King Rat" Wright, leader of the LVF. Wright was serving an eight-year sentence in the Maze prison. The INLA gunmen smuggled weapons into the prison and shot him five times at close range. Wright's assassination drew an immediate response from his LVF colleagues. That same evening LVF members hijacked buses and set them on fire in Portadown, Northern Ireland. On 28 December three LVF gunmen opened fire on a hotel frequented by Catholics, killing one person and wounding three, including a teenager. At the end of 1997 the Ulster peace process included parties from both Unionist and Republican camps, including Sinn Fein. Pressure is building for the parties to reach some agreement before the deadline for a settlement in May 1998.

17

Terrorism and Its Impact on South Asia

Terrorism is not a new phenomenon. The world has experienced it, in different faces and different demonstration, since ancient times. Particularly, the twentieth century, which is certainly the most blood-ridden century in human history, saw a persistent increase and evolution in the terrorist activities. However, it had never enjoyed the status of being the foremost challenge for the international community. This transformation of the status of terrorism is obviously the outcome of the attacks of 9/11 on the twin-towers of World Trade Center and Pentagon- the chief symbols of American economic and military supremacy. Wounded at the time of its zenith as the sole super power of the world, America understandably decided to strike back and to launch a global campaign against terrorism. It was a very unpleasant decision. What this American resolve to initiate a world wide war could have implied for the dynamics of international relations could be well- judged by what President Bush said in his address to the joint session of the US Congress on September 20, 2001. "Our response involves far more than instant retaliation and isolated strikes.

Americans should not expect one battle, but a lengthy campaign. We will starve terrorists of funding, turn them one against another, and drive them from place to place, until there is no refuge or no rest. And we will pursue nations that provide aid or safe havens to terrorism. Every nation, in every region, now has a decision to make. Either you are with us, or you are with the terrorists." It shall be more than clear from this policy statement of the American President that what America was going to start was not to be a limited military action; rather America would take the war to the doorstep of every nation in every region. Thus, every nation and every society had to bear its share of the impact of this global war. Stephen P. Cohen has said, no part of the world has more affected by the terrorist attacks of September 11, 2001 than South Asia. 1 Today, if we look back at the five years history of the war on terrorism, it becomes clear that South Asia had to endure the strain of the consequences of the war. Perhaps it has been the centre of enormity in this unusual war.

There were a number of factors which made South Asia a central point in the US war. First and prime, the alleged suspects of these attacks were traced back to the mountainous wilderness of Afghanistan. The propinquity with a Taliban-ruled Afghanistan brought the war on terror to the doorstep of South Asia. As we know Pakistan shares border with Afghanistan and was among the countries which had a formal diplomatic relations with Afghanistan. Secondly, and more importantly, perhaps, there was no other state in the world that knew the radical regime of Taliban better than Pakistan. The ample treasure of reliable intelligence, the ability to launch air strikes from adjoining Pakistani airbases, and the Cold War confidence in its pledge made Pakistan, and therefore South Asia, a sort of field headquarters for American military campaign. It may be said that General Pervez Musharraf calculated that if Pakistan did not cooperate with USA his nation at the very least would be marginalized and isolated by the US and the international community, at worst Pakistan itself could be targeted because of its support and relationship with

Taliban Thirdly, a deep study of the American foreign policy thinking in the last decade will reveal that Americans began to develop a feeling of threat from the Islamic revivalism, after the end of Cold War.

South Asia happens to be home to quite a number of active Islamic revivalist movements. Accordingly, the presence of militant organizations in South Asia was an open invitation for the American war on terror. Fourthly, the danger of nuclear terrorism also was a factor for the revival of American interest in South Asia. In the last decade, a major and drastic challenge to international security has been the rise of the non-state actors and the stem possibility that the nuclear weapons may fall to their hands. The presence of strong radical elements in a nuclear South Asia made this threat highly plausible. It was for these, besides other reasons, that South Asia was so pervasively involved in the American war on terror. As the United States prepared to launch its global war, it put a tough choice before the states of the region "Either you are with us or against us". It was not only a decisive message but also an indication of the future course of Pak- USA relations. India, stimulated by the hope of strategic gains offered its all-out support, in every possible way. Pakistan, given its historic ties with the elements in Afghanistan was caught in a predicament, for some time, whether to join the war or not.

Nevertheless, when Pakistan was presented the famous list of seven demands, it did not take much but a call from Colin Powell, for Pakistan to take the bold decision of joining the American war, unconditionally. Pakistan became an indispensable allay after 9/11 when President Pervez Musharraf broke with the Taliban and Al-Qaeda to join in the US- led war against terrorism. On January 12, 2002 President Pervez Mushraff said," we have decided to join international; coalition against terrorism. We took this decision on principles and in our national interest. He further said Pakistan will not allow its territory to be used for any terrorist activity any where in the world. It may be stated that whatever President Pervez Musharaff has done to help the US in its war against terrorism was to avert the grave consequences of saying 'no' to the US. Pakistan's support was vital for the US because it not only wanted to use the territory of a country which shares the border with Afghanistan but also to avert the support which was being given to the Taliban government by Pakistan.

The proactive role of US in South Asia posed challenges for Pakistan .Pakistan wanted to safeguard its strategic assets, the Kashmir cause and economic recovery. However there is a sense of dissatisfaction and a belief that the US and its allies did not live up to the promises and pledges made to Pakistan for its support in the war against terrorism. It may be argued that as far as South Asia is concerned, the post 9/11 development worsened the security environment of the region. The South Asian countries decided to join the US led war against terrorism because of their own interests. India was prompt in offering its support in the hope that such a configuration of the situation in South Asia. Pakistan decided to join because of predictable economic incentives, the need to save its strategic assets and salvaging its Kashmir policy from total destruction. President Pervez Mushraff acceptance facilitated America's military needs of the moment and led to yet a commitment of aid to Pakistan, has earned the country the title "key ally". But it is imperative to note that America has seen the wisdom of building up India as counterbalance to China.

We may agree with Moisi Dominique that thirteen years ago, Samuel Huntington argued that a "clash of civilizations" was about to dominate world politics, with culture along with national interests and political ideology, becoming a geo-political fault line .... Today the world faces what might be called a "clash of emotion" as well. The western world displays a culture of fear, the Arab and

Muslim worlds are trapped in a culture of humiliation and much of Asia displays a culture of hope. Now almost 5 years have passed and the profound effect of the war is gradually unfolding. As we have mentioned in the beginning, the impact of the war on the South Asian region has been particularly at three levels—regional level, at the level of bilateral relations among regional states and at the domestic level. At the regional level, the important impact has been the resurgence of South Asia as the region of highest priority for America. While during the closing decade of Cold War, since 1979, South Asia remained the highest point in American foreign policy thinking, it lost its prominence with the Cold War.

While the first Clinton Administration wanted to establish a rapport with India, but South Asia did not figure heavily in American interests. However, the start of the global war on terror has rediscovered South Asia for America. With the presence of two nuclear power friends, and an Al-Qaeda-strewn Afghanistan, South Asia assumed a strategic status in American eyes. The rebirth of South Asia prominence was not limited to America, rather for whole the world. There was a long chain of Heads of States, and highest officials visiting the region every alternative day were evidence of long term strategic interests of the US in the region. The main objective of the US during the stand off was:

(1) That the prevailing tension between India and Pakistan should not escalate into a nuclear exchange

(2) That the deteriorating situation should not affect Pakistan's support to the US war against terrorism in Afghanistan.

According to Vanni Cappelli, the Bush administration presented President Pervez Musharraf with an ultimatum abandon support of Taliban and commit to the American -led war on terror or face the consequences of being considered an enemy of the US. Moins Ahmer says that," there is no overwhelming strategic framework for South Asia and being against "terrorism" doesn't provide one" neglecting both the regions enduring historical relations and our most pressing current security challenges. Resolution of the Kashmir issue was important for us to maintain good relations with Pakistan and India. It is imperative to note that the US later played a proactive role in the normalization of deteriorating Pakistan –India relations. It became the centre of global attention in the global media and the central battle- ground where the global war was either to be lost or won. Secondly, the war on terror has had a lasting impact on the regional stability. There are opposite views in this regard.

One viewpoint is that the war on terror has improved the regional stability. The source of regional instability mainly has been the irregularly rising tension between the nuclear archrivals—India and Pakistan. The war on terror and the American military presence is a factor of stability for the region. This has been fully proved during the 2002 militancy standoff. Following the December 13 attacks on its parliament, India had pushed the war hysteria up. There was an unprecedented mobilization of armed forces on a large scale. The armed forces stood eyeball to eyeball for several days, on both sides of the borders. Even nuclear threats were exchanged. An outbreak of war was believed to be certain. Then the American military presence entered as a stabilizing factor. America perceived that a war between India and Pakistan will certainly subvert, and disrupt its campaign against terror. Its war on terror could only be saved by avoiding the outbreak of a regional conflict. So America initiated a whole- hearted effort to defuse the situation. The tension came down. Those who believe that it was American diplomatic activism which prevented an outbreak of war and nuclear holocaust believe that the US war on terror is a factor for regional peace and stability.

On the opposite, a viewpoint upholds that the US war on terror has made the region highly unstable. There are many aspects of this instability. Firstly, the Taliban had been successful to restore a kind of stability in Afghanistan for the first time after a very long period of unrest. America, by dripping to pieces the Taliban regime, once again pushed Afghanistan into a new phase of insurgency and civil war. This unstable and troubled situation will not remain confined within the Afghan borders; rather will soon spread into the neighboring states. We can see for ourselves that the unrest and turbulence in Afghanistan has leaked out into Pakistan. The second aspect of war created instability in the region is related to the Indian effort to manipulate the situation in its favor with full vigour. India equated the self- determination movement in Kashmir with terrorist and accused Pakistan of support and cross border terrorism.

Lal Krishna Advani warned that Bush doctrine could be used against Pakistan. The situation provided an opportunity for India to justify its previous allegation against Pakistan before the world community. India planned to capitalizes on the emerging world wide focus against terrorism, which gave New Delhi an opportunity to portray Pakistan a state sponsoring Jihad and terrorism. It may be said that in this way after 9/11 Pakistan India relations took a new turn when New Delhi offered full support to the US war against terrorism and tried its best to establish a linkage between Pakistan support to the Muslim struggle in Jammu and Kashmir and struggling elements in Afghanistan but India failed to stop Pakistan from joining the US –led coalition against terrorism. India's purpose was to discredit the Kashmiris freedom movement and declare Pakistan as a terrorist state. Consequently Pakistan initiated measure to launch a crackdown on terrorist elements especially those having connection with Al-Qaeda and Taliban. It indicated a change in government's approach on supporting Kashmiris freedom struggle.

It is imperative to note such measure did not result in de-escalation in tension between Pakistan and India. It may be stated that even though Pakistan is, currently the frontline state in the US war on terror, it is America who is essentially reaping benefits from the situation, conditions in Indo-Pak hostility, to materialize its own selfish design vis-à-vis the south Asia region. The Indo-US nuclear deal is a proof of the fact that US has given a military edge to India making Pakistan more apprehensive than ever as to what real motives of US friendship with Pakistan. Convinced of American support, India tried to manipulate the American doctrine of pre-emption to pressurize Pakistan. India had been accusing Pakistan of waging cross border terrorism in Kashmir. It gambled to justify a possible attack on Pakistan by borrowing the preemptive doctrine and bringing the Kashmir insurgency into the realm of US definition of terrorism. The Indian effort to built pressure on Pakistan on the unjustified pretext of doctrine of pre-emption threatened to destabilize the region.

The third aspect in which the war on terror generated regional instability is even more important and sensitive. The chief source of regional instability is the hostility between India and Pakistan. On the western border, Pakistan always likes to feel secure through the presence of a friendly regime in Afghanistan. The war on terror has brought the Northern Alliances to the power in Kabul. The Afghan government is extremely antagonistic to Pakistan. This has made the western border of Pakistan highly troubled, thus adding to the regional instability. Apart from its impact on the regional environment, the war on terror has largely influenced the bilateral relations of the countries in the region. The bilateral relations between India Pakistan, in the last decade of the 20th century remained as tense as ever, except for the temporary relief of Lahore Declaration.

The nuclear tests in May 1998, and then the Kargil crisis in 1999 worsened the relations to the worst levels. However, after passing through the litmus test of the 2002 military standoff, the ice began to thaw. The peace process, starting after the friendship offer by Vajpayee on April 18, 2003 marks the dawn of a new era in the bilateral relations between India and Pakistan.

The composite dialogue has completed its three rounds. Although, it has not been able as yet to produce some meaningful progress on any of the major issues with India, nevertheless, the general normalization of relations and decrease in tension is no mean achievement in itself. It may be said that the success of composite dialogue could make both countries abandon wars and cherish peace. The long range of CBMs is accomplishing their objective of reducing the trust deficit. Resumption of road, rail and air links, exchange visits by the parliamentarians, media men, and students, the opening up of trade ties, and the growing people to people diplomacy will ultimately make the task of final resolution of all disputes including Kashmir, much easier to achieve. One can hardly deny that this peace process and the CBMs is not inclusively a product of the realization on part of India or Pakistan, rather the role of third party is of key importance. America, keeping in view the demands of its war on terror, has been decisive in the initiation and continuation of the present peace process. On the third level, the war on terrorism has had its effects on the domestic political dynamics of the South Asian states. The impact has been most evident and vital at the domestic level. It has been either a direct result of the American military activities, or indirect fallout of the policies adopted by the United States in the region. Perhaps no other country of the world, except America, has been as deeply affected by the war on terror as Pakistan. Pakistan's geographical location, its nearness with Afghanistan, its close relations with the Taliban regime, its deep knowledge of the rugged terrain of Afghanistan, and its history of Cold War alliance made Pakistan obviously the most important strategic asset for the United States.

As Pakistan was chosen to once again fight an American war, it had to make a number of difficult choices, which changed the course of its history. Pakistan had to take a U-turn on its Afghan policy by accepting the new regime; both parties' relations could not become cordial just on pretence. Pakistan was forced to leave its longstanding search for the strategic depth in Afghanistan. It made forceful efforts to convince the Taliban to act in accordance with the demands of international community, but as the Taliban were insolvent, Pakistan had to withdraw its hand from all kinds of support to the regime. With this major shift in its Afghan policy, Pakistan lost whatever influence it had in Afghanistan, Karzai's government was of the opinion in 2006 that it was a kind of hidden invasion propped up by outside interference .... Intended to tarnish the national identity and historical of Afghanistan.

For decades it was policy of Pakistan to support and sponsor the militant organizations in quest of its bleed-India policy. However, the US war on terror forced Pakistan to rethink its priorities, because America believed that these militant organizations formed a pool of terrorists as well as a ready-made basis for its organizational facilities for the Al-Qaeda network. So, Pakistan at once attacked at the militant organizations. Some of the organizations like LAT, JEM, TNFJ, SSP, and TNSM were banned. Their bank accounts were frozen, and their offices were closed. That Pakistan's participation in the war on terror has come at a heavy domestic price is clear from the later tussle between the government and the militants. The militant organizations were not ready to diaper so easily. They put up a firm resistance, and the government had to face a severe backlash. Law and order situation go worse. The banned organizations re-surfaced under new names. The frequency of terrorist activities multiplied.

There was a sharp increase in the suicide attacks on the government officials and assets. The President himself narrowly gets away two suicide attempts at his life. This backlash has been most alarming in the North West of Pakistan. The North Western mountainous terrain, the ethnic ties between the Pashtoons on both sides of the border, and the tribal traditions combinely offered the region as an ideal safe haven for the Al-Qaeda and Taliban fighters running from Afghanistan. The prevailing religious extremism and the large chain of madarssas spread all over the area welcomed the fugitives Mujahideen with open arms. As the pressure mounted up on Pakistan to trace and capture the fleeing terrorists, the government was faced with the difficult choice of launching a military operation in the tribal region.

The state forces initiated a full-fledge military campaign to drive out the Taliban scraps in mid-March 2004, when the armed forces came upon an Al-Qaeda shelter at Kaloosha near WANA, in South Waziristan. Since then, a high tension clash between the state forces and the foreign militants, along with their local supporters is going on. The government had to concentrate as many as 80,000 troops in its effort to bring the troubled region under control. It was almost impossible terrain despite countless raids siege and search operations as well as large scale arrests the high value targets were still away from the iron hands. Thus the military operation failed to deliver required results at the expense of bloodshed by country men of their brothers. No Al-Qaeda figure of any note was caught, except their Pakistani supports. Few observers have pointed out that Kabul is not a free agent and that they would not have done all this without the approval of Americans.

The terrorist put up a daunting resistance, claiming the lives of above 700 army men. The indiscriminate shelling on the non-combatants by security forces, have also caused a large-scale displacement of tribesmen from the violence-hit areas. Hundreds of families are forced to live with relatives in the neighboring towns. The Government has alternatively tried various forceful and appeasing strategies. The turbulence originating in the restless west has penetrated into the far and wide of the country. Major Urban centers have been targeted by the irritated militants. Pakistan feels itself unjustly targeted as the pressure from America continues to go up without reason for doing more. While Pakistan has started its military operation into the Northern areas at a very heavy domestic price, the Karzai Government in Kabul, and the aggressive elements in American think tanks continue to show lack of trust on Pakistan.

Besides the military clashes in the tribal agencies, the war on terror is making its impact on the more peaceful cities as well. There is a clear cut polarization in the society on the question of Pakistan's desirable role in the war. This polarization has further deteriorated the perennial challenge of national integration and social cohesiveness in Pakistan. One school of thought believes that it is a battle that Pakistan is fighting for its own sake. The militant organizations have become Frankenstein, and turned against their creator. Therefore, such forces need to be controlled by the government. The opposite viewpoint upholds that the government is unjustified for lashing at these very organization which it established by itself. It is, for them, unethical on the part of government to unleash terror on the Jihadi organizations, by surrendering to the American pressure. This sharp divide has displayed itself emphatically in public protests and media opinion.

It needs to be emphasized that while Pakistan is genuinely committed to a war against all forms of terrorism, the United States is making the task difficult for the Government of Pakistan, with its unintended actions. The heartless adventures like the gruesome air strike on the village of Damodola on13th January, 2006 is but only one of the many examples of the American actions which make it more difficult for the Pakistan government to justify their stance before the masses. Similarly, the way Karzai government continues to cast aspersions on Pakistan's role in restraining the militants further complicates the situation. It may be said that five years after 9/11, Pakistan's Islamist parties are growing stronger; the continuous violence in Kashmir has as far as Mumbai. All along this, we must not forget the heavy economic cost that Pakistan is paying for the war on terror. The adverse situation generated by the war has discouraged the foreign investors and impeded the domestic economic activity due to political uncertainty.

No doubt Pakistan has been taking substantial financial inflows from outside, but this temporary aid and assistance cannot be a substitute for the genuine inflow of investment, and resulting industrialization of a backward economy. One may argue that the political compromise on the constitutional engineering in Pakistan and the game being played with the democratic ideals is also a result of the war on terror. Had it not been but for his all out commitment to the American war on terror, who knows what, would be the American level of tolerance and support for the military regime of Pervez Musharraf.

This is a compromise that the west in general and America in particular, are willing to make, for the sake of their war on terror. In this way, the analysis at the various levels—regional, bilateral, and domestic— makes it sufficiently clear that the war on terror has been a factor of utmost importance in the political, strategic and military dynamics of the South Asian region. It has left a lasting impact on the regional strategic environment, on the nature of relationships among the various states in the region, and on their domestic politics. What we must not forget is the fact that the war on terror is still not coming to an end. Therefore, its consequences and implications for the region of South Asia will continue to be gradually known for an indefinite period of time.

18

Nuclear War and Famine

The use of nuclear weapons will grow increasingly likely by 2025, US intelligence warned in a report on global trends that forecasts a tense, unstable world shadowed by war. "The world of the near future will be subject to an increased likelihood of conflict over scarce resources, including food and water, and will be haunted by the persistence of rogue states and terrorist groups with greater access to nuclear weapons," said the report.

> "Widening gaps in birth rates and wealth-to-poverty ratios, and the uneven impact of climate change, could further exacerbate tensions."

Called *Global Trends 2025 - A Transformed World,* the 121-page report was produced by the National Intelligence Council, a body of analysts from across the US intelligence community. Officials said it was being briefed to the incoming administration of president-elect Barack Obama. A year in the making, the report does not take into account the recent global financial crisis. "In one sense, a bad sense, the pace of change that we are looking at in 2025 occurred more rapidly than we had anticipated," said Thomas Fingar, deputy director of National Intelligence.

One overarching conclusion of the report is that "the unipolar world is over, (or) certainly will be by 2025," Mr Fingar said. But with the "rise of the rest," managing crises and avoiding conflicts will be more difficult, particularly with an antiquated post-World War II international system. "The potential for conflict will be different then and in some ways greater than it has been for a very long time," Mr Fingar said.

The report has good news for some countries:

- A technology to replace oil may be underway or in place by 2025;
- Multiple financial centres will serve as "shock absorbers" of the world financial system;
- India, China and Brazil will rise, the Korean peninsula will be unified in some form, and new powers are likely to emerge from the Muslim non-Arab world.

Risk of Nuclear War

But the report also says some African and South Asian states may wither away altogether, organised crime could take over at least one state in central Europe; and the spread of nuclear weapons will heighten the risk they will be used. "The likelihood that nuclear weapons will be used will increase with expanded access to technology and a widening range of options for limited strikes," it said.

The report highlighted the risk of a nuclear arms race in the Middle East where a number of countries are thinking about developing or acquiring technologies that would be useful to make nuclear weapons. "Over the next 15-20 years, reactions to the decisions Iran makes about its nuclear program could cause a number of regional states to intensify these efforts and consider actively pursuing nuclear weapons," the report said. "This will add a new and more dangerous dimension to what is likely to be increasing competition for influence within the region," it said.

The report said it was not certain that the kind of deterrent relationships that existed for most of the Cold War would emerge in a nuclear armed Middle East. Instead, the possession of nuclear weapons may be perceived as "making it safe" to engage in low intensity conflicts, terrorism or even larger conventional attacks, the report said. The report said terrorism would likely be a factor in 2025 but suggested that al-Qaeda's "terrorist wave" might be breaking up.

"Al-Qaeda's weaknesses - unachievable strategic objectives, inability to attract broad-based support and self-destructive actions - might cause it to decay sooner than many people think," it said. "Because history suggests that the global Islamic terrorist movement will outlast al-Qaeda as a group, strategic counterterrorism efforts will need to focus on how and why a successor terrorist group might evolve during the remaining years of the 'Islamic terrorist wave'." The report was vague about the outcome of current conflicts in Iraq, Afghanistan and nuclear armed Pakistan.

In 2025, the government in Baghdad could still be "an object of competition" among various factions seeking foreign aid or pride of place. Afghanistan "may still evince significant patterns of tribal competition and conflict". "The future of Pakistan is a wildcard in considering the trajectory of neighbouring Afghanistan," it said.

Nuclear Program- a Matter of National Pride

Having used a legal loophole to enrich uranium, Iran is loath to give it up under US pressure. If you want to experience nationalism wrapped in nuclear power, this is the place. Officials, professors, and taxi drivers all would tell a visitor that Iran does not want "the bomb," but only "nuclear technology" or "the fuel cycle" – needed to run power reactors. Indeed, nuclear weapons would make Iran vulnerable and isolated, insist officials and regime opponents alike. Iranians want nuclear technology to show the world that their nation is advanced, fully developed, and strong – that Shiite Iran is the greatest society in Southwest Asia. Enriching uranium and generating electricity within the rules of the international nonproliferation system satisfies these objectives better than bombs.

Civilizational pride makes Iranians loathe being seen as rule-breaking, lying aggressors in quest of nuclear weapons. Cannily putting their shady nuclear past behind them, they now project themselves as a sophisticated, law-abiding member of the international community seeking nuclear fuel-cycle capabilities. But Iran's recently uncovered nuclear practices, and its unsettled neighborly relations, deepen many people's conviction that new rules are needed to manage nuclear technology.

A promotional videotape from Iran's atomic energy organization trumpets the call for Iran's acceptance in the existing nuclear elite. Pictures of nuclear installations are interspersed with blooming flowers and snow-capped mountains in a paradisiacal montage. An enthusiastic narrator (speaking English!) trumpets, "Iran is a country of intelligent people." A young worker at the uranium conversion plant in Isfahan holds a small canister of uranium hexafluoride (which can be processed into fuel for power plants or bombs) while other young men reach to touch it as if a sacred artifact. "Our people feel great pride because our young Iranian scientists can produce nuclear fuel, the most important part of the fuel cycle, despite all of the sanctions and pressure from the West," explains Iran's chief nuclear negotiator, Hassan Rohani.

Another official notes privately, "US pressure has unified the people in wanting nuclear technology, even more because the US says we can't have it." Rather than prepare the public to accept a backing away from nuclear technology, Hashemi Rafsanjani, Chairman of the Expediency Council the driving force behind the nuclear program since the late 1980s, stokes nationalist resistance. He says Iran is willing to apply unprecedented monitoring and control on its nuclear activities, but the United States rejects this because Washington truly aims to keep Iran from becoming a developed country. Oil will run out soon, he argues, and countries like Iran will need nuclear technology in order to be developed. Washington's attempt to deny this is payback for its dependence on Persian Gulf oil in this narrative.

Iranians want US respect, but not on terms imposed by Washington, especially if those terms reflect a dim view of Iranian civilization. Iranians displayed inside and outside the government a injured pride at the idea of international pariahdom. How can the United States treat Taliban-infected Pakistan as an ally, and indulge its careless possession of nuclear weapons, but regard Iran as the world's worst menace? "Pakistan – is that a country?" an influential Iranian conservative asked me when I said I was on my way there.

Iranians see Japan as a model for their future: "We want what Japan has," a leading Tehran professor insists. "If Japan can have the fuel cycle and stay happily in the NPT, why can't we?" Because Iran is not Japan. Japan recognizes all its neighbours; Iran does not accept the existence of Israel. Japan does not support organizations engaged in violent struggle and targeting non-combatants; Iran does. Japan has not been lying about its nuclear activities for the past 20 years. Differences between Japanese and Iranian approaches to human rights and global economic integration also explain international confidence in Japan's nuclear responsibility – and doubts about Iran's.

Even if Iran were more like Japan, the world cannot accommodate more nuclear Japans. Terrorism and unstable global security dynamics make it too risky to allow new factories for separating plutonium and enriching uranium, as Iran seeks. Iran's insistence on purely peaceful intentions may be genuine, but intentions can change too quickly for comfort in states with nuclear weapons capabilities. The Bush administration, Mohammed El Baradei of the International Atomic Energy Agency (IAEA), and Kofi

Annan agree that the interpretation of nonproliferation rules must be updated in order to keep additional states from acquiring facilities to produce potentially dangerous nuclear materials. The Non Proliferation Treaty's vague Article IV right "to develop research, production, and use of nuclear energy for peaceful purposes" should not be interpreted to endorse additional states' acquiring uranium enrichment or plutonium separation facilities.

Lacking the temperament to build an international consensus on better rules, the United States aims to unite a coalition of willing "good guys" to keep "bad guys" like Iran from acquiring potentially dangerous technology. According to this logic, bad guys are illegitimate by definition, so their interests need not be recognized or accommodated. And if bad guys have sympathizers, they, too, should be ignored. The problem, of course, is that the United States alone – or even with the UK, France, and Germany – cannot coerce Tehran to accept an interpretation that neither it nor a majority of the world thinks is fair .Coercion of a state as proud and powerful as Iran only works if the vast majority of its neighbors and counterparts are unified in pressing sanctions and isolation. (No significant coalition will support US or Israeli military force.)

And that unity will come only if the "rule" being enforced appears fair enough to encourage voluntary compliance. The Iranian strategy now is to play by the rules and demonize Washington for trying to change them. Tehran presses the IAEA to certify its compliance with nonproliferation standards, and therefore allow it to resume uranium enrichment and plutonium programs without sanction. Iranian officials hint they will accept any European-suggested verification measures, in order to prove Iran's peaceful intentions. Iran will do anything but give up its "right" to enrichment capability. As chief negotiator Rohani put it, "termination of fuel cycle activities as demanded of Iran means you have killed the NPT. If you take out Article IV, all developing countries will step out of the treaty.... Termination is war between the North and the South. The Americans say forget about Article IV, forget about the disarmament promised in Article VI....The US today is trying to create a second discrimination, one between those that have peaceful nuclear technology and those not allowed to have peaceful nuclear technology."

Washington's challenge is to prevent Iran from isolating it! The United States and EU are right on the substance, but to garner international support they must make trade-offs that the Bush administration resists. If options for national nuclear fuel-cycle development are to be constricted, then concessionary international energy cooperation needs to be expanded – perceptions of neocolonialism must be debunked. If controls on proliferation of dual-use technology to new countries are to be tightened, then commitments by nuclear-weapon states to dismantle their arsenals and quit building new nuclear weapons must also be tightened. Iran is mounting a fairness campaign; the United States and EU must counter with a better one.

The Challenge of Terrorism

Although terrorism was one of the least plausible causes for the recent U.S. war in Iraq and there was a surprising lack of terrorist acts aimed against the United States or U.S. interests during the war, the predicted upsurge of terrorist attacks in postwar Iraq occurred sooner than many expected. Terrorism generated by the conflict in Iraq might have been overshadowed by a stronger and more massive form of resistance—an uprising against the occupying forces that has gone beyond both terrorism and guerrilla warfare— but remains a long-term security problem whose potential negative regional and international ramifications may well exceed those of Afghanistan.

Domestic and "Imported" Terrorism

Even prior to the Shi'a uprising that signified a truly massive nationwide resistance to the U.S.-led coalition, post-Saddam Iraq was in a postwar, but not a post-conflict, stage. At the earlier postwar stages, armed resistance simply took the shape of an asymmetric low- intensity conflict and employed several tactics from guerrilla attacks against coalition troops and collaborationist security forces to terrorist acts against foreign and local civilians. The attacks against civilians occurred almost on a daily basis and demonstrated mixed tactics (suicide bombings, explosive-laden pushcarts on roads, mortars, automatic weapons fire, and, since the beginning of the Shi'a uprising in April 2004, a massive hostage-taking campaign directed against foreign civilians, particularly against the citizens of the coalition member-states).

In the terrorist attacks, the use of relatively standard weapons and explosives was usually coupled with sophisticated coordination, targeting, and planning. Even with multiple sources of terrorism in post-Saddam Iraq, it is still possible to identify both a strong domestic anti-coalition element and an international dimension. The dominant pattern of terrorism in Iraq has been one of homegrown conflict-related terrorism, with the fight against foreign occupation as its main rationale. Domestic forces that employed terrorist methods ranges from nationalist elements of a relatively secular nature, best described in terms of anti-neocolonialism and extending far beyond ex- Baathists and ex-security professionals of Saddam's regime, to Sunni radicals and a growing Shi'a religious element.

Foreign civilian targets clearly have been more vulnerable, both as objects for attack and as potential hostages, than coalition military targets. In addition, collaborationist Iraqis of all kinds have been used as substitute or even supplementary targets—from people working directly for the occupational regime to those simply loyal to the U.S.-sponsored interim Iraqi government, and from those profiting materially from the occupational rule to purely accidental victims. One of the main sources of instability and a cause of various forms of violence in Iraq, including terrorism, has been the coalition-sponsored government's lack of legitimacy, coupled with disagreements over the type and composition of the future governing arrangement as well as widespread popular skepticism about its viability.

In this context, terrorism has not only been used as a powerful mechanism of internal destabilization, demonstrating the inability of occupying forces and the pro-U.S. Iraqi administration to provide elementary security, but also has become integrated into the inter- and intra-community struggle. The latter was evidenced by the diversification of targets to include Shi'ites (the killing of the top Shi'a cleric Ayatollah Sayed Mohammed Baqr al-Hakim in a massive car bomb explosion in Najaf in August 2003 and the targeting of the Shi'a Shrines in Kerbala and Baghdad in March 2004) and Kurds (Kurdish targets included the offices of the Kurdistan Democratic Party and Patriotic Union of Kurdistan).

As for the international dimension, the primary rationale behind the influx of foreign fighters into Iraq (which even the U.S. administration does not view as sponsored by any particular Muslim state) remains the presence of Western, and particularly U.S., targets, including coalition military forces and international civilian personnel, on Iraqi territory. By moving these potential objects of attack to the conflict area itself, the U.S.-led occupation has thus far stimulated mainly the import of terrorism into Iraq rather than the export of terrorism. Although often attributed to the "Iraq factor," several high-profile terrorist attacks with a clear international connection, such as those in Istanbul (November 2003) and

Madrid (March 2004), instead should be associated with Al Qaeda's broader strategy of using each and every manifestation of U.S. anti-Islamism and "imperialism" as a pretext for advancing Al Qaeda's own agenda and ideology— developed long before the war in Iraq and supported by a range of radical Islamic groups, not necessarily associated formally with Al Qaeda.

The few direct and proven cases of terrorism being exported from Iraq (the shooting of a religious procession in Quetta, Pakistan in March 2004, for example) have so far been mainly limited to the states of the region. Although not all of the foreigners joining the resistance in Iraq are Islamists of some variety, many appear to be professional jihad fighters migrating from one conflict area to another. Some of them arrived during the war in response to Saddam Hussein's call to non-Iraqi Arabs to help defend Iraq and have remained in the country under the occupation. The involvement of foreign jihad fighters in attacking coalition and other international targets in Iraq, including civilian personnel and objects, is highly probable, but their role in using terrorism to incite inter-communal and inter-ethnic violence in the country is less likely.

Both the scale of the threat posed by the import of terrorism to Iraq and the potential cooperation and coordination between transnational and local armed groups may have been overestimated, particularly by top U.S civil officials (in contrast to assessments by military commanders on the ground). The threat itself, however, cannot be written off until postwar Iraq fully overcomes regime collapse and ceases to be an externally imposed embryonic state, lacking both functionality and legitimacy.

Furthermore, as the conflict intensifies and the goal of turning Iraq into a second Palestine starts to materialize, the prospects of the spread of terrorism to the wider region and even to the United States or Europe might increase and its link to anti-American, especially Islamic, extremism in the Middle East and elsewhere may become more evident. In this context, the potential scale-down of the U.S. military presence, coupled with the more active transfer of security responsibilities to Iraqi structures, poses a serious security dilemma, as it may help weaken the initial motivation for terrorism, but also might physically facilitate the export of terrorism from Iraq.

Russia's Anti-terrorism Experience

The prospect for Iraq to become a major rallying point for terrorists is of deep concern to Russia, in terms of the country's broader security agenda as well as its anti-terrorism strategy and experience. Despite Russia's opposition to the war in Iraq and disagreements between the U.S.-led coalition members and key European states, including Russia, over the post-Saddam arrangement for Iraq, one common interest related to the situation in that country has been shared by almost all external actors: the need to prevent Iraq from becoming a new source of terrorism and Islamic extremism.

Otherwise, the coalition's inability to secure law, order, and stability in Iraq serves as an additional post hoc political justification of Russia's staunch opposition to the war. The limits placed by high levels of insecurity on the remaining Russian business presence in Iraq (particularly those concerning the safety of personnel, such as 'collateral damage' and possible kidnapping, if only by accident) are compensated by Russia's financial gains from high oil prices to which the instability in postwar Iraq, limiting the flow of Iraqi oil to international markets, is certainly a contributing factor.

Anti-terrorism, however, is a different matter. Russia has been confronted for a decade with the challenge of terrorism generated by an armed conflict on its own territory and is concerned about terrorist threats to its Commonwealth of Independent States (CIS) neighbors, particularly the Central Asian states, another hotbed of Islamic terrorism located not far from its own southern borders and emerging as a new potential trigger that could at any time re-activate the southern arc of instability is most undesirable.

As noted earlier, problems created by the U.S. intervention and occupation of Iraq are of a long- term nature and are not likely to be solved effectively by the coalition itself. Sooner or later, these problems will have to be addressed by the broader international community in cooperation with an Iraqi postwar government that has not been imposed on the country and people. At this point, rather than bitterly lamenting the illegal nature of the U.S.-led war against Iraq and simply trying to keep pace with the rapidly changing political environment in that country, thinking about the potential ways to combine anti-terrorism with postwar reconstruction that might be utilized in future attempts to find a way out of the continuing Iraqi crisis might be much more useful.

In technical terms, Russia's growing experience in anti-terrorism, particularly in dealing with complex terrorism as a mix of domestic, conflict-generated resistance, and international influences and connections, compensates for its non-involvement and lack of operational experience in post-Saddam Iraq. More generally, unlike the United States and its former and current coalition partners, Russia has not been a direct party to an armed conflict in a Muslim-populated state since the end of the 10-year Soviet military presence in Afghanistan. (In fact, in some cases Russia has contributed to a peaceful resolution of such conflicts, as in the case of the civil war in Tajikistan, which involved an Islamic opposition.)

In the eyes of radical Islamic organizations, however, this point is fully undermined by the fact that Russia remains the only major European state that has been fighting an insurgency in a Muslim-populated part of its own territory. Despite the wide disparity between the terrorist challenges posed by the conflict in occupied Iraq and those posed by the still unstable post conflict environment in Russia's North Caucasus, as well as the respective responses, some parallels can be traced. First, both conflict areas directly concern important or even vital security interests of the respective states—establishment of direct U.S. control over one of the world's major oil-producing areas through the demise of a "rogue" regime in the former case and preservation of the territorial integrity of Russia as a federal state in the latter.

This means that the interests at stake in each case are high enough to not be undermined easily by the negative political and public consequences of the armed opponent's extensive use of terrorist means alone. Secondly, in shaky postwar environments that can easily degenerate into a full-scale armed conflict, the range of threats and of security measures that need to be undertaken to meet these threats always goes beyond the terrorism/anti-terrorism dichotomy. In the case of Iraq, this has been demonstrated by the Sunni guerrilla campaign reinforced by the Shi'a uprising against the coalition forces.

The U.S.-led occupation of Iraq remains to a large extent a military affair, with elements of a large-scale counterinsurgency campaign so that most of the problems it raises, the operational tasks it poses, and the methods employed (including, among other things, high-altitude massive bombing of certain areas and long-range missile strikes) have little to do with counterterrorism in a more narrow sense. Under such circumstances, the functional division between traditional military duties and other tasks taken on by the security forces, such as law enforcement and counterterrorism, may become very blurred. Russia's experience in fighting an asymmetric war on its own territory, as well as those of other states facing similar problems (i.e., the United Kingdom in Northern Ireland), demonstrate that it may not be easy to reconcile tasks that are more specifically focused on and tailored to counterterrorism needs (intelligence assistance, intelligence sharing, special and covert operations), on the one hand, and more regular enforcement and policing measures, let alone military operations, on the other.

Terrorism, however, is a very specific form of asymmetrical violence that involves a combination of political motivation and a civilian/non-combatant target. It cannot be countered adequately at the operational level just by improving general security conditions and thus requires specifically tailored counterterrorist tools and instruments and special operations that must be effective without provoking more terrorism. As applied to Iraq, these difficulties can be illustrated by the coalition's postwar prioritization of increased border security and control of border regions. Although important as a general security measure, border control is less valuable as a specific anti-terrorist tool, as it is based on a misleading perception that terrorism in Iraq comes primarily from outside the country.

Also largely ineffective as an anti-terrorism tool are most aspects of the U.S.-sponsored formation and reform of the Iraqi security sector, which is not only part of the externally imposed state apparatus lacking popular legitimacy, but also does not stand up to the task of anti-terrorism in operational terms. In particular, the lack of a single chain of command, the multiplicity of security structures with overlapping functions, and the excessive reliance on tribal security networks perceived as loyal or neutral (particularly in Kurdish and some Shi'a areas) have both impeded the formation of the post-Saddam national security structures and complicated rather than facilitated counterterrorism in Iraq.

The problem, however, goes much deeper than the need for better demarcation of various security tasks and for coordination and proper division of responsibilities between the military, law enforcement and intelligence/ counter-intelligence sectors. As most vividly demonstrated by Russia's experience in countering terrorism generated in the North Caucasus, the key issue is to what extent counterterrorism in a postwar but not yet post conflict environment should be viewed and undertaken as an enforcement-type activity. In fact, what distinguishes counterterrorism from other security tasks is that its central goals and the main indicators of success are prevention and preemptive disruption of terrorist activities and networks, rather than post hoc retaliation or coercion, particularly when the latter takes the form of massive collective punishment. Although coercive measures may be used selectively in support of counterterrorism, they are not the core of counterterrorism.

The most pro-active and effective counterterrorist policy is never the most offensive and retaliatory one. In particular, operations whose influence extends beyond the terrorists themselves—so-called collective impact measures, such as closures and mopping-up (zachistka-style) operations, which have also been employed frequently by U.S. forces in Iraq—can only serve counterterrorist goals, when they are implemented for a pre-defined period of time, in a limited area, based on very solid intelligence, and for specific operational purposes, not when they are used as punitive measures or as a substitute for other security activities, such as regular patrolling and policing.

Finally, it must be recognized that whether part of a formal peace process or not restoring and strengthening state control or, in failed states, (re)building national state institutions and authority, appears to be the most effective long-term anti-terrorism strategy. The centrality of effective post-conflict state-building as a long-term anti- terrorist strategy has been vividly demonstrated in the case of Russia, where earlier attempts to delegate state-building to armed separatists have failed, leading to more conflict and instability. In its subsequent Chechnya policy, the Russian government simply had no viable alternative to prioritizing the need to build-up a new Chechen administration loyal to the federal government and the Russian constitution and gradually transferring administrative responsibilities to this administration.

No doubt, the state-building process in a chaotic war-torn area or country involves many dilemmas, such as that between the more rigid security-oriented approach to state-building, focused on centralization of power, strict hierarchy, and formal institutional mechanisms, and a more flexible approach that might involve more informal political arrangements and not make absolute the centralization of power. Other crucial dilemmas include the constant trade-off between the functionality and legitimacy of the structures being built and an uneasy compromise among various, often-conflicting state-building agendas. In this sense, post-Saddam Iraq is no exception and the key to anti-terrorism in Iraq lies in the formation of functional state institutions that will enjoy both local legitimacy and broader international, particularly UN, recognition.

Thus far, the mainstream, official political process sponsored by the United States and its allies is increasingly contested not only by military means but also by alternative political and state-building initiatives, such as the one declared as early as the fall of 2003 by Moqtada al-Sadr. Prior to the anti- coalition uprising of Iraq's radical Shi'ites in the spring of 2004, it appeared as if the optimal scenario for postwar Iraq might have resulted from a coalition-sponsored political process centered on the creation of a relatively loyal Iraqi administration coupled with the gradual scale-down of coalition presence and visibility, thus stimulating the transformation of the conflict into an increasingly internal matter.

However, because the coalition has faced armed confrontation against both Sunnis and Shiites, united by anti- Americanism and the common goal of driving the occupying forces out of the country, the prospects of building an externally imposed Iraqi state that can play an arbitrary role in a relatively fragmented country divided by religious denomination and ethnicity may wane. It is worth noting that, as the key resistance leader, al-Sadr has already started to position himself as a political figure with nationwide rather than purely Shi'a appeal. Ironically, for post-Saddam Iraq, it is anti-Americanism that can play the long-needed role of uniting Sunnis and Shi'ites around a common platform and creating the conditions for the emergence of post-Saddam nationalism that, in turn, could potentially serve as a powerful ideological basis for a new unified Iraqi state.

Bibliography

Adams, James. *The Financing of Terror,* New York: Simon & Schuster, 1986.

Alexander, Yonah and Richard Latter, eds. *Terrorism and the Media: Dilemmas for Government, Journalists & the Public,* Washington, DC: Brassey's, 1990.

Andersan, Sean and Stephen Solan. *Historical Dictionary of Terrorism,* 2nd ed. Lanham, MD: Scarecrow, 2002.

Atkins, Stephen E. *Terrorism: A Reference Handbook,* Santa Barbara, CA: 1992.

Bell, J. Bower. *Transnational Terror, Washington,* DC: American Enterprise Institute, 1975.

Burton, Anthony. *Urban Terrorism: Theory, Practice, Response,* London: Cooper, 1975.

Chaliand, Gerald. *Terrorism: From Popular Struggle to Media Spectacle,* Atlantic Highlands, NJ: Saqi, 1987.

Comb, Cindy C. *Terrorism in Twenty-First Century,* 2nd ed. Upper Saddle River, NJ: Prentice Hall, 2002.

Crelinsten, Ronald D. and Denis Szabo. *Hostage- Taking,* Lexington, MA: Lexington Book, 1979.

Crenshaw, Martha. *Terrorism, Legitimacy, and Power,* Middletown, CT: Wesleyan University Press, 1983.

Gay, Kathleen. *Encyclopedia of Political Anarchy,* Santa Barbara, CA: ABC-CLIO, 1999.

George, Alexander, ed. *Western State Terrorism,* New York: Routledge, 1991.

Gurr, Ted Robert. *Handbook of Political Conflict: Theory and Research,* New York: Free Press, 1980.

Harmon, Christopher C. *Terrorism Today,* London: Frank Cass, 2002.

Hoffman, Bruce. *Inside Terrorism,* New York: Columbia University Press, 1998.

Jenkins, Brian. *International Terrorism: The Other World War,* Santa Monica, CA: RAND, 1985.

Kushner, Harvey W. ed. *The Future of Terrorism: Violence in the New Millennium,* Thousand Oaks, CA: Sage, 1998.

Laqueur, Walter. *History of Terrorism,* New York: Transaction Publishers, 2001.

Lesser, Ian O. et al. *Countering the New Terrorism,* Santa Monica, CA: RAND, 1999.

Lewis Bernand. *The Political Language of Islam,* Chicago: University of Chicago Press, 1988.

Miller, Abraham H. *Terrorism and Hostage Negotiations,* Boulder, CO: Westview, 1980.

Moss, Robert. *Urban Guerrilla Warfare,* London: International Institute for Strategic Studies, 1971.

Netanyahu, Benzamin. *The Terrorism Reader,* New York: Meridian, 1986.

O'Neill, Bard E. *Insurgency and Terrorism: Inside Modern Revolutionary Warfare,* Washington, DC: Brassey's, 1990.

Peters, Rudolph. *Jihad in Classical and Modern Islam,* Princeton, NJ: Markus Wiener, 1996.

Picard, Robert G. *Media Portrayals of Terrorism: Functions and Meaning of News Coverage,* Ames: Iowa State University Press, 1993.

Pillar, Paul R. and Michael H. Armacost. *Terrorism and U.S. Foreign Policy, Washington,* DC: Brookings Institution, 2001.

Rashid, Ahmed. Jihad: *The Rise of Militant Islam I Central Asia,* New Haven, CT: Yale University Press, 2002.

Rosie, George. *The Dictionary of International Terrorism,* New York: Paragon House, 1987.

Schamis, Geraldo Jorge. *War and Terrorism in International Affairs,* New Brunswick, NJ: Transaction Publishers, 1980.

Segaller, Stephen. *Invisible Armies: Terrorism in the 1990s,* San Diego, CA: Harcourt Brace Jovanovich, 1987.

Sofaer, Abraham D. and Seymour E. Goodman. *The Transnational Dimension of Cyber Crime and Terrorism,* Stanford, CA: Hoover Institution, 2001.

Sonn, Richard D. *Anarchism,* New York: Twayne, 1992.

Stern, Jessia. *The Ultimate Terrorists,* Cambridge, MA: Harvard University Press, 1999.

Tanter, Raymond. *Rogue Regimes: Terrorism and Proliferation,* New York: St. Maytin's, 1998.

Tucker, Jonathan B. *Toxic Terror: Assessing Terrorist Use of Chemical and Biological Weapons,* Cambridge, MA: MIT Press, 2000.

U.S. Department of State, *Patterns of Global Terrorism,* Washington, DC [Annual].

Venzke, Ben N. *First Responder Chem- Bio Handbook,* Alexandria, VA: Tempest, 1998.

Wardlaw, Grant. *Political Terrorism: Theory, Tactics, and Counter-Measures,* New York: Cambridge University Press, 1989.

White, Jonathan R. *Terrorism: An Introduction,* 3rd ed. Belmont, CA: Wadsworth, 2001.

Whittaker, David J. *The Terrorism Reader*, London and New York: Routledge, 2001.

Zinn, Howard. *Terrorism and War*, New York: Seven Stories, 2002.

Index

Q

R

S

T

U

V

W

Y

Z